I, JOURNALIST

Coping with and crafting media information in the 21st century

Edited by:
Lee Duffield PhD
and
John Cokley PhD

With contributions by:
Lee Duffield PhD
John Cokley PhD
Mark Hayes PhD
John Herbert PhD
Elaine Ford B.Jour (Hons)
Rebekah Van Druten B.Jour (Hons)
Kasey Glazebrook B.Jour
Janice Holland BA (Jour)
John Flynn B.Jour
Bill Harper BAppSc. (Comp)

Pearson—SprintPrint is an imprint of Pearson Education Australia. It has been established to provide academics throughout Australia and New Zealand with fast and efficient access to the printing, warehousing and distribution services of Australia's leading educational publisher, ensuring a smooth supply channel to your campus bookseller.

For more information about the **Pearson—SprintPrint** service, contact the Editorial Department, Pearson Education Australia, Unit 4, Level 3, 14 Aquatic Drive, Frenchs Forest, New South Wales, 2086. Telephone: 02 9454 2200.

Associate Editor: Jill Gillies
Project Editor: Chris Richardson

Printed at the Pearson Australia Demand Print Centre

ISBN 10   0 7339 8403 7
ISBN 13   978 0 7339 8403 7

Pearson Education Australia
Unit 4, Level 3,
14 Aquatic Drive
Frenchs Forest NSW 2086
www.pearsoned.com.au

 An imprint of Pearson Education Australia (a division of Pearson Australia Group Pty Ltd)

Dedications

To Alice and Arnold Duffield

To Pip Hanrick, Liam Cokley and Erin Cokley.

Brisbane, April 2006

The editors

Dr Lee Duffield is a journalism lecturer at the Queensland University of Technology in Brisbane. He was a journalist and overseas correspondent during more than twenty years with the Australian Broadcasting Corporation. His research interests include the roles of journalists and mass media in historical crises and international relations.

Dr John Cokley lectures and researches in journalism, media and communication at the University of Queensland specialising in news delivery to remote communities; he is also convener of the Australian Convergent Journalism Special Interest Group (the Australian affiliate of the NewsPlex research complex, University of South Carolina). A reporter and editor with independent magazines and News Corporation newspapers between 1981 and 2002, he has taught and researched at four universities; has worked as a volunteer presenter in community radio, run successful small communication businesses with his wife Phillipa Hanrick, and is a member of the Society of Editors (Queensland) and the Small Island Cultures Research Institute.

The contributors

John Flynn spent most of his first 15 years in journalism in Queensland regional television news. One of the first video journalists, he did pioneering work with new technologies before starting out as an independent. He is a sports specialist contributing to international online services, and a journalism graduate from the Queensland University of Technology.

Elaine Ford began career life in journalism as a freelancer but moved quickly to her present position as a journalist and new-media producer with the state-owned broadcaster *ABC News Online* in 2001. Graduating with first-class honours in journalism from the Queensland University of Technology, she received a major international Golden Key (Adult Scholar) award.

Kasey Glazebrook is a journalist with Prime television in New South Wales. She graduated in journalism from the Queensland University of Technology in 2004. Her preparation for journalism included student exchange experience overseas and advanced studies in French. Her research at university included work on developments in freelance journalism.

Bill Harper is a public service information technology specialist with an Applied Science (Computing) degree from Charles Sturt University. He has done further study in creative writing and journalism to support activities as a regular podcast consumer, planning to create his own podcast (though still with 'no idea what the hell to talk about').

Dr Mark Hayes is a sociologist, journalist, and writer on mass media who has taught journalism at four Australian universities and the University of the South Pacific in Fiji. He is currently following specialist interests and engaging in research on cultural issues and mass communication in the South Pacific.

Professor John Herbert is an Australian broadcast journalist and academic who has worked in broadcasting, newspapers and journalism education for all his professional life, split between Britain, Australia, New Zealand, Singapore and Hong Kong. He co-founded the UK's first postgraduate diploma in radio journalism in London; was Head of Radio Training for the BBC; in charge of radio journalism training for the ABC; started print and broadcast journalism, both undergraduate and postgraduate, at Staffordshire University and was foundation Professor of Journalism there. He now specialises in researching, writing and speaking about many aspects of journalism and journalism education.

Janice Holland graduated in journalism at the Queensland University of Technology, and then progressed to an MA (research) degree where she has examined the street-press phenomenon and its implications for journalism practice. She has worked freelance and in corporate communication, has edited business and industry magazines, and publishes *Your Pet* magazine.

Rebekah Van Druten is a journalist with the Australian Broadcasting Corporation. She is a first-class honours graduate of the Queensland University of Technology [B.Jour, 2004] and continues there as a tutor. Her research on international news and correspondents has included extensive interviews with practitioners in Australia and Europe.

Note on referencing styles:

In deference to our general position that journalism is becoming freer, the editors have chosen not to hog-tie contributors to the same style 'post'. Accordingly, varying recognised academic referencing styles – all rigorous, of course – have been allowed within these pages, which readers in different markets around the world will find accommodating according to their tastes.

Introduction

I, Journalist looks at some facts and theories about the new economy of the world, with its heavy component of information technology across the whole range of economic and also social activity. This is done with two principles in mind: firstly, the changing world communication and mass media scene is viewed from the perspective of media practitioners, specifically the journalists; and secondly, we confine ourselves to discussion about technologies and technology-driven changes that are already strongly in evidence, documenting changes in the making instead of speculating about futures.

One prime reason for *I, Journalist* is to assist journalists to locate themselves in the new terrain of global media and media organisations this century. There is certainly considerable writing already on where mass media is going, much of which will suppose it means the end of the news business, and will celebrate the prospect of a world where media professionals will be replaced by a 'democratised' free exchange of information. In truth our collective research for this book suggests that demand for journalistic ways of thought and professional media skills stands to increase. Such demand for journalists, or at least journalistic abilities, may well enter new fields and new industries, where there is much more communication going on than before, and where accurate and well-formed communication becomes vital to many forms of production. For example, the convergence of audio-visual systems, mass media and telecommunications, puts sophisticated communication tools in the hands of many people in many kinds of enterprise, as we will hope to show in the following chapters.

The actual profiles of journalists and their journalistic practices can be expected to change suddenly. The professionals have begun the new century by losing their near-monopoly on communication tools, from licensed television frequencies to satellite transponder space, and their near monopoly on expertise in mass communications practice. From now on, virtually everybody can become as materially well equipped as the professionals, if they want to. They can certainly obtain and process large wads of information and use it to publish their own interesting news products, if they want to. This means that professional journalists can expect to be dealing with extremely aware audiences who know how communication is done and who will take full advantage of the systems available to interact with them freely.

Therefore we propose in this book that citizens generally should consider getting a journalistic education as a very effective way to come to terms with the new world. We identify the ways of thought that have characterised professional journalists, especially those which are applicable to the demands of the new technology and global media. We suggest that these will be of great use to all, for example, in handling huge amounts of information, as journalists must do; in making products for communication, such as reports, features, presentations of many kinds; and especially, in making sense of a confusing world environment. Here we argue that ordinary ways of dealing with information, crafting and representing it, and putting it into an individual mental context, actually are unsuitable for coping with powerful media instruments. It is far better to take up some applied ways of managing them – and journalism is a very relevant choice.

We also identify ways in which the model of the professional media worker needs to change in response to the demands of the times. For example, interactivity has arrived and must streamline journalists' understanding of their markets, and their relations with the public, in a radical way. Likewise, as another example, producers of television are confronted with the option of breaking a chain of historical developments in their craft, over centuries, to adopt new production values, new forms of representation, born of new software and equipment.

The method we adopt for making this argument and showing how things are progressing in our world of media is to stick very close to actual experience. Where there is discussion about burgeoning technology and the confusing array of options it presents, we take a walk into the streets to note the array of communication activities going on, check it in a knowledgeable way, and make an inventory of the systems in use. Where we see journalists having to make adjustments, specifically elite practitioners found in overseas reporting or in television current affairs, we ask them directly about their experiences. Where we see journalists exploiting fresh options to set up new enterprises, with new kinds of production facilities, targeted audiences they can get to, novel approaches in the way they organise their work and finances, and the way they design and make products, we report on their progress as case studies.

In the conclusion we will suggest that projects such as *I, Journalist*, just like journalism, are here to stay. More activity and new forms must come up to be documented, as is being done here. The book is intended as a forum for self-conscious reflection by media professionals on their situation and their on-going practices. It offers one way in which people both within media professions, and those affiliated with them through being their clients, audiences, customers, interlocutors, correspondents, collaborators and friends, can get a sound understanding of how the media world is progressing.

Contents

Preface

Professor John Herbert

There are five important concepts (there may of course be many more) which I believe the journalists of the 21st century have to get to grips with:

1. Economic matters cannot be ignored when deciding on news values. Publishers and indeed editors won't let that happen.
2. Technology is changing the world of the media, communications and therefore journalism in a way never known since the introduction of Caxton's printing press.
3. The age of the *citizen journalist* is upon us, arising out of technology and the ease of communication but also out of an increasingly disparaging attitude by consumers to the world of the journalist.
4. The inexorable rise of 24/7 broadcast news in which the concept of deadline no longer exists.
5. Increasing lack of respect between politicians and journalists.

The inescapable logic of these concepts is that journalists themselves must do something to prove their worth; to prove their need; to help consumers realise that a world in which everyone is a journalist in fact means that no one is a 'journalist' any more.

And the logic of that argument is, inescapably, that there must be, possibly for the first time, an introverted discussion, an inward looking self-criticism of the role of the journalist by journalists themselves. It is too late to leave such analysis to others; to the politicians, the media analysts, the communication studies specialists who may be able to look from the outside in, and therefore not achieve the credibility and usefulness that journalists themselves require to change the habits of hundreds of years. This book points us in this direction, and is therefore important both for its content and concepts.

The age of this new communication technology, decline in reading and viewing habits of consumers across the world, the ability to test with a click of a mouse the Google take on what journalists say, requires a new type of journalist. And it requires a new type of journalism education.

Hence this book, and the importance of this book. These days there are far too many books saying the same thing in different or even not-so-different ways, looking at journalism with a fifty-year old view, stressing the importance of how. This book is genuinely new in its approach to the problem of journalism credibility. It is new because amongst trades and professions, the least willing to look inwards on itself is journalism. Those of us who have practiced journalism either as a reporter or as an editor in the highly pressurised world of broadcast news and current affairs know this well. There is no time for introspection. There is time only for the next story. All of this means we as journalists need to stop and re-evaluate, or perhaps, sadly, evaluate for the first time what it is we do, how we do it, whether the concept of freedom of speech as it relates to modern communication processes needs a different approach both to ethics and the right to publish. Professional journalists, if they are to continue as a race, need to look at their responsibilities and find a new reason for existence.

At the moment external regulation of journalism is hotly contested by journalists and editors, and this is a tradition going back several hundred years. The idea is that journalists are ethical enough and professional enough to self regulate. That will only work if we highlight the 'self' and look inwards at ourselves first.

Of course the age of new forms of communication, citizen journalists and the need to curb the rampant commercialism that increasingly plays a part in what is news has an insidious side. Take Google's decision in January 2006 to omit Web content that China's government finds objectionable so that it would be given a licence to be used in China. Murdoch did similarly when trying to get his Sky satellite system into China by taking off BBC News from the service that would be seen in Asia. Market forces override freedom of reporting and freedom of speech.

This causes some cynicism and a result is the rapid growth of citizen outlets, independent news operations already showing they can survive while observing high standards by any measure. For just one example: A Korean based citizen journalist organisation, ohmynews.com, has been operating for more than six years. Their concept is that every citizen can be a reporter. They have over 40,000 citizen reporters posting 200 articles a day. And they check the facts first. www.ohmynews.com (Korean, translation). So, welcome the rise of citizen journalist, and as this book so persuasively comments: everyone can be a journalist, but that means everyone should first learn journalism, or at least some basic parts of it. I would go further: the modern university should make an understanding of journalism and how to operate journalistically with an ethical professional framework a compulsory part of every syllabus for every discipline in every course. Ideas, philosophy, democracy, society, freedom, news control. A brave new world of journalism: ethical, responsible and thinking. These concepts are necessary for anyone wanting to change the world of journalism and communication practice and scholarship. That means all of us. And that's the lesson from this book.

In the past Journalism and the Public have been related mainly within the watchdog formula; aggressive Journalism that aims to protect the Public. But there are signs that the public isn't responding and is putting journalism at the bottom of the pile in terms of what readers and viewers think of its trustworthiness, its intrusiveness and its lack of authority. Journalism has to change its philosophy, its approach both to newsmakers and to news readers.

It can begin by relaxing its traditional close accommodation with the political establishment. The mutual dependency of journalists and politicians has in any event been on the wane, suggesting the time is right for a different mood, less tension in the news. Nick Robinson, the BBC Political Editor, commented in a speech at Oxford in 2006, that: 'politicians are increasingly convinced that the media are obsessed with personality, trivia and divisions while ignoring what really matters – policy. We all too often retort that they offer up only spin, sound bites, or obfuscation.' (Robinson 2006, http://blogs.bbc.co.uk/nickrobinson 1.2.06)

Students entering the journalism field these days need to understand how different media – written words, audio, video, graphics, photographs, interactivity – work together to tell a story. Yet they need to know much more than just how to do these things.

Refocusing journalism is a massive task, and not one that by and large J-Schools are terribly good at. By and large we focus on the 'now', educating journalists for their first job in a couple of years time. Our job has been to guard the existing; our job in the future is to show where existing practices are wrong or have drifted away from the ethics of journalism, and swing the ship back to its proper direction of information that is credible, accurate and balanced. When we believe journalism is on the wrong path we should say so; otherwise, who will?

The exciting and important thing about the thoughts expressed throughout this book is the contribution they make to journalists' understanding of themselves and their environments. The editors and contributors are to be congratulated on undertaking such an important task. My message to all readers of this book: Let there be more of this explorative, introspective, indeed theoretical work by journalists about journalism. That's the way to improve the professionalism of journalists and their standing amongst their customers.

References

Robinson N (2006), *Television and Democracy: a troubled marriage*, the Phillip Geddes memorial lecture, Oxford, January 24, 2006, urn:schemas-microsoft-com:office:smarttags, retrieved from
http://blogs.bbc.co.uk/nickrobinson/ 1.2.06
www.ohmynews.com

Executive summaries of chapters

Part one: the new media environment

Chapter 1: *Thinking like journalists: how journalists and the general public can work together in the information economy.*
Dr Lee Duffield draws on some popular sociology to set out a context for journalism in the 21st century economy. He identifies journalistic practices and habits of thought very relevant to the demands of this century and in the process suggests that 'thinking like a journalist' becomes an actual form of knowledge.

Chapter 2: *The mirror-ball effect: investigating channels, messages and participation levels.*
Dr John Cokley conducts a survey of digital networks and appliances used to deliver news and information, and suggests an analysis of participation levels among journalists and their audiences. An earlier version of 'The Mirror-ball Effect' appeared in the peer-reviewed international online research journal *eJournalist*, 4(2) 2005.

Part Two: adjusting to change

Chapter 3: *Neo-firefighters: a new model for international news correspondents in the changing context of world journalism.*
Rebekah van Druten looks at the trend for media organisations to reduce their international services after the end of the Cold War and identifies an awakening of activity among foreign correspondents, who are finding new ways to do their work, often for new masters … themselves.

Chapter 4: *Making television current affairs in Australia: are the flagships flagging?*
Elaine Ford examines the presentational style of national current affairs television programs and the competition they are experiencing for audiences. She questions leading producers and presenters about their options and inclinations to learn whether they are ready to meet demands for major change.

Part Three: new models

Chapter 5: *Doing journalism in and from Dot TV: isolated Tuvalu adapts new media to its own ways.*
Dr Mark Hayes visits the so-called 'sinking' Pacific country Tuvalu regularly and portrays its media workers in this chapter, showing the world how the country faces bombardments from the sea. The workers provide 'mass' media services for their own community and so offer some cultural protection against bombardments from outside media.

Customary ways are seen as valuable but they also complicate the business of communication with the world outside.

Chapter 6: *Podcasting: giving control 'back to the masses'.*
Bill Harper provides an up-date on the democratisation of mass media through the 'podcasting' revolution, cataloguing services already drawing in millions of users. He details how the podcasters operate and finds this do-it-yourself media format is accessible and affordable although not yet a totally easy ride.

Chapter 7: *Trends in freelancing: a difficult road may now lead to success.*
Elaine Ford and Kasey Glazebrook investigate the options for journalists as sole traders in the freelance market. They identify a community of workers sharing information and comparing notes on business models, markets and technologies. Things may be opening up for freelancers living with the eternal two-part challenge: doing what you want to be doing, and struggling to make it pay.

Chapter 8: *Your Pet and Jofly Media: two case studies.*
John Flynn and Janice Holland have created their own media businesses: one producing video reports for specialised markets, usually delivered on line; the other exploiting an idea that pet lovers would sustain their own magazine. In this case study review with Dr Lee Duffield, each attests they could hardly have done it without the new-found availability of high-grade production tools that an individual entrepreneur can now afford.

Part Four: conclusions

Chapter 9: The editors of *I, Journalist* recapitulate on the social and technological environments of journalism in this century and the prospects for new forms of journalism emerging now.

Thinking like journalists: how journalists and the general public can work together in the information economy

Lee Duffield PhD

Journalism is seen to be responding to its changed environment in the 'new economy' of the 21ˢᵗ century, as audiences obtain communications skills and equipment as sophisticated as those available to the news media themselves. Media professionals are confronted with the opportunity – or necessity – to take advantage of the new order to operate more as sole traders not corporate employees, and so grasp at more professional autonomy. Amid prospects for citizen-produced media services and more interactive relations among professional media workers and public, a proposal is made here that everybody could do well to become a journalist. This refers to the adroitness of journalists in grappling with floods of information, making products with it, and forging relationships with a market for those products. This chapter also examines the proposition that for people to adopt a journalistic approach will mean coming to think like journalists; and it considers what that might mean. It treats the state of being a journalist as possessing certain ways of thought, and as a form of knowledge; to be studied in an epistemological way. By way of definition, epistemology is the very 'theory of knowledge, especially the critical study of its validity, methods and scope.' (Collins)

Introduction

Epistemology is not a word journalists can readily use in copy but it is defining their collective future. An argument is being made here that journalism can be seen as a form of knowledge, one that can be valuable for society at this time in history. It begins with a look at the circumstances of journalism at the start of the 21st century.

Communications technology is the well-recognised determiner of change in many areas. With growth in that technology there is a large and always growing component of information and communication activity now inherent in virtually all social life and all economic production. The argument is made that because of this change in circumstances, media workers have started moving into new roles that will permit them more professional freedom of action. It may reduce their traditional role as corporate servants, but build on their traditional place in intellectual and cultural leadership. The technologies themselves, especially communication satellites and videotape, more lately digitisation of all systems – for text, images and sound – have been expanding the range and productivity of journalists' work in dramatic ways.

A new economy as the context for media workers' employment

This study of journalism has a very wide context of social and economic change. Perceptions of radically changing times have been articulated and promulgated, most prominently by Charles Leadbeater (*Living on Thin Air*) and Richard Florida (*Rise of the Creative Class*) in their best selling texts and lectures. They have identified a synthesis of changing production styles, industry structures, job designs and loosening socio-economic class categories, all part of a more integrated global economy, to describe a new world with new needs and social relations. They posit cause and effect relationships, linking technological development with other drivers of change and re-ordering, e.g. couples having fewer children or none at all, mobility in a more flexible world labour market that undermines racial discrimination, ever-expanding consumerism, new industries permitting growth of new cities or the re-birth of old ones as cultural hubs – a necessary supporting environment for creativity (Florida, 2004: 22). All this is seen as stimulating higher productivity, with emphases on efficient systems and advanced design work; hence the strong marketability of creative talent, the 'rise of creativity as an economic force' (23).

The new world so depicted is congenial to entrepreneurship and freelance forms of work; contracts over careers. There are parallel

2

changes in modes of employment going on inside corporations, which hitherto cultivated hierarchical, stable work patterns, but are seen as changing, to stimulate innovation. These arguments cannot be too boosterish; there must be qualifications; the change process is incomplete and in the meantime has brought unresolved problems. Most recent concerns of the two principal writers referred to here are to do with the opening of enormous disparities in wealth, many representatives of the new creative classes being among the big winners (Leadbeater, 2000: 12-13). Leadbeater has proposed reform of institutions to overcome a 'trust deficit' (150-51), or that public-spirited giving will provide investment for the social good (Leadbeater, 2005); Florida is concerned about dissatisfaction among blue-collar workers and others associated with the 'old economy' falling behind: 'something's got to give', he has forecast (Florida, 2005). Yet, beyond doubt, work with a heavy creative input in this century is bringing high returns. It is a field where venture capital can be found for new enterprises. For the present discussion, that does mean forms of work for journalists outside of the corporations, which by tradition were commonly seen as hand-to-mouth freelancing, now can be taken as potentially most viable.

Descriptions of the new jobs being occupied by a new class are specific, well grounded in public statistics, though the data may require some re-configuring and interpretation (Reich, 1992: 173). Often called the knowledge workers, portfolio or information workers (Leadbeater, 2000: 1), Florida's Creative Class had 38 million members in the United States, 30% of all employed people. It was an assembly of those engaged in new industries, from computer graphics to digital music and animation, and those in re-made professions and roles:

> *I define the core of the Creative Class to include people in science and engineering, architecture and design, education, arts, music and entertainment, whose economic function is to create new ideas, new technology and/or new creative content. Around the core the Creative Class also includes a broader group of creative professionals in business and finance, law, health care and related fields. These people engage in complex problem solving that involves a great deal of independent judgment and requires high levels of education or human capital ... The key difference between the Creative Class and other classes lies in what they are primarily paid to do. Those in the Working Class and the Service Class are primarily paid to execute according to plan, while those in the Creative Class are primarily paid to create and have considerably more autonomy and flexibility ... (Florida, 2004:8).*

Reich produces similar lists in a class categorisation of routine production workers (25% of jobs), an expanding in-person services group (30%), and a 'creative class' category providing symbolic-analytic services (20%, expanded from 8% in the 1950s). The latter group trade in the manipulation of symbols, being data, words, oral and visual representations; and will include production designers, publishers, writers and editors, public relations operatives, and journalists. This treatment provides both an indicator of the kind of social change which has been taking place, and also a reminder that more traditional forms of work and social organisation have persisted in strength (Reich, 1992: 174). The 'new economy' is a strong growth sector.

Working in corporations and as sole traders

The argument here is that the new order is providing a distinctive field of activity, and field of knowing, that seems made for journalists to occupy. It is possible by registering actual developments, like the advance of new modes of industrial production, and the proliferation of communication tools throughout the community, to identify two main impacts: on one level, consolidation and intensification of corporate-based media management, news gathering, news production and distribution of products; on the other hand, a co-existent empowerment of practitioners as individuals or small groups becoming able to handle more and able to do business on their own account. Furthermore the availability of new communication tools to all people, not just regular media workers, is having special impacts for the media professionals best able to use them, with implications for a common good.

The emergence of journalists in business as sole traders becomes a key theme in this debate. Already the effectiveness of small organisations in some branches of mass media – typically small film and television production companies – is well recognised. These provide models, while they stand to develop further on their own account, and the vision can now be extended. It will take in stand-alone operations which can operate across a wide range, delivering services in diverse media fields. For instance a small firm, maybe a partnership, can now provide at any one time: general news updates from its chosen service area, in text, images and sound; reportage or commentary in specialised fields, e.g. regional commerce; archiving and research services; interactive forums; and customised services for private subscribers.

The difference between an agency of that kind, and precedents like the independent television producers, or small regional news agencies as found in the United Kingdom, is that the technology now allows private operators to handle a greater volume of output and across a broad range.

Technologically driven, their productivity is very high. Investment of editorial sense, professional craft skills and creativity can be turned to better effect. It will not need such major-scale investment and organisation that only large corporations can afford. Furthermore the strength of such small firms is enforced by their being able to publish. The online option, and its variants, will mean that a journalistic operation can sell direct to the public, e.g. as subscribers, and so have some independence from corporations as clients. Similarly small magazines are popular and have become economical to produce at a high standard. In publishing a product, as the core service of the business or to promote other services, the important battle of getting known in the market place is half-won. Quality of the product, good fortune and effectiveness in moving it then become the next issues for producers to address, but at least they are in the game on their own account.

So the argument progresses towards the promise of more pluralistic daily services; here corporate, there independently run. In this symposium, *I, Journalist*, some case studies are given that show how sole traders can make their own media products, whether in the field of iPod publications, short documentaries for television, or magazines. Such work is usually done by a younger generation of journalists; some would have been working in elite corporate areas; all are receptive to possible ways of doing their professional work scarcely thought of in the past century.

Everybody could do well to become a journalist

So far, however, the discussion does not say an entirely new kind of journalism is on the way, only that journalistic practice as it is known is likely to go through further radical change. The next step is to say that some fundamental adjustments will be involved, especially in the way that journalists engage with publics, and at the heart of the argument is the idea of journalism as knowledge available to all. A proliferation and democratisation of the supply of daily information creates a new information order with new demands on the individual, and introduces the proposition that everybody could do well to become a journalist. Here it is proposed that learning to be journalists is in fact a key life skill for private citizens this century. Principally, coping with vast floods of information, like a journalist, is first base for coping with workaday and private life. Information may well be, and is, continuously catalogued, indexed, edited, illustrated and served in manageable portions, for example by commercial databases; yet coping will demand more. It will demand habits, skills and intuition for using the information with effect. Put another way, information handling alone will not do. Information handling alone is about the processes of finding out then cataloguing, while what is required for life in this world, is to have also the different intellectual faculty of retentive knowing, and knowing how to use. After that, the requirement becomes to craft something new out of what you have been finding out. At issue is finding a mechanism for coping with copious information through actively using it, by publishing and communicating with it.

In this argument, for anybody to possess specifically journalistic knowledge will mean their being disposed and also able to simultaneously craft their own products while assembling and evaluating information for the purpose. A bundle of facts and ideas, if expertly got together, judged expressly in terms of what might be crafted out of them, and used to make a product accessible to its audience, is different from ordinary information, handled ordinarily. Time is a key element. Thinking and crafting in such a way is geared to be done expediently, suitable for the pace of contemporary life; suitable for any purposes that require prompt but precise handling, such as, for the base model, preparing the daily news. There is an obvious creative element in such a distinct process of communication; working with facts as materials for products in all the media. Functioning in this way gives the outlines of a 'knowledge psychology' of journalists; it is cognitive and creative; it is learned but must become habitual; it affects the identity and personality of the possessor. Where citizens will want to make use of opportunities available in the information society, a leading option is to learn to share to some degree the mind of a journalist, as information handler and as producer of artifacts; setting up facts to provide tidings, entertainments and ideas.

Characteristics of journalists' mode of work, and thinking

A point warranting more discussion: the journalist's product is the original in the chain, 'first cab off the rank'. Repurposing, reworking, repositioning of material – for instance being able to make an update on one of the great tsunami, hurricane, earthquake disasters of 2005 – of itself is not enough, because in the end it is only rehashing what already exists. When it comes to making a product, like a feature published on line, the task is to take a step into the unknown. Researching off the web, reworking copy from public sites, lifting and remaking images, are actions that journalists perform, but with that process going on, the creative act of the working journalist is to locate the new advent, to write original paragraphs, prepare original graphics and images; which in turn others might come along and re-use. This has value because of the intrinsic quality of the new element, which is recognisable by all, reads true, and traditionally, 'sells papers'. Being adept at making something out of information got from constant floods of material is the first aspect of journalistic thinking. It is journalists' capacity for routinising what they do, while yet creatively groping for the essence of a story – the lead, the line, the angle, the main point to put up. Tuchman gives a most recognised treatment of the way journalism makes a routine of the processing of new material: 'routinising the unexpected' (1997). Her critique concentrates on the enactment of this on an industrial scale; the information machinery, the news machine, concentrates on low risk, high return operations, which on the down-side can exclude the participation and valid interests of many in society.

In the case being argued now, as befits an emerging new economy with mixed modes of production, we can put a focus on the autonomous work of journalists, within or outside of large industrial settings, and study their routines. These are the standard practices, which are also the characteristics of a journalistic way of thought. For example we have the checklists and tests journalists employ as they do their surveillance, select and prioritise, research, write and review – in a simultaneous thrust. They ask: Is it true? Is it new? Who is it for? Where has this information come from? How did it get to us? Who is responsible for it coming out? Construction of the news product follows its formula; questions begin with the gap stoppers: who, what, how, when, where and why. Other identifiable aspects of journalistic thinking include: establishing facts, in order for those facts to be realised on as the core of every product; immediacy, dispensing with tasks on a short-term basis; keeping a focus almost exclusively on new material; high transparency of operations, certified by the fact that after all, to publish is the central objective; targeted research practices; and a focus on essentials to enable sense-making out of the phenomena of the natural world – the social goal of a journalist's vocation.

The device of objectification is employed – a notion plagued with misunderstanding. Many practitioners proclaim a habit of 'saying what they see', which is to say, to ignore any personal consequences to themselves of saying it, or writing it. Striking an attitude of unengaged observer is the standard device for being able to grasp, live with and reconcile different perspectives, when writing about them. It is a device for handling, to be learned. It is not put forward as a characteristic of the product, as if to make the news report, or other product, definitive and incontestably true; let alone that 'objectivity' should be an actual characteristic of the writer as a person, as if unfeeling, morally neutral, unconnected with the world.

A further habit cultivated by journalists, involving some denial of the self, is disrespect for the imagination gap. It means, being first to confirm a piece of news, to go ahead with publishing it, even if finding it difficult to assimilate in your private mind. A well-archived example was the struggle of Walter Cronkite announcing on CBS the death of President JF Kennedy on 22 November 1963. Journalists were not alone with this on 11 September 2001; millions were able to confront their own imagination gap watching the World Trade Centre begin to collapse, on live television. A classic, well-reported discussion on the theme of reporting against the frame of expectations is provided by Halberstam (1965; 66-77, 185-220, 266-76) and Knightley (2000; 409-440), on the experience of American reporters sent to Vietnam in the early 1960s. The great majority in their private outlook had begun generally supporting the United States government position. They quickly came to see it was tenuous; overcame their own hesitancy and sent back reports to that effect; then encountered very strong resistance, from their home desks refusing to believe the news, and from government sources prepared to exploit that incredulous response in badmouthing the reporters to their employers.

Where objectivity fails to satisfy, transparency becomes the proffered antidote to bias or distortion of news products. News products are by definition ones amenable to inspection; sources are identified as much as possible; open verification is a value for journalists to cultivate. In recent debate, the American Committee of Concerned Journalists has been associated with a study to review issues confronting journalists in regard to bearing witness, evidence and verification. If faith in 'objectivity' had declined as a means of taming distortion from any source, conscious or unconscious, journalists were being encouraged to persist with an evidentiary approach able to take over where objectivity left off, to develop 'a consistent method of testing information, a transparent approach to evidence, precisely so that personal and cultural biases would not undermine the accuracy of their work' (Kovack and Rosenstiel, 2001: 72). A third journalistic habitude, after objectification and transgressing the imagination gap, is being habituated to high accountability. The work is well exposed, by definition published material open to public scrutiny, more than the work of other professions; so journalistic habits of thought provide ways of coming to terms with a critical environment. Writing becomes non-judgmental, or will take an evidentiary approach, or will be highly eclectic in its featuring of views and ideas. Accountability stands to become more organised and thorough with growing inter-activity among news media and audiences.

A final aspect in this treatment of journalistic thought can be called comprehensiveness. Journalism entails knowledge of the processes of discovery and management of facts across a broad range. It will grasp and pass on an understanding of many phenomena. While it will conduct intensive research, e.g. journalists investigating war crimes and advocating trial, it does not have custody of any exclusive body of knowledge external to its own processes and craft skills. There are practitioners prepared to argue that in their professional activity they hold only one opinion strongly, that they should not indulge in strong opinions. Journalists in intellectual life are the knowing spectators and interpreters; they are sense-makers.

Journalism's contribution is that it offers a way to apprehend the world. This is close to the heart of the epistemological argument, the proposition that journalism stands as a certain form of knowledge and way of thinking.

Journalism defining itself, resisting social prescriptions

In this argument, the definition of journalism is drawn from a description of journalists in terms of how they need to think and what they do. It is actually independent of social prescriptions of what they, and news media, should do; what society may be said to expect of them. For example, with the famous 'four theories' (Siebert et al, 1956) and their various adaptations, as in Kovach and Rosenstiel (2001), the notion of 'social responsibility' will be accepted mostly by journalists as a description of their most conscientious work. For an actual guide however, the journalistic process sets its own terms, and in the present era, as indicated in this discussion, the process is influenced by a changing mass communication environment.

A three-point slogan is useful for understanding this concept of journalism defined by its own processes:
1. wetware,
2. software and
3. skills.

As 'wetware', the way of thinking defines the journalist, as knowledgeable and adept at getting knowledge, being engaged in finding what is new and true, from a plethora of sources, and in the process, at all times crafting new products.

In regard to 'software', the functions of journalists are enhanced by new communication technologies, with the clear potential to revolutionise their situation, from the point of view of productivity and professional autonomy.

For 'skills', it requires deployment of intellectual skills and craft abilities at special levels of capability, in order to manage, reduce and process material into new products, at rather high levels of accountability, even though in very tight time frames.

Audiences informed and equipped to participate in journalism

This sketch of a form of knowledge called journalism, and journalists' style of knowing, a habit of inquiry and wide scope of interests, is put forward as being central to the needs of a new economy and new society. In fields of information, members of the public able to avail themselves of journalistic knowledge and the associated skills can do much more work for themselves. If they want to report the news in any particular field, when educated to do it, they will be able to. Such participants – who are delving into the great volume of messages and information made available through the power and impacts of new technology – can be empowered also as discerning buyers of services provided professionally. They may not want to hack away at finding out and crafting new products for themselves, but might want some control over production of their news, at very least some streamlined feed-back mechanisms where their own educated input can count. After all, having an advanced education is a characteristic of members of the Creative Class. Journalistic products may become like others that consumers can make for themselves but would find it more useful to buy in. Do-it-yourself journalism should have much in common today with home brewed beer, dress-making or keeping chickens in the coop; while the quality may be good, it is time consuming to bring off, and easily replaced or supplemented by a product professionally manufactured outside.

Journalism can expect to work to an attuned market, a situation invoked by the new commonality of means of communication. Media professionals in this decade will have access only to the same facilities – hardware and software – as their clients. Only twenty years ago they had prime, often exclusive access to virtually every material means of media production, from extensive use of long-distance telephones, to satellite exchange of materials, multi-channel information feeds, quick access research databases, broadcast quality cameras, editing facilities for images or sound, and publishing platforms with promotional facilities for drawing attention to them. Maybe the new situation will be welcomed as an extension of the conventional insistence of journalists that they require no more, but no less than every citizen's private right to information, such as access to an open court of law. It is a democratic notion which in the information society offers some evident, positive implications for social communication and accountability – at least among those not information poor.

Journalists for a century and a half have been mostly corporate employees of mass circulation outlets moving their products in a one-way flow to consumers, with whom they would seek – with varying success – to have common understanding, not least in order to find stories of greatest public interest, and so make better sense out of their world. The customers in these situations, reading the press or following network news bulletins, can respond only indirectly, as sources, as subjects of market research, as talk-back callers or letter writers, as consumers who will buy or ignore the product. For the most part they are only equipped to receive; do not know about how the product is made; and have few resources for feeding back to the monolith. By contrast, in a new information order journalists stand to have access to publics who are physically able to communicate with them, extensively, commonly operating at close to their own level of media proficiency, able to get information from many other sources, and being well versed in the way that journalism functions.

The capacity for trading in such super-feedback may give a practical expression to ideas about democratising mass media on a large scale, proposals such as that of Renckstorf and McQuail (1996:60) for 'media use as social action'. Renckstorf, considering descriptions of media impacts to be weak, unconvincing and highly speculative, concentrates instead on self-initiative on the part of audiences, foreshadowing a model where media users are seen as handling media messages efficiently, in line with their own interests. 'For the mass media and their messages this means that the media form but a part of the meaning-producing symbolic environment of human actors', and, 'media users are active individuals who interpret media messages' (Renckstorf and McQuail, 1996: 63-64).

It almost goes without saying that markets for journalistic products have become global and diversified. It is no secret to monitors of media trade publications that advertisers and media organisations alike are wondering each year about the characteristics of audiences, far more than before, and ways of reaching them through diverse media options. The question of where to place advertising is unprecedentedly complicated: which media to choose, in what proportion of the spend in relation to other media, for which demographic segments? The diversity and fragmentation of audiences, where 'information workers' or the 'creative classes' are found, together with a proliferation of media vehicles (taking in internet services, digital television, and many others – see Chapter 2), is demanding the use of more advanced technology to keep the ratings and profile the customers (Danaher, 2002: 42). Advertisers want deeper investigations of the availability of alternative outlets to find sectoral or niche markets (Ellen, 2002: 83).

Futures for communication, media and journalism

For media corporations, a little paradoxically, the economic variables tend to demand the creation of rather standardised products for these diversified, globalised markets; with syndication of news, pooling of raw product, network consolidation, reuse of standard formulae for game shows, reality or drama; safeguarded by a vigilant maintenance of corporate intellectual property rights. Yet that is not always the case. Large corporations can see that by encouraging individuality among employees, they may obtain more innovative work, and so be able to produce more diversified and marketable new products – for very discriminating consumers. Niches abound; new markets are available to be made; the world is a big place, and accessible; opportunities are available to diverse players, whether ensconced in corporate settings or operating as independents. Cultural differences from market to market, or within national audiences, are a challenge in providing services for audience members who have much in common but much dividing them, not least different languages. Yet cultural differences also provide opportunities; the 'exotic' is accessible and can be made properly intelligible to large numbers of new participants, with the availability of sophisticated communication media of all kinds. Only a limited deployment of imagination is needed to show how communication across cultures may open the prospect of mobilising a vast array of resources, for example in human organisation and work management, or in product design and style.

Like leading pursuits in international cyber trade at this time – finance, pornography, gaming – the movement of all manner of 'journalistic' fare, being information treated in a journalistic way, has no boundaries. This universality can be attained because of one other determining feature of the journalistic process which is traditional, that being the eternal news principle: all gets tested to see if it qualifies as news. It has to be new, based on a fact, cultivating a quality that can spark the curiosity and interest of several humans at one time.

So it comes back to autonomy and creative inspiration. Journalism seen in this way is the system of thought, it might be said once more, made for the information society, highly adaptable to its demands. The adaptations have begun, in the organisation of major mass media services run by corporations, supplemented by the emergence of new possibilities for sole traders and other smaller operators; and in the continuing adoption and proliferation of new communications technology, an ongoing process where the most-used systems of the coming century, obtainable off the shelf, are just becoming known. With such a movement there are emerging prospects for greater autonomy in forms of work for journalists and others in mass media, among the 'creative classes'. Practitioners can expect to be affiliated more closely with audience members, readers and clients, perhaps less with media corporations as their employers. It has implications for their professional preparation, their modes of work and way of life, and the quality of their products.

References

Collins Concise Dictionary, 3rd edition, 1998. Sydney: Harper and Collins.

Danaher P., with M. Balnaves 2002, 'Beyond Exposure, Interactive Television and the New Media Currency', *Media International Australia-Culture and Policy*, No. 105, November: 40-48.

Ellen J., with L. Ferrier 2002, 'Media Buying and Planning: An Insider's View', *Media International Australia-Culture and Policy*, No. 105, November: 66-76.

Florida, R. 2004. *The Rise of the Creative Class and How It's Transforming Work, Leisure, Community and Everyday Life*. New York: Basic Books.

Florida, R. *The Flight of the Creative Class*. Public lecture, QPAC Brisbane, 24.2.05.

Halberstam, D. 1965. *The Making of a Quagmire*. London: Bodley Head.

Knightley, P. 2000. *The First Casualty, The war Correspondent as Hero and Myth-maker from the Crimea to Kosovo*. London: Prion.

Kovach B. and T. Rosenstiel 2001. *The Elements of Journalism, What Newspeople Should Know and the Public Should Expect*. New York: Three Rivers Press.

Leadbeater, C. 2000. *Living on Thin Air, The New Economy*. London: Penguin.

Leadbeater, C. Australian Broadcasting Corporation (ABC). Interview, Radio National, 10.3.05.

Leadbeater, C. *Open Innovation and the Creative Industries*. Address, Queensland University of Technology, Brisbane, 2.3.04.

Reich, R.B. 1992. *The Work of Nations, Preparing Ourselves for 21st Century Capitalism*. New York: Vintage Books.

Renckstorf K., D. McQuail and N. Jakowski 1996. 'Media Use as Social Action, a European Approach to Audience Studies', *Academia Research Monograph* 15. London: John Libby.

Siebert F.S., T. Peterson and W. Schramm 1956. *Four Theories of the Press: The Authoritarian, Libertarian, Social Responsibility and Soviet Communist*. Urbana, Ill.: Univ. of Illinois Press.

Tuchman, G. 1974. *The TV Establishment, Programming for Power and Profit*. Englewood Cliffs NJ: Prentice Hall.

Tuchman, G. 1997. 'Making News by Doing Work, Routinising the Unexpected', *Social Meanings of News*, a Text-reader, ed. D. Berkowitz. Thousand Oaks, Calif.: Sage.

Chapter 2

The mirror-ball effect: investigating channels, messages and participation levels

John Cokley PhD

Journalists have always used equipment which has been generally available in the communities in which they worked. This has been a result both of economy and necessity, since they found they had to connect with their audiences using means that were available to the audience, not just to the sender. Newspapers sold on street corners in the very early media days; SMS and email have become the rule for the early 21st century. This development also admits the possibility of the roles of the communication professional and the community merging during the 'public journalism' process, and has become most recently evident in the areas around the Bay of Bengal, struck by the tsunami on December 26, 2004, especially in the Indonesian province of Banda Aceh, and in the Andaman and Nicobar Islands, where tiny portable radios, featuring solar panels and hand-cranked dynamos, have suddenly become part of a vital news media channel. In this article participant-observation and personal interview techniques are used to record and compare many of the digital channels used by news and information senders up to 2005. It also investigates the level of genuine participation which these new technologies have brought to the communications process.

Introduction

The chapter documents an audit of new 'general-purpose technologies' (GPTs, Forman et al, 2003:113) conducted from 2001-2005. The audit covered GPTs which have been applied to the task of transmitting journalistic messages since the late 1970s, the period when newspapers began to change their production processes from 15th-century Gutenberg methods (Man 2002:1) and to digital computing methods of production and delivery. Journalists have always used equipment which has been generally available in the communities in which they worked. They have instinctively understood that they have had to use technologies available and amenable to their audiences in order to make an effective connection with members of those audiences. Newspapers sold on street corners in the very early days; SMS, news feeds and email (and many others) are used in the 21st century. This is the physical embodiment of the traditionally close link between journalists, their audiences and the technologies which bring them together; the same link noted by Romano (2001:44):

> ... *Journalists attempt to reflect the diversity of community opinions about ... issues and questions in a way that allows community members to assess and appreciate the respective merits and weaknesses of each.*

If 'reflecting the issues in a way that allows community members to assess and appreciate' them means getting on the mobile, or texting someone or even displaying news on a roadside billboard or a computer touch screen, then the modern journalist needs to have those skills. Northrup (2003) notes that the average consumer in the United States in 2002 spent 3,599 hours using all forms of media, an increase of 1.8 percent from the previous year: 'That works out to about 9.9 hours per day reading, listening, watching and surfing for any combination of professional and personal purposes'. Northrup said this figure was expected to increase 1.5 percent annually, to at least 10.6 hours per day in 2007, but instead of reflecting a 'mass-media' audience watching just a few channels, this reflected an 'aggregate audience media model' (Northrup 2003):

> *Forward-thinking news organisations are responding to this growth opportunity with strategies that invariably involve combining content formats and delivery channels to tap into the new aggregate audiences and to better mirror the way contemporary news consumers integrate print, video, online and mobile to satisfy their need to be informed.*

But the application of these *in situ* technologies also must recognise Shannon's 'Information Theory', as explained by Schramm (1966) and more recently by Benkler (2003), so that the mere presence of the technology with both senders and receivers is insufficient for truly effective communication; both ends of the communications process must know how to use the technology effectively, and the signal itself must travel through the connections well and arrive clearly enough to be understood. If understanding does not take place – and allow a meaningful response – then the information process will take on the nature of a disco 'mirror ball', a meaningless parade of flashing lights intended to illuminate a community but which succeeds only in showing itself off. Measurement of this understanding and the capacity for response among receivers constitutes measurement of the level of genuine *participation* – 'the process by which all stakeholders ... negotiate power and openly reach collaborative decisions' (Griffin 2003, n.p.) – which new technologies and their diffusion through communities (Rogers 1995) have brought to the news communication process. The processes and technologies documented here are introduced to highlight the presence or the lack of – but in any case the importance of – these central features of the communications process. A limitation in this audit is acknowledged, in that it captures a snapshot of a particular geographical communications environment, Australia, along with some of the global computer mediated environment of the World Wide Web.

Theoretical background

In the 17th and 18th centuries, public sphere activity took place in the coffee houses, salons, clubs, English magazines such as *The Spectator* and *The Tatler*, reading societies and lending libraries (Poole 1989:14). This activity in the public sphere, defined in Habermasien terms as 'a discursive, institutional, topographical space, where people in their roles as citizens have access to what can be metaphorically called societal dialogues, which deal with questions of common concern' (Dahlgren 2002:196) should logically have been enhanced by the emergence of relatively inexpensive communications technologies using the Internet. This progression had been true in the past, as verified by Kielbowicz (1989:180) who reported that postal subsidies for political journals had a direct and positive effect on the growth and influence of the newspaper industry in the United States during the 18th-19th centuries. The impact of price as a positive communications driver was further demonstrated when those same postal subsidies for political journals were extended to the popular press, magazines and eventually books (Kielbowicz 1989:180). This is supported by economist Eckert (2002) who demonstrates that price decreases result from battles over market share. That price is an important driver of demand even across commodities and services has also been demonstrated by Voxi and Amavilah (1995). These sources indicate that competition for market share in the technological communications sector drives down prices of technology items such as Internet-equipped computers, PDAs and mobile phones, and consequently drives up innovation-adoption rates and future hardware sales. In practice, this is observed in the continual fall of computer, Internet and communications hardware prices since the advent of television in the 1950s in Australia. It is also demonstrated in the observed market response to practically all subsequent electrical and digital hardware, in which computers, game consoles, and mobile phones, PDAs, DVD and media players launch on to the market as expensive then quickly reduce in price and remain relatively inexpensive. As Voxi and Amavilah's research suggests, a controlling factor on these prices would be the final connection and communications cost to the user. In the Australian market up to 2004, falling connection costs epitomised by the 2004 ADSL price war between Telstra and its wholesale Internet customer-competitors demonstrated the theory accurately by driving prices down and adoption upwards.

So now, instead of just coffee houses, salons, clubs, journals, newspapers and books, there are home Internet terminals, Internet cafes, chat rooms, discussion forums and email lists on the Internet, as well as a widening range of diversified digital production and delivery channels such as mobile phone, chat, and picture and audio-file swapping. The potential power of such modern public sphere activity can be judged quickly by a simple comparison. The number of coffee houses in 18th century London was between 2000 and 3000 establishments (Poole 1989:14), to serve a population of 600,000 (Old Bailey Online 2004), a ratio of one coffee house for every 200-300 individuals. In 2002, the number of individual Internet users, and thus possible chats, personal email transactions and discussions in larger forums, was 605 million worldwide (NUA 2004), in a world population of about 6,000 million (Population Reference Bureau, 2004). This suggests a ratio of one possible Internet connection for every 10 individuals, 20-30 times greater than the coffee-house coverage in 18th century London.

The scale of potential participation is magnified when the variety of opportunities for individuals to communicate and respond online is considered. As well as home connections, Internet users can visit Internet cafes in their home towns or while travelling. At just one EasyInternetCafé at Times Square in New York in 2002, Internet users could choose between 800 computer terminals, all rigged for chat use around the clock (Eng 2002). In the city of Shanghai, with a population of 170 million residents, there were 1,325 Internet cafés (BBC World News 2004). In Australia, the CyberCafé website (2004) listed 144 Internet cafés around Australia, with the greatest number, 40, in Queensland, followed by New South Wales (39) and Victoria (31). My observations put the number of available Internet terminals in such cafés at from 8-50 in each place, charging $2-$7 per hour for use. The audit documented here was conducted to investigate how much and how effectively new technologies have been applied in Australia and on the World Wide Web to the process of communicating the specific product called 'news'.

The audit

In order to track and document some of the latest digital technologies available and appropriate to journalistic use, the international newspaper research association Ifra conducts the 'Advanced Journalist Technology Project' (Ifra 2004). The 2004 edition of the project report lists 15 appliances which it says 'assembles a complete package of cross-media capabilities into a custom technical backpack that today's multi-skilled journalist could carry into any news coverage situation' (Ifra 2004). Those 15 appliances were: a Toshiba Portégé M200 Tablet PC; an Apple *iSight* video-conference camera; a Sony DCR PC330 digital camera; Serious Magic Visual Communicator Pro; Archos AV320 video recorder; Nokia 6600 imaging mobile phone; Emergecore IT-100 network hub; D-Link DCS-1000W wireless webcam; DaKine Pod 1 urban backpack; Canon BJC-55 portable printer; Visioneer Strobe XP100 scanner; SmartDisk FireWire CardBus PC card; Logitech 'Bluetooth' mouse; Zip-Linq retracting cables; and a Logitech QuickCam for Notebooks Pro (Ifra 2004). The total retail budget needed to acquire and set-up the NewsGear 2004 backpack (including the backpack itself) was $US9,030, equivalent in February 2004 to $A11,314. The present audit explores, outlines and explains some of the vast range of other digital news and information delivery channels which have already been adopted (or at least, announced) by media organisations or individuals. It should be noted that since modern developed societies, and many which still sit in the 'developing' list of world economies, have become enmeshed in digital technologies, it is for this reason that the observations included here follow only a general, speculative order, not any order of importance, theoretical or otherwise. Also, as the diffusion of news technology is taking place so quickly, this audit does not claim to be definitive; merely a snapshot in time and place.

2.1. Media players (Windows, QuickTime and RealPlayer) and associated digital applications for program production

Media players are software applications which allow users of computers and other general-purpose technologies to listen to audio, or view and listen to audiovisual news and entertainment content, both online and offline. Listening and viewing is the most appealing of the World Wide Web experiences, and the most common versions of media players are supplied by Microsoft ('Windows Media Player'), Apple ('QuickTime') and Real Networks ('RealOne Media Player'). Delegates to the 2003 International Consumer Electronics Show in Las Vegas, the United States, were told that 'more than 40 new devices supporting Windows Media are being unveiled by leading consumer electronics manufacturers' (Microsoft 2003). In a press statement Microsoft officials said the 'total number of devices that support Windows Media (is now) more than 200 ... (including) DVD players, CD players, car stereos and portable audio devices' (2003). Portable audio devices called *DiscMan* retailed in Australia in December 2003 for $179, with the sought-after ability to play compressed MP3 files downloaded from the Internet. I frequently listen online to classical music and news broadcasts from the Australian ABC as well as the BBC. A feature of both players which is not shared by other domestic general-purpose software is the 'visualiser' or 'audio analyser' which allows users to choose from a range of colourful patterns which display in synchronisation with the audio. While serving no audio function whatever, this feature displays the entertainment function which is common among many general-purpose technologies. (During experiments I have conducted on a new Apple Macintosh notebook computer, however, the 'visualiser' function has not been available.)

Media players also let computer users (including those with mobile phones and PDAs) watch and listen to audiovisual presentations such as games and news bulletins, by decoding and displaying special file types such as RealMedia (*.ram* extension) or SMIL (synchronised multimedia integration language, with the *.smil* extension). By 2004, games had become an integral part of publishing and marketing of entertainment as well as news and informational content. The movie *Van Helsing* was released theatrically in May 2004, at the same time as game versions were released for the PlayStation 2, XBox and GameBoy Advance game platforms. Marketing took place using an interactive website www.vanhelsing.net which demonstrated all the features by launching media player software.

The Australian Broadcasting Corporation's online news bulletin for Monday May 10, 2004, provided an example of how an Internet user would view a news bulletin using RealOne media player.

Artists and journalist-producers are able to capture audio and video for these presentations using digital video recorders and mini-disk audio recorders, then edit and combine them with other material using digital tools such as *Flash, Director,* and *Fireworks* distributed by the Macromedia Corporation (2004), or Adobe *Premier* and Avid *ProTools.* Still pictures and graphics including text can be incorporated after editing in products such as Adobe's *Photoshop* and *Illustrator* (Adobe 2004).

Once complete as multimedia productions, these journalistic artifacts can be incorporated into hypertext mark-up language (HTML) using HTML editors such as Microsoft *FrontPage* and Macromedia *DreamWeaver* before being uploaded to websites using file-transfer protocol (FTP) software. This allows the development of what is now known as 'rich-media' websites (see 2.15, *below*) as well as news and informational content for automatic teller machines and computer kiosk displays (see 2.16, *below*).

Apple *QuickTime* has been expanded with a plug-in known as VR (Virtual Reality) which has been applied by (among others) the Australian Antarctic Division (AAD). The Division's website www.aad.gov.au/default.asp?casid=1966 (2004) allows Internet users to display panoramic pictures of scenes at Australian bases on the south polar icecap, taken and produced by photographer and artist, Wayne Papps (who died while filming in 2003).

This application of digital photography and media player technology shows the way for journalistic photographers who could display murder scenes, courtroom scenes and crowd scenes online using these techniques (Fig 2.1 *below*).

1. → → → → → → → → 2. → → → → → → → → 3.

Figure 2.1 Stills from a QuickTime VR show displayed on the Australian Antarctic Division's website, May 2004. Produced by Wayne Papps, the panorama allows computer users to see a 360° view of the Mawson base in one sweep, controlled by the user's mouse and cursor. Users can also zoom in and out. Panorama by Wayne Papps, Australian Antarctic Division Multimedia, © Commonwealth of Australia 1999 (used with permission).

Notwithstanding all the advantages which digital computing brings to a publisher's ability to manipulate editorial, illustrations and advertisements quickly and relatively easily into website packages, the technology has not changed one problem which print journalists have been aware of for decades: the possibility of unfortunate juxtapositioning of a breaking story with advertising on the same topic. The May 31 edition of the *Sydney Morning Herald* website www.SMH.com.au provided a timely example of this problem, when a report of an Australian citizen being killed in a hostage crisis in Saudi Arabia appear below an animated advertisement for the Bahrain-based company Gulf Air (May 31, 2004).

2.2. PDF publications

'PDF' refers to a kind of computer file marketed by the Adobe Corporation which mimics characters and fonts available in most commercial word-processing applications but which stores them in a 'read-only' format, barring ordinary readers without the more sophisticated programs such as Adobe Acrobat from making any editorial changes. As the Adobe corporate website (2004) explains:

> *Portable Document Format (PDF) is the defacto standard for the secure and reliable distribution and exchange of electronic documents and forms around the world, with a ten-year track record. PDF is a universal file format that preserves the fonts, images, graphics, and layout of any source document, regardless of the application and platform used to create it. Part of the success of the PDF format has been due to the successful diffusion tactics which Adobe adopted since the mid-1990s.*

Adobe PDF files are compact and complete, and can be shared, viewed, and printed by anyone with free Adobe Reader software. To date, more than 500 million copies of the software have been distributed (Adobe 2004).

The chief tactic which the corporation adopted was to distribute PDF as what's called 'an open file-format specification', which allows 'anyone who wants to (to) develop tools to create, view, or manipulate PDF documents'. More than 1,800 vendors now offer PDF-based solutions (Adobe 2004).

One of those 1800 vendors is a news service called TEAM*talk*, operating in England, which has used Adobe PDF format to transmit regular bulletins to subscribers around the world, including to ships at sea and to Australian researchers in Antarctica. More fully known as

TEAM*talk* Satellite the company is based in Liverpool, England, with a subsidiary office in Fort Lauderdale, Florida (Henney 2002).

TEAM*talk* Satellite is part of the TEAM*talk* Media Group, also based in Liverpool but with offices in Charlotte, Chicago, Glasgow, Fort Lauderdale, Leeds, London, Munich and Stockholm (TEAM*talk* 2002*)*. TEAM*talk* Media Group was taken over in July 2002 by UKBetting Plc and now promotes TEAM*talk* as one of the brands with which it intends to drive revenue, which, for the six months to June 30, 2002, was reported at £17.5 million (then $A49.5 million). The company was formed as 'IMC' in Liverpool in 1985 by Bernie Thomas and Tim Whalley. Both men were ex-seafarers and had been Maritime Studies lecturers at Liverpool Polytechnic (Henney 2002) and conducted government-funded research on use of communications systems and computers by ship crews. This resulted in the development of a ship-to-shore messaging system and, later, a news service for cruise companies including P&O Cruises and Cunard, using material sourced from Associated Press, the Press Association, Agence France-Presse and Australian Associated Press. Stories are selected by editors who then impose computer coding on them to form collected bulletins in the various languages offered in the service. The TEAM*talk* subscriber list for 2002 included 55 news products daily, in 10 languages. They claimed approximately 85 percent of the world's cruise line companies as clients and also sent news to crew on cargo ships, to some remote hotels and to safari camps in Africa, as well as to the Australian Antarctic stations Mawson, Davis, Casey and Macquarie Island (Henney 2002).

An Australian equivalent editorial service, albeit serving a different market, is the *GoAuto e-news*, developed and distributed by publisher John Mellor in Melbourne. Mellor's background (Mellor 2004, personal communication) includes 37 years as a publisher and writer. Having founded the *Automotive Business* section in *The Australian* newspaper in 1990 and producing and editorially directing it until 1998, his motoring team was then appointed to produce the automotive content for the Yellow Pages web site: 'GoAuto Online was launched three years later'. He notes (2004, personal communication) that *GoAuto e-news* had grown to circulate to about 22,000 subscribers: 'Our syndicated online service provides content to 13 web sites and delivers between 130,000 to 160,000 stories and car reviews a month to readers'.

Mellor said (2003, personal communication) that Adobe PDF technologies had allowed him to transfer the biggest costs to his customers and by doing so, reduce his own production costs and stay in business: 'The main change (in our business) has been that the customer now pays for the ink and the paper'. The use of digital technologies such as network channels, PDF and HTML technology to develop websites, allowed Mellor to control variable business costs such as ink, paper, transport and delivery, as well as some of his fixed costs, such as office infrastructure and wages. They also allow him to embed hypertext mark-up links within those PDF documents so that when Internet users receive and view the Mellor publications online, they can click on advertisements and visit marketing and other corporate websites seamlessly. This illustrates Brill's proposition (1999:159), that 'the integration of editorial matter – "news" – and advertising has long been an accepted practice in the United States and much of the democratic world'. Finally, journalists (including Mellor) are able to work from distributed locations such as home offices and at times which suit them and the business, rather than turn up for regular office hours. Mellor (2004) had 12 journalists and artists on staff; by the end of 2004, only three of these would work from the central office.

Also in Australia on a larger scale, newspaper publishers were able to centralise the production of national tabloid and other-sized magazines in Sydney and Melbourne and distribute them around the country as PDF files using FTP software. Previously teams of reporters and editors had been employed to produce similar versions of these magazines in each capital city.

Worldwide, the NewsStand Inc organisation (2004) has adapted the PDF format to enable it to distribute and sell online more than 50 newspapers, magazines and newsletters, ranging in size and reach from the US daily *The New York Times* to the Townsville monthly *Fish and Boat*. The special 'NewsStand Reader' – a variation on the Acrobat Reader used to decode standard PDF documents – allows a subscriber to save and read editions online for up to a year after publication. It also incorporates a useful new feature which allows readers to operate a 'pen tool' and complete crossword puzzles in the same way a traditional newspaper reader would do so. Readers of *The New York Times'* NewsStand Edition can thus directly compare this method of completing their favourite crossword with the Java-script and Cookies method described below (see 2.11 and 2.12, *below*).

2.3. Telephony, radio and television

Residents of Australia have been going through a complicated and potentially confusing process of shifting from analogue to digital systems for control of its mobile telephony, and radio and television broadcasting. Between 1987 and 1993 the only mobile phones available in Australia operated on the so-called Advanced Mobile Phone System (AMPS) in the 825-890 megahertz range (Australian Academy of Science n.d.). In 1993 the 'Global System for Mobile Telecommunications' (GSM) digital system was introduced to run alongside AMPS. Then in 2000, AMPS was withdrawn, leaving only GSM and another new digital system, Code Division Multiple Access (CDMA) which runs in the same frequency range as AMPS. At that time, AMPS users were compelled either to migrate to GSM or CDMA or go without mobile telephony.

Users of the Australian domestic television signal, which began analogue transmissions in 1956, face similar changes and challenges. These analogue transmissions continued unchanged until the late 1960s when the Phase Alternating Line (PAL) system of analogue transmissions was introduced, a system not compatible with the United States' National Television Standards Committee (NTSC) system. In 2001, Australian television stations began broadcasting binary (digital) television signals concurrently with existing analogue (waveform) signals. This procedure has been set down to change again in 2008, at which time analogue signals are due to cease and digital only will become the standard (Ritter 2000). On March 14, 2004, pay-TV operator Foxtel (a joint subsidiary of the US-based News Corporation and the Australian telco Telstra) launched its own version of digital television in Australia for its subscribers. The system offered 44 video channels (16 of them new to the Foxtel network) in the 16:9 wide-screen format, including 12 channels featuring enhanced sound quality employing the Dolby Digital 5.1 surround system, and 30 digital audio channels (Walsh 2004:5-6). Industrial disputes among Foxtel installers acted as an immediate, if temporary, impediment to the diffusion of this innovation.

2.4. Radio

The transmission technology of news on free-to-air radio changed little between the earliest days (Miller 2002) and the late 1930s, when Frequency Modulation (FM) broadcasters joined Amplitude Modulation (AM) radio. Australia caught up with FM in the mid-1970s. Short-wave radio, with its higher frequency, allows a longer range and has persisted throughout the history of radio news broadcasting but with relatively small audiences. The latest moves by the Australian Government until 2004 included running a series of operational tests on the new delivery channels available, including Eureka 147, IBOC, Digital Radio Mondiale and digital satellite and hybrid satellite/terrestrial services (Australian Broadcasting Authority 2004a). These tests were being conducted during 2004 on VHF channel 9A in Sydney and Melbourne for up to 18 months (Australian Broadcasting Authority 2004a).

I have observed that VHF (very-high frequency) and UHF (ultra-high frequency) radios have another quite different interpretation in rural areas of Australia. Most pastoral property homes in the outback contain as standard equipment a VHF and a UHF radio transceiver, as well as television, telephones, AM/FM radio and fax machines (not to mention

Internet connections in some areas). UHF is used for communications between vehicles in localised conversations and for communication between families on properties or in vehicles, while VHF is used for more distant or formalised communications or across a wider network, such as for fire fighters and emergency workers including police, as Cripps (2004) explains:

VHF was used for bushfires once – you can speak to people zillions of miles away and thru (sic) smoke. Its downfall was that Rural Fires Boards controlled its use and there was just one channel so it wasn't much good for other communication: messages from the shearing shed, requests for smoko brought out to the lamb markers, etc. Not everyone wanted to hear everyone else's business. So property and townspeople started using UHF, which has 40 channels and that's still not enough. It has a 'line-of-sight' range so repeater stations are needed if you want to contact someone on the other side of the shire. Some shire councils have installed repeaters in strategic locations for this purpose. We have a base set in the house, two mobiles mounted in each vehicle and two handheld sets for (husband) Bill mustering on a bike, and whomever he might employ.

Yet another radio band has also been used for information delivery in the Australian Outback – HF (high frequency) radio – used to deliver education as part of the 'School of the Air'. This was phased out in 2004 in favour of telephone and online delivery of classes (Cripps 2004).

Scientists at the Research School of Physical Sciences and Engineering and the Faculty of Engineering and Information Science of the Australian National University report that they are developing a new wireless technology to exploit the above VHF capacity in rural Australia: the Bush Local Area Network, known as 'BushLAN' (Conboy 2002). As the scientists explain (Australian National University 2004): 'BushLAN allows a one-hop route to connect remote users … There would be no large-scale infrastructure (since) VHF TV does not need expensive repeaters or satellites!'

Radio took on a crucial developmental communications role in the countries around the Bay of Bengal after the December 26, 2004, tsunami disaster. Hogan (2005) reports that aid agencies made extensive use of small, inexpensive hand-cranked dynamo radio receivers, with solar collecting capacity as well, in the Indonesian province of Banda Aceh, and in the Andaman and Nicobar Islands, to revive community media networks during the disaster recovery period.

2.5. Free-to-air, satellite, cable and digital television

Transmission of news, current affairs, entertainment and advertising by television arrived in southern Australia (Sydney and Melbourne) in 1956 and extended north to Brisbane in 1959. For the next 17 years, Australians saw their news and television entertainment in shades of grey on a monotone signal. But when change came, it came with a rush: black-and-white pictures acquired colour using cumulative patterns of coloured pixels of varying intensity (in 1976 in Australia but earlier overseas); the previously single-channel sound signal developed to allow stereophonic reception; and in 2001 the largest Australian transmitters moved to dual-signal, carrying analogue as well as the new digital, 'wide-screen' signal. Current Australian legislation dictates that the analogue signal will be discontinued in 2008 in favour of digital signals but industry sources maintain that the dual signal could continue for several years beyond that deadline (Ritter 2000; Nash 2002). Other 'television' opportunities for news delivery include Direct-to-car TV (telematics) and Web TV, neither of which had diffused to Australia at time of writing. Television signals also contain the capacity to deliver teletext and closed captions.

2.6. Teletext and closed captioning

In the early 1970s a new kind of delivery channel opened up on television screens around the world: teletext (Cook & Brown 2004). It was delivered as lines of crudely designed text scrolling from bottom to top of the receiver's television screen, and controlled by what was known as a 'decoder'. The customer's experience – indeed the sales pitch – was of information being sent 'in a hitherto unused part of the television signal' (Cook & Brown 2004). It was the first time Australians had been offered the chance to buy extra content on their free-to-air televisions. This occurred around the same time as the Whitlam Labor Government abolished the practice of television and radio owners having to pay a licence fee to the government (Caslon Analytics 2004) and offers one reason why the networks offering teletext in Australia saw a commercial opportunity to take up that revenue stream. The experience of most people, however, was that teletext was every bit as 'popular and successful' as the Beta videotape format and 8-track cartridges for home music (i.e. so *un*popular they became commercially unviable media systems). There has been a revival of teletext in the digital TV environment both in Australia and Great Britain (Cook & Brown 2004) and I observed advertisements for teletext services begin to air again in Australia during 2003. Robson writes: Closed captions 'present the dialogue and sound effects of television programs and pre-recorded movies as text on a television screen' (2004). Elsewhere he continues 'closed captions are captions that are hidden in the video signal, invisible without a special decoder' and 'open captions are captions that have been decoded, so they have become an integral part of the television picture, like subtitles in a movie. In other words, open captions cannot be turned off.' (Robson 2001). Both open and closed captions are used on many television transmissions including news but open captions are used exclusively on the Qantas in-flight news and entertainment video service 'On Q' (see below).

2.7. News tickers on billboards and websites

Outdoor advertising retains one of its major assets over other advertising media by being available to thousands of viewers per hour on national and local road networks, or on buildings in high-traffic locations. In Brisbane, a large billboard, inbound near the corner of Ann Street and Commercial Road, Newstead, had been hired by the Nine Network to publicise its nightly television news service. As a value-adding component, a light-emitting diode (LED) electronic strip at the bottom of the billboard displayed current Channel 9 news headlines for the passing traffic. Another of these ticker-boards had been installed outbound from Brisbane on the Warrego Highway near Gailes, in the city of Ipswich.

Further innovative possibilities are being explored by outdoor media companies, such as the French company JCDecaux (2004a), now with offices in England and Australia. JCDecaux, which claims to have built the first bus shelter sponsored by advertising (JCDecaux 2004b), has placed moving and illuminated advertisements on bus shelters in Sydney as part of its launch into Australia. Its website, however, reveals far more adventurous projects in Europe and the UK, including bus shelter panels which viewers can touch to activate media-player software to listen to popular music, advertising spiels or telephone ring-tones (for the mobile phone client Nokia) and in some cases view short movie clips (including *Star Wars*), also using media-player technology (JCDecaux 2004b). Other players in the outdoor advertising market – and by extension, the outdoor news and information delivery market – include Australian Provincial Newspapers' Digital Division in Australia, and a group of students at the University of Western Sydney, who supplied short movies in 2003 to the New South Wales CityRail network at the Wynyard railway subway station in Sydney. These movies were projected from above the platform on to the subway wall when trains were not in the station.

2.8. Fax

During a study of how Australian researchers in the Antarctic received their news services in 2002 (Cokley 2003), survey data showed a strong first preference for the relatively old-fashioned method of having 'printed newspapers copied and sent or distributed to you' (mostly by fax). Of the 80 researchers surveyed, 16 said they mostly received news 'relayed by fax or letter'. Fax is the exact kind of equipment often found at scientific research stations, as well as at remote pastoral properties. Information in written, diagrammatic or pictorial forms can be transmitted easily and this suits the newspaper format precisely. Before the introduction of the large digital network, and indeed before news pages were distributed using PDF technology, the preferred method for distributing broadsheet or tabloid news pages around large continental distribution regions (used by *The Australian* newspaper between Sydney and the other capital cities) was the 'press-fax' system which I observed in operation regularly during production work for News Ltd publications.

Information can also be retrieved from distant databases using the fax procedure known as 'polling', in which the intended receiver dials a number on his or her fax and a fax is sent back from the remote database and call and fax costs are debited to the initiator's account. The Australian Bureau of Meteorology (2004) gives detailed instructions about how to use this aspect of its service. Cooking and gardening television shows often distribute recipe and planting information using poll fax services. Before such electronic services were available, I often included this kind of reader adjunct-news information in newspapers and magazines on which I worked as a journalist.

2.9. Corporate radio and television:
2.9.1: 'On Q' (Qantas)

Qantas aircraft have been showing a video-based service and a tape-based radio presentation called 'On Q' on its aircraft since 2001. I have observed the video presentations on long flights between far north Queensland and Hobart, Tasmania but they go all over the world. I recall a similar service on Ansett Airlines but that stopped when the airline collapsed in 2001. 'On Q' includes news bulletins prepared by TCN9 (the Nine television network) and television entertainment programs from various other distributors' networks (including *The Nanny* and *Everybody Loves Raymond* from the Ten Network). The executive producer of Qantas in-flight entertainment, Mr Michael Freedman, said that the service was produced in two parts: (1) news and (2) non-news material (2004). The news segments were produced at TCN9 Sydney by 'reversioning' daily news bulletins emanating from Channel 9 in Sydney. Three bulletins were supplied daily at 5am, 12.30pm and 2pm. The 5am and the 2pm bulletins were packaged for the Qantas domestic fleet and the 12.30pm bulletin was packaged for the international fleet. Mr Freedman said the two domestic bulletins ran in 40-minute packages with 20 minutes of news at 5am and 10 minutes of news at 2pm (2004). The international bulletins ran in 30-minute packages with 25 minutes of news. The non-news Qantas and 'On Q' material packaged with the news was delivered to TCN9 at the start of each week for inclusion in the pre-mastered packages. Delivery of the packages from TCN9 to Qantas took place by real-time video feed, either by fibreoptic cable or by satellite uplink from the Nine Network studios in Sydney. Qantas staff at each of nine Qantas ports (Brisbane, Sydney, Canberra, Melbourne, Adelaide, Perth, Cairns, Gold Coast and Townsville) used a satellite-dish downlink facility on the terminal roof to retrieve program content and record it directly to video cassette. Mr Freedman noted (2004) that Darwin was omitted because the airport was considered a defensive zone and as such a satellite footprint has not been permitted by the military. 'It saves time if staff members retrieve the satellite feed by playing it direct to the video cassette,' Mr Freedman said (2004). Other non-news programming outside the bulletin slots was produced and mastered at Qantas facilities in Sydney and delivered to airports weekly and staff at terminals placed this onboard aircraft over weekends. Sometimes things go wrong, as happened on one flight on December 3, 2003, when I observed 'On Q' host (and Channel 9 presenter) Deborah Hutton urge viewers to enter a competition for seats to the Rugby World Cup final, which had been held on November 22, more than a week previously. 'On Q' also includes open captions on the news programs.

Audio-only content is supplied by 'On Q radio', delivered to passengers by head-sets, and carrying 'news content' other than the Nine Network bulletins. Mr Freedman said the radio content was produced in Sydney and shipped on cassette tapes monthly and played in a two-hour loop (2004). The cassette tape format was being phased out during 2004 in favour of compact-disk storage and delivery. On December 3, 2003, an onboard radio segment called *The Qantas comfort zone* displayed the system's potential to deliver health news. A segment was aired featuring a Sydney physiotherapist Anna-Louise Bouvier instructing passengers in some simple exercises designed to reduce discomfort on long-distance flights. Anna-Louise Bouvier had recently published spoken-word tapes through the network of ABC Shops (ABC 2004). Health news and information is now routinely presented on Qantas flights, especially focusing on the dangers of deep-vein thrombosis. As one means of evaluating the quality and effectiveness of the programming, 'On Q' won the World Airline Entertainment Association's 'Avion Award' for best in-flight entertainment in 2002 (from 41 entrants) and again in 2003 (from 43 entrants). The award announcement said prizes were 'determined by a 22-member international media panel that evaluated in-flight audio, video and print entries from 43 leading passenger airlines worldwide' (WAEA 2003). Mr Freedman compared the 'On Q' service with another terrestrial video/radio service he said was operating on New South Wales government buses, in which 'little television monitors drop from the ceiling of each bus and passengers can view and listen to programming during their trips' (2004). 'Everything is easy on the ground,' he said. 'It's the movement of the content into the air that makes things hard.' (2004)

2.9.2: 'Channel C' (Commonwealth Bank)

The Commonwealth Bank has been presenting video programs inside its branch offices since 2003. I observe that these programs include no entertainment content or news content outside the bank's sphere of operations, but are restricted to promotional and advertising segments designed to sell the bank's financial products and services. However they are presented in a quasi-news, documentary style, clearly using journalistic and filmmaking techniques to increase customer interest. The merchandising manager in the Commonwealth Bank's Marketing & Information Services section, Lisa Whelan, said 'Channel C is simply a VHS tape played through a VCR and TV monitor. Channel C is used to both inform and entertain our customers whilst they are in a queue. Originally it was more corporate in style and more recently has changed to the more "lifestyle" feel. We aim to give our customers information and tips on financial management. We also use Channel C to demonstrate the bank's sponsorships within the community.' (2004)

2.9.3: Kmart radio; SuperCheap Auto Radio, SkyBus video

In December 2003 I observed that both Kmart (a part of the Coles Myer Ltd retail chain) and SuperCheap Auto retail chains had begun broadcasting what each called 'radio' within stores. Branded 'Kmart Radio' and 'SuperCheap Auto Radio' the programs carried music, news and promotional-sales segments. In the time I devoted to making these observations I was unable to detect any news network affiliation for the journalistic content: news was read by the same presenters who played the music and read the advertisements.

It wasn't until much later (Roberts 2006, personal communication) that I learned that this content was produced and supplied by a Brisbane company called Australasian Retail Radio Network Pty Ltd, based in the outer northern suburb of Aspley. General manager Noel Roberts said the company began providing live in-store radio in Australia in November 2002, first to SuperCheap Auto, then Kmart at the end of 2003 (when I first observed the phenomenon) and later to 1st Choice Liquor stores (another Coles Myer chain) early in 2005. 'We are launching 3 new networks in Australia in March this year (2006),' he said. All services were broadcast 'live' via Optus satellites to every Kmart, SuperCheap

Auto and 1st Choice outlet in Australia and the company provided a pre-recorded service to SuperCheap Auto and Kmart in New Zealand.

A five-minute 'live' news service is broadcast to each of the above networks every hour, using content purchased from the Australian Associated Press radio service: 'most stories are broadcast "as is" without any local editorial input' (Roberts 2006). A dedicated news reader was employed for the Monday to Friday services but on weekends the bulletins were read by the duty announcer. Time calls were not included in any of the bulletins:

> *The reason we don't mention the time is because of the time differences across Australia. The service is not delayed for those states on DST (daylight savings time) or for Western Australia, so we completely avoid mentioning the time (even references to morning and afternoon can be difficult). Brief capital city weather details are provided at the end of each news bulletin.* (Roberts 2006)

Roberts said his company provided all the content for each program, sourcing and auditioning every music track to ensure each met quality and content criteria for what he called the 'retail environment (no swearing or offensive lyrics)'. A similar filtering process ensured that 'every track we play is appropriate to the particular demographics of the typical customer in our clients' stores':

> *For example, there are many tracks that we play on SCA radio that are unsuitable for Kmart Radio because of the different customer profile.* (Roberts 2006)

> *Live, in-store radio is relatively new in Australia (although it's been around overseas for many years) and to our knowledge, we're the only ones providing this service in Australia. ARRN is staffed mainly by ex-commercial radio staff and we run our services as professionally as we can. Surveys of Kmart staff and customers have overwhelmingly endorsed the concept and content – so we figure we must be doing something right.* (Roberts 2006)

In June 2004, I also observed the same kind of news, advertising and music 'radio' being played inside the HMV music store at Carindale in Brisbane, indicating that the phenomenon was spreading, since 'HMV Radio' was not playing in December 2003.

On December 3, 2003, I observed a news and promotional video presentation on a *SkyBus OnBoard* transit service between Spencer Street railway station in Melbourne and the city's Tullamarine Airport. The program (which I later observed was the 'outbound' version and different from an 'inbound' version) started with a male announcer introducing himself and the SkyBus service. This was followed by an advertisement for a shopping centre in Melbourne and what appeared to be a community service announcement urging Melbourne residents and visitors to conserve water. Hard on the heels of this 'community service announcement' was a segment entitled *A Minute with the Minister*, in which a man who might have been a Victorian Government minister but who carried no identifying caption spoke about tourism in Victoria. Finally in the presentation, the male host returned and introduced passengers to the facilities at Tullamarine Airport, telling passengers which terminal to choose to alight from the bus, according to which ticket they held: Virgin, Qantaslink or Qantas. The program was well timed and concluded on schedule just as the bus stopped at the first (Virgin and Qantaslink) terminal. The program credits said it had been produced by Sauci Marketing Services, apparently of Melbourne. According to the website Destination Melbourne (2003): '(the) 12-minute audio-visual program … (would) be aired on a four-weekly cycle on the new Super Shuttle rapid transit link between Melbourne Airport and Melbourne CBD'.

The same website said 'the program will be both entertaining and informative and will be limited to six product segments in each cycle' (2003). It said the SkyBus OnBoard offered advertisers 'a captive and targeted audience' and identified that audience as including more than 30,000 inbound customers each month. The website explained: 'The majority of travellers are international (35.3 percent) and NSW (22.4 percent) visitors with over 84.1 percent from outside Victoria. Nearly 60 percent are aged between 21 and 40 years of age. The major reason for travel is Holiday (53.4 percent) and VFR (visiting friends and relatives, 34.6 percent) with an average stay of 5.14 days and over 55 percent staying in city hotels' (Destination Melbourne 2003).

The cost to advertisers for participation in this targeted campaign ranged from $5,750 for a 1-minute segment on the bus for 12 weeks, to $33,000 for a 3-minute segment run for 24 weeks.

2.10   Mobile phones:
2.10.1   Email to SMS (and vice versa) – short message system, 160 characters

On Wednesday, February 18, 2004, staff on the Seven Network morning news television program *Sunrise* announced that they would be launching 'new technology' to allow viewers to send SMS messages direct to the show's producers and have them displayed on screen at the same time. They called the technology '7smsTV' and said viewers could 'now interact with live Sunrise broadcasts in real time using SMS on your mobile phone' (Seven Network 2004). In the weeks following, the 7smsTV service was displayed as a scrolling type array in a colour box to one side of the television screen, while announcers David Koch and Natalie Barr continued with a commentary (including sometimes reading what was on the 7smsTV screen) at the same time.

A variation on the web-mobile interaction took place in the first week of March 2004, in which mobile phone users and web participants attempted to create a fantasy 'treasure hunt' called *I like Frank* in the streets of Adelaide, explained by a press release from the federal Minister for Communications, Information Technology and the Arts, Daryl Williams (2004):

> *I like Frank is a cross between a treasure hunt and hide-and-seek and connects participants across the country via mobile wireless technology. Players explore Adelaide using voice messages and SMS to communicate with their online counterparts using 3G Motorola handsets.*

Williams said participants in the m.Net network included Adelaide University, Agile Pty Ltd, DSpace Pty Ltd, the Playford Centre, Telstra Corporation, Austereo, the City of Adelaide and the University of South Australia (2004).

2.10.2 *News on mobile phones*

News is now commonly available delivered to consumers' mobile phone and wireless devices, such as handsets, Personal Digital Assistants (PDAs) and wireless-equipped laptop computers. I observed three mobile phone networks' offerings and report that Telstra (through its Communic8 service) offers the PocketNews text and picture service (Communic8 2004a), Optus offers what it calls MmsVideoNews (Optus 2004) and the newer '3' network offers text, audio and video news to its subscribers (Three.com 2004). Short audio messages and short multimedia messaging are included in many mobile phone customer packages, subject to network availability and bandwidth.

Conversely, news content can be delivered by reporters, photographers and even members of the public *back* to news publishing organisations as events happen. In May 2004, a fire started at the Morrison Hotel in Brisbane and *The Courier-Mail* newspaper reported the next day (Thompson 2004:9) that many of its readers (as well as a reporter who lived nearby) took photographs of the fire on their new mobile phones before sending those pictures straight to the newspaper's email address.

The transnational sports news agency, Infostradasports.com, based in Nieuwegein, Holland, but with an office in Sydney, Australia, run by former Australian Associated Press journalist Steve Dettre, collects and supplies news and information from more than 60 sports worldwide, and publishes this using FTP, XML and database, potentially for 'Web, WAP, SMS, I-mode/GRS, multimedia CD-ROM, digital television, MMS or print' (Dettre, personal communication 2004; Infostradasports.com 2004). Along with students and other journalism educators, I encountered Infostradasports.com and Dettre in 2003 during the Rugby World Cup events in October and November. Dettre had managed the media information system at the Sydney 2000 Olympics, and since then had worked on other large-scale events such as the Manchester Commonwealth Games and the Soccer World Cup in Korea and Japan during 2002. The organisation had been commissioned by the Australian Rugby Union to supply player biographies, sports details and training and match reports, known as the Rugby News Service (RNS), for distribution to ARU-accredited media organisations other than the host broadcaster Channel 7, which had acquired 'access-all-areas' rights. During the three Townsville matches (Japan v Scotland, France and Fiji) four of my James Cook University journalism students, a freelance journalist from Melbourne and I attended training runs, pre-match and post-match press conference and the matches themselves to compile our reports. Like other groups at match venues around Australia, we then connected (using dial-up laptop computers or hard-wired desktops in the stadiums) to the RNS network, with username and password privileges to create and edit stories. This network was part of a national grid, controlled from an office in Sydney where Dettre's sub-editors (averaging four on match nights) worked on copy from the venues and published the stories to a web-based interface used by accredited 'news' journalists at each venue and, occasionally, on the web at their offices. In practice, RNS journalists would obtain and publish quotes and story leads before, during and after matches, which subscribing journalists could then incorporate into their stories for news bulletins and publications, or at least use them as background for further interviews.

2.10.3 Vending machines operated by mobile telephones

In 2001, the Coca-Cola company formed a relationship with Telstra to allow rail commuters in Sydney to purchase soft drinks from a vending machine at Sydney Central Station using their mobile phones (Communic8 2004b). The transaction was executed by the mobile phone holder standing in front of the drinks machine and dialling a number displayed on the machine. The purchaser was able to follow electronic prompts on the mobile phone to instruct the drinks machine to deliver a can of Coke and debit the price to the caller's mobile phone account (which was also debited for the price of the call). Since then the facility has been extended to 20 locations around mainland Australian states (Communic8 2004b). There is clear potential for the same dial-up sales process to deliver a thermal printout of the latest news headlines to commuters. Brenda Maddox foreshadowed this 30 years ago when she forecast the delivery of daily newspapers to the domestic home by fax (Maddox 1972:16).

2.11. Java

The *Sydney Morning Herald* newspaper's online site has had to deal with developing technologies, or at least the availability of those technologies to all its readers and screen viewers. In February 2004 I observed that the *SMH Online* site was presenting the following FAQ (*Frequently Asked Questions 2004*) information to its crossword followers:

> *The crossword software uses the java language. If you cannot see the crossword, then the Java software is probably not present or working properly on your computer.*

I sampled the SMH.com.au 'premium crosswords' offering on May 26, 2004, and learned that I could input answers simply by typing into the clue grid, a different and easier process than that offered by the NewsStand PDF (described in 2.2, *above*). Simplicity helps in delivery, since crosswords are among the most traditional and popular pastimes for newspaper readers. Although they carry no news content at all – in common with the daily astrology column, bridge notes and the comic strip, among others – they are often placed into the newspaper pages by journalists. Having to explain how these 'new crosswords' work is a task that editors less than 20 years previously would never have imagined. I know I didn't, and managing the crosswords page at *The Sunday Mail* newspaper in Brisbane was just one of my editorial roles in the 1990s (along with the bridge notes, the comics, the social and weddings pages and the index section at the front of the newspaper, all of which remained journalistic roles at QNPL at least until 2003). Other 'services information' which journalists are required to include in editorial sections of newspapers includes obituaries, tide and weather information and forecasts, sports results, turf and dog racing results and future fields (in tabulated details form) law lists, historical events (*Today in History*), lottery results, the newspaper index, shipping and flight arrivals and departures, stock reports and agricultural market reports. In the first years of the 21st century, every one of these types of information became available online independently of newspaper organisations and began to attract audiences in their own right. Journalists at publishers such as News Ltd were able to receive data from racing, weather, the stock market, agricultural and transport authorities via Internet file transfer (FTP) or were given digital permissions to allow them to enter secure corporate sites to harvest materials themselves for inclusion in the relevant publications.

2.12. Cookies

The New York Times Online website producers encountered a similar problem with their crosswords and in 2004 presented the equivalent of 'pages' of information and instructions about how to load and install the appropriate software to view its crosswords (New York Times 2004a). The *New York Times Online* also had to explain to its Internet audience the meaning of the computing term 'cookies' and how these little pieces of code affected their experience of the online newspaper, because it is possible for computer users to exclude cookies from their systems and thus defeat the delivery mechanism intended by the newspaper publisher:

> *A 'cookie' is a small piece of information that a Web site can store in a designated file on your computer. It can be used, among other things, to identify you when you log in to a Web site. When you visit a site, that site can access only the information which it stored in your cookie – not information put in your cookie by other sites. The New York Times on the Web is one of many sites that use cookies. The cookie helps us determine, for example, whether you are a paying subscriber to our crossword puzzles. (New York Times 2004b)*

2.13. PowerPoint presentations

In October 2001, as part of the editorial development team at Queensland Newspapers Pty Ltd, I participated in a novel journalistic publishing venture involving the use of the Microsoft PowerPoint application and image capture devices. A reporter on *The Courier-Mail*, Michael McKinnon, presented the development team with a problem: how to capture more than 280 pages of legal documents and publish them unedited within three days. McKinnon had specialised in reporting topics discovered under Freedom of Information legislation and had been fighting a court battle with the Australian Tax Office for documents. As he related to us in the newsroom, and later reported in *The Courier-Mail*, October 25, (2001:1), the Tax Office defence in the Administrative Appeals Tribunal hung on its contention that News Ltd would selectively edit any documents the Tax Office handed over and would possibly distort the facts contained therein. McKinnon chose not to argue whether or not any distortion would take place; instead he argued to the tribunal that the newspaper would indeed publish articles about the documents but would also publish the entire, unedited set of documents, and quickly, so that the public would be able to see the Tax Office's information for themselves and arrive at their own conclusions. He argued this position having discussed the feasibility of this strategy on *The Courier-Mail's* website with myself and the online editor at the time, Mr John Grey. I said it would be possible to obtain the documents – no matter how many pages – and scan the information into TIFF (tagged image file format) computer files. Once the TIFF files were secure in the Queensland Newspapers Pty Ltd network, we could compress ('optimise') the image files so as to occupy less computer data space without distorting the typescript, and then include them in a simple Microsoft PowerPoint document, resulting in the equivalent of an online slide show. We would then upload the PowerPoint document to the QNPL website and invite the web audience either to run the PowerPoint online or to download and save it to their own computers and view it at their leisure. The tribunal agreed with McKinnon's (and our) novel proposal and the entire set of documents (approximately 286 pages A4) was scanned by the newspaper's computer graphics operators, optimised and installed into a PowerPoint by me and published to the World Wide Web by Grey within two days. The methodology for the above innovative approach to publishing news was developed by my students and I during the 'East Timor Press project' at the Queensland University of Technology in 2001 (Cokley et al 2000; Tickle 2002). The staff-student team came up with the idea of scanning and optimising copies of the struggling *Timor Post* newspaper so that the images could be published in indigenous and local languages on the World Wide Web. The task was completed successfully.

2.14. *Streaming data and internal networks such as Corporate, Educational and government intranets*

The commercial website AustralianIntranets.com (2004) describes 'intranets' as 'a private space that gives employees in a company the ability to organise information, readily access that information, manage documents, share calendars and enable efficient collaboration, all in a familiar, browser-based environment'. In 2006 the above concept of an intranet was familiar to many people who work inside companies, educational institutions and wide area networks. But according to Rhonda Garmo, Bill Hagar and Meghin Wojtowicz at the University of Michigan-Dearborn (Garmo et al 2004) the earliest printed documentation of the existence of 'intranets' was as recently as 1995. Now large intranets in such organisations as government departments, universities and news publishing corporations stretch across whole continents and connect tens of thousands of people. When I performed design and editorial development work on the News Ltd intranet in Brisbane from 1999-2002, I had a very clear understanding that the words and pictures I was publishing could be seen from Perth to Townsville and nearly every large and small News Ltd site in between (possibly also by News Corporation chairman Rupert Murdoch in New York). The distributed network it used allowed for quick and easy – and essentially accurate – publication of company and general interest news to employees, all within the safety of password-protected environments.

2.15. Rich media promotions and advertising

At the same time as journalism has been developing and adjusting to new digital technologies, advertising has been doing the same, but using far more advanced tools, especially a range of technologies known as 'rich media' which John Bowen describes as 'the use (or combination) of video, voice, data, and other technologies, such as animation over IP networks, to create an otherwise unattainable user experience' (Bowen 2001). These applications have become well known to users of the Eudora email client software, especially the free version available to academic users, which delivers messages complete with coloured, moving and sometimes audio advertisements. Rich media is also employed on many free email websites, such as Yahoo and MSN, to allow the delivery of exciting and different styles of advertising.

2.16. ATMs and kiosks

Around the turn of the 21st century, the National Bank began serving text and coloured graphics and images to its automatic teller machines in Australia along its national network. I observed this at the branch on the corner of Abbotsford Road and Montpelier Road, Bowen Hills, Brisbane. Other banks have followed suit in ensuing years, depending on the colour and graphics capacity of each machine. Some banks in north Queensland still displayed only yellow text on a black field in 2004. The field of kiosks with touch-screen facilities is developing much faster. I have observed touch screens delivering: historical information at the Hyde Parks Barracks Museum in Sydney and at the Museum of Tropical Queensland in Townsville; community land-care information in the council offices of the Burdekin Shire; and most recently (2004) in Shell petrol stations installed with the new 'Shell Touch' kiosks (including one observed at Aspley, on Gympie Road). These kiosks have come the closest I have observed to news delivery stations because they feature regularly updated fishing and recreation information as well as movie screenings … of course, customers can convert this interest into cash by purchasing tickets online there and then.

2.17. Other web casts (also streaming media)

The world knows about web casts thanks to comedian Lenny Henry who appeared at the Royal Jubilee 'Party at the Palace' celebrations in London in June 2002 and waved to the crowd … then waved jerkily again and said 'that's how they're seeing me on the Internet!' Web casts are commonly used for corporate meetings instead of videoconference meetings, and can be used to deliver product announcements as well as training seminars such as those hosted by Microsoft and the OSISoft Corporation (2002). Web casts typically are delivery channels rather than interactive channels of communication.

2.18. Keno and lottery networks

According to the Jupiter's website (2003), Keno was launched in NSW registered clubs in September 1991 and it is now one of the largest networked Keno games in the world, operating in more than 1000 clubs in NSW and at Star City Casino. Keno now operates in most Australian states and has been observed operating in the Wrest Point Casino in Hobart, Tasmania, for example. Since mid-1997, Jupiter's Keno has spread to clubs, hotels, TABs and casinos throughout Queensland. The Jupiter's website said Keno was available in more than 1800 clubs and hotels in NSW and Queensland and played in most states and territories. The clear demographics of the Keno gambling audience make it an attractive news delivery vehicle for journalistic publishers. The audience can reliably be described as aged 18-80+, including both male and female participants, and possessing a level of disposable income which can be measured by Keno turnover at any venue and across the whole network. I have observed Keno players and they are highly focused viewers who are able to participate in a complex game at the same time as they watch a screen filled with moving numbers, complete betting coupons, talk to their friends and drink beer, wine or other beverages. They are attracted to the Keno screens by the lure of winning money as well as the sense of participation with their friends. They can participate while consuming legal drugs (alcohol and in some parts, tobacco) and since Keno games are transmitted from 9am-2am daily (except Christmas) there is an audience watching almost round-the-clock. The delivery device is a cable television network onto standard television screens, with text and colour image capacity. The Cowboy's Leagues Club in Townsville has already integrated its Keno screen with a sports news television station on a separate screen just below the Keno device. At Wrest Point in Hobart, a space at the bottom of the Keno game screen has been converted to display scrolling information about hotel events and conference news for guests, and at the Mount Gravatt Hotel in Brisbane, the same crawling 'news ticker' space has been devoted to displaying special bargains in the hotel liquor shop.

2.19. Game Boy Advance, PlayStation 2, XBox, Game Cube

Gaming and news are still largely at arm's length but researchers at the University of Indiana Mime Project (Gillespie, Thom n.d.) have produced unusual and thought provoking storytelling websites such as *The Zone* (www.zonecomics.com). However, chief among the capacity of game consoles such as the Sony PlayStation 2 is its ability to read and play back DVDs, the medium on which video and even news clips are best stored. Game consoles are portable, less expensive than televisions, and have a built-in draw for younger audiences. Willcox (2002:75) argues for the adoption of computer gaming within journalism training itself, noting that 'fun, fast-paced computer gaming, complete with full sensory feedback, missions and guilt-free actions' might engage students' imagination while 'teaching them the tools and skills necessary for modern journalism'. Willcox's proposal is generally supported by the learning theories described by Biggs, especially 'constructive alignment' (1999:25) and would be a fertile area for future research.

2.20. USB Memory Sticks and 'Thumb Drives'

I have observed people using the 21st century phenomenon of the thumb drive – also known as memory sticks and by other names (Direct Connect CD 2004) – to share information and other data around schools and university lecture rooms. Owners of these devices, which feature a single-click installation into the Universal Serial Bus (USB) ports of computers in both the Windows and the Macintosh environments, view them and use them as the latest and easiest way to carry and share information. The capacity of such devices had reached 2GB by mid-2004 and would probably increase with time. I suggest that these devices could easily be used to capture daily news content for a fee at your local news agent's shop, replacing some newspaper sales.

2.21. Register docket and EFTPOS bulletins

Large supermarket chains such as Woolworths have used register-docket tape carrying advertisements since the mid-1980s. The advertisements mostly come pre-printed from advertising wholesalers such as the Shoppadocket company. I have observed that other retailers such as Coles have switched to thermal printed register dockets and EFTPOS machines such as those from the ANZ Bank and the National Bank also use thermal printed paper for their customer receipts. Since modern supermarket and large retail checkouts (such as Coles Myer [Mahler 2003] and Bunnings Warehouses) are actually enormous integrated digital networks with the capacity to deliver all kinds of different information, I suggest these would make the ideal delivery system for instant news headlines delivered to customers as they proceed through check-outs. Marketing potential exists for such companies to offer current news headlines to their customers as they leave the stores, as it does for news delivery services such as Australian Associated Press (AAP) as well as the Australian Broadcasting Corporation (ABC), News Ltd and Fairfax to supply that news to those retailers on a subscription basis. This is already the practice among (and even between) some of these companies. Both the Nine television network and News Ltd publish AAP reports on their online sites, preferring the pre-packaged and edited agency copy for breaking stories to those from their own in-house journalists.

2.22. CD-ROMS and DVDs (passed hand-to-hand, rented, or posted)

Meadows (1993) relates how remote groups of indigenous Australians in the 1980s passed video tapes from community to community to transmit but at the same time preserved the integrity of sensitive cultural material. I suggest less remote metaphors for this observed practice include the suburban (or rural town) video and DVD rental store and the videos and DVDs available for loan at municipal libraries. In fact people have been sharing information using video tapes, CDs and DVDs since these units became available in the mid-1970s and it remains a popular mechanism for children and others to share music, electronic games and movies. There is clear potential for application to news delivery.

2.23. Email, discussion lists and forums, World Wide Web browsers and hypertext

While many people in Westernised and non-Westernised countries now communicate almost effortlessly using email, Internet discussion forums and by publishing information on HTML-driven web browsers, others have been putting their now-mundane software applications to specific uses. One such operation is the People First Network (Biliki n.d.) in the Solomon Islands, north-east of Australia, which applies short-wave radio signals as the transmission channel for email and Internet data to be carried between central and remote, or remote-to-remote points in the distributed island group of the Solomons. The power comes from aggregated solar panels connected to batteries. A simple example of how this works in the community sense is that while an email passes between two computers, recipients can further transmit the contents of each email, discussion posting or web page orally to a much wider community group according to local traditions and customs. Journalists at the *Timor Post* in Dili, East Timor, have also applied simple email and World Wide Web browser technologies since the successful completion of the 'East Timor Press' project at the Queensland University of Technology in 2002 (Cokley et al 2000; Tickle 2002).

The Google Corporation operates a news division, at http://news.google.com/, which claims to use advanced computing and web browsers to augment and publish news which it says is customised for readers in various territories around the world. In this way it follows the lead established by Gruhl and Bender (2000) who proposed computerised filtering of news articles based on metadata and other filters applied to the articles by human editors. This proposal proved a popular one among respondents to that survey conducted among researchers in Antarctica (Cokley 2003).

2.24. *Online database retrieval systems such as news-media pay-per-view archives*

Journalists in major newsrooms around the world have become accustomed to paying for access to large database retrieval systems, such as LexisNexis in the United States. In Australia, journalists working at the larger newspaper publishers such as News Ltd and Fairfax Ltd enjoy the use of a large suite of databases containing articles published in both participating news stables and all their affiliates, making a search of most of Australia's newspapers possible as well as many in New Zealand, the UK and several in the US. Since 2002 this has become a small but important revenue stream for both publishing companies as they are selling access to stories as far back as 1984 to the web-browsing public. These are at www.newstext.com.au for News Corp and http://newsstore.f2.com.au/apps/newsSearch.ac for Fairfax. Such database mining of news reports is well known among US and UK newspapers companies as well.

At the News Corporation affiliate in Brisbane, Australia (Queensland Newspapers Pty Ltd) journalists have also enjoyed access to a range of more complicated, password-access level private and government operated databases such as ABR (Australian Business Research), ASIC (the Australian Securities and Investments Commission) and CITEC, the Queensland-government owned but corporatised database which allows journalists to look up land titles and car registrations (at least until early 2001 and the Sheppardson Inquiry) and other otherwise confidential details about people and organisations such as land valuations.

ABR, for instance, allowed journalists (and other users who paid a subscription) to investigate whether named individuals owned shares in particular of any companies, or in reverse, who were the principal shareholders and/or office bearers in named organisations. There are privacy issues involved in the handling of this kind of information. Journalists at QNPL had been in the habit of searching for motor-vehicle registration details using CITEC and during 2001 managed to collect 'incriminating' evidence (in the light of other evidence at the Sheppardson Inquiry) on several top political figures in Queensland. Soon after, the motor-vehicle registration searches were dropped from the available menus on the CITEC site and officials told journalists such data would no longer be available 'for privacy reasons'.

Discussion

Poole (1989:14) notes that while it was a convention of the coffee house that differences of rank did not count and that all within had the right to speak, the social organisation of the time excluded working class men and all women and was merely a bourgeois public sphere riddled with competitiveness and discrimination (Poole 1989:15). This happened in the United States as well, documented by Kielbowicz (1989:180) who notes that postal subsidies initially extended only to political journals because 'Congress deemed publications other than (such) newspapers less deserving of support'. The realisation that social organisation within the public sphere was restricting membership of that space eventually moved Habermas to retreat to a more specialised understanding of the public sphere as the 'ideal speech situation' (Poole 1989:16). This has prompted more recent commentators to move even further away from the topographical, spatial nature of Habermas' idea to something more notional called 'public life' (Craig 2004:53). As Huesca notes (2003:281), the 'ideal speech situation' is also compatible with participatory communication research. However, even the modern public 'sphere', 'life' or 'domain' (Craig 2004:53) is not an 'ideal speech situation'. Recent information-technology research in Australia by Hallinan (2003:1) demonstrates how Internet chat exhibits some of the hegemonic problems of the coffee houses:

> *A self-organised social network derived from Internet Relay Chat (IRC) channel interactions exhibits measurable hierarchical modularity, reflecting an underlying hierarchical neighbourhood structure in the social network.*

Meyer (2002:120) notes wider negative aspects of the technological revolution, the largest of which has become known as the 'digital divide', predicted by Umberto Eco and identified by Australia's National Office for the Information Economy (2002) as a key inhibitor of economic development. The digital divide is also the great enemy of the effective diffusion of communications innovations, since 'in all likelihood a considerable number of people will lack the skills and willingness to develop basic competence in the use of network communications' (Meyer 2002:120). In the long run, many people will find themselves shut out of the Net, either by lack of competence or lack of equipment, and this will encourage a two-class society of users and non-users (Meyer 2002:121). The Internet tends to be used as an additional means of communication by previously existing social and political networks (Meyer 2002:121) rather than a new forum for the otherwise disenfranchised:

> *Even when conversations in the interactive zone of net communications include many people, they still have the air of exchanges between private persons. What is missing is the opportunity for the individual to emerge from the private sphere into a public space, and join in discussions guided by the social rules regulating discourse about public affairs.*

These private/public discussions need to be 'subject to rational debate and criticism' and 'to the extent that they are informed by this process, and survive it, they cease to be merely private and become matters of public opinion' (Poole 1989:13-14). But Meyer (2002:123) also notes that broad-gauged, intensive Internet use leads to the fragmentation of the public sphere into a series of partial publics. Habermas himself recognised that 'truth-oriented conversations among the denizens of the life-world do more than merely build consensus on issues of common concern ... the social act of trying to reach consensus by deliberation also generates social cohesion or solidarity' (Meyer 2002:135-136). Dahlgren takes this solidarity a step further and says civil society can begin 'to stimulate both a renewal of the mass media in the direction of more appropriate reporting and the emergence of other complementary forms of public communication' (Meyer 2002:137). This leads to a discussion of the place of modern journalism in public sphere activity.

Craig (2004: viii) notes that 'public life is a mediated phenomenon' and that 'the media are not "outside" observers but ... integral components of politics and public life' and involved in the various performances which take place within the public sphere, because as Dayan and Katz demonstrate, 'media events are organised by public bodies with which the media co-operate' (in Craig 2004:119). In many parts of rural, regional and remote Australia and elsewhere, however, this performance has lately adopted the message-transmission characteristics of Plato's Cave (Cohen 2002) in which chained audiences facing away from the entrance to a cave see messages as shadows projected on the wall of the cave by diffused sunlight filtering in from the outside world. Cohen writes (2002, explaining Plato):

> *The prisoners may learn what a book is by their experience with shadows of books. But they would be mistaken if they thought that the word 'book' refers to something that any of them has ever seen.*

This is also the situation of people on 'the wrong side' of the digital divide in the world of 2005: they might think that they can participate in public sphere activity but it's really an illusion.

Conclusions

It is clear from the preceding audit that in 2005, 'state-of-the-art' refers not to upgrades or incremental changes – or even new backpacks and equipment for reporters – but rather to a difference of kind in the systems available both to journalists and their audiences. Instead of journalists and their corporate bosses using what was previously called 'advanced technology' to produce newspapers, radio or television broadcasts, the journalistic world of 2005 is embroiled in a game of 'catch-up', trying desperately to connect with the general-purpose technologies their audiences are already using, such as mobile phones, digital gaming consoles and PDA handheld computers. News providers have been forced to adopt technologies as soon as they hit the showroom floor, and sometimes before they're completely suited for the traditionally understood journalistic environment. The audit has demonstrated just how tightly the processes of communication are bound up with the technologies used to carry that communication (Silverstone 1998) and how dependent modern civilisations have become on them (Ball-Rokeach and DeFleur 1976). Mobile telephony and wireless communications head the list of technologies that have acquired strong cultural meaning, especially among teenagers and the business communities, and these communities have emerged as the biggest sales market for companies supporting these technologies. However, the penetration of mobile audio and video signal carriers into everyday life – into banks, billboards, vending machines, shopping centres, aircraft and government-operated public transport – suggests that this sector is the next one deserving of further research, especially the development of news delivery environments for touch screen kiosks, gaming consoles and on gambling networks such as Keno. It is also suggested that, notwithstanding the roll-out of technologies which provide the potential for general two-way participative communication, there is still no strong evidence of this participation in the news media field.

References

ABC Shop (2004) http://shop.abc.net.au/, <viewed 02.04>

Adobe website (2004)
www.adobe.com/products/acrobat/adobepdf.html; also
http://www.adobe.com/products/main.html <viewed 02.04>

Australian Academy of Science website
http://www.science.org.au/nova/022/022key.htm <viewed 02.04>

Australian Broadcasting Authority (2004a) website
www.aba.gov.au/radio/digital/index.htm, <viewed 02.04>

Australian Broadcasting Authority (2004b)
www.aba.gov.au/tv/research/projects/pdfrtf/DigitalTVinAustralia.pdf
<viewed 02.04>

Australian Bureau of Meteorology (2004) website
www.bom.gov.au/other/wbf/wbf.shtml <viewed 02.04>

Australian Intranets (2004) www.australianintranets.com/ <viewed
02.04>

Australian National University website (2004)
www.rsphysse.anu.edu.au/bushlan/background.html <viewed 19.02.04>

Ball-Rokeach, S.J. & DeFleur, M.L. (1976), 'A Dependency Model
of Mass Media Effects', *Communication Research*, vol. 3, pp. 3–21.

BBC News World Edition website, http://news.bbc.co.uk/2/hi/asia-pacific/3648813.stm <viewed 22.04.04>

Benkler, Yochai (2003) 'Some Economics of Wireless
Communications', in *Rethinking Rights and Regulations*, MIT Press,
Cambridge, Massachusetts, pp.149-192

Biggs, John B (1999) *Teaching for quality learning at university*,
Society for Research into Higher Education & Open University Press,
Buckingham

Biliki, Randall PeopleFirstNet manager (n.d.) website
www.peoplefirst.net.sb/ <viewed 02.04>

Bowen, J. (2001) *Emergence of rich media*, www.RedHerring.com
<viewed 24.01.01>

Brill, Ann (1999) 'Online Newspaper Advertising: A study of format
and integration with news content', in Schumann, David; Thorson,
Esther, *Advertising and the World Wide Web*, Lawrence Erlbaum
Associates, London: 159-173

Caslon Analytics (2004) Ketupa Project website
www.ketupa.net/austnetworks1.htm <viewed 02.04>

Cohen, S. Marc (2002) *The Allegory of the Cave*, Washington
University, http://faculty.washington.edu/smcohen/320/cave.htm <viewed
03.04>

Cokley, John (2003) 'Staying in touch – News Delivery to Australian

Researchers in Antarctica', *Southern Review* (RMIT), 2003, 36:1

Cokley, John; DaCosta, Aderito Hugo; Lonsdale, Jamie; Romano, Angela; Spurgeon, Christina & Tickle, Sharon (2000) 'Media, Democracy and Development: Learning From East Timor' in *AsiaPacific Media Educator* (#9, July - December 2000)

Communic8 website (2004a) website www.communic8.com.au/fun/pocketnews/index.asp <viewed 02.04>

Communic8 website (2004b) website http://www.communic8.com.au/promo/dialacoke/index.asp <viewed 02.04>

Conboy, Nelson (2002) personal communication

Cook, Mark & Brown, Mike (2004) Teletext timeline, website http://teletext.mb21.co.uk/timeline/ <viewed 02.04>

Craig, Geoffrey (2004) *The Media, Politics and Public Life*, Allen & Unwin, Sydney

Cripps, Sally (2004) grazier at Blackall, central western Queensland, email communication, February 2004

CyberCafes.com <viewed 23.04.04>

Dahlgren, Peter (2002) 'The Public Sphere as Historical Narrative', in *McQuail's Reader in Mass Communication Theory*, McQuail, Denis (ed), Sage, London, P. 195

Destination Melbourne website (2003) www.destinationmelbourne.com.au/marketing/skybus-onboard-entertainment.asp <viewed 02.04>

Dettre, Steve (2004) personal communication

Direct Connect CD (2004) www.directconnectcd.com/memorystick_products.html <viewed 02.04>

Eckert, Andrew (2002) 'Retail Price Cycles and Response Asymmetry', *Canadian Journal of Economics*, Vol. 35, pp. 52-77, 2002, abstract viewed at the Social Science Research Network http://papers.ssrn.com/sol3/papers.cfm?abstract_id=308963 <viewed 03.04>

Eng, Paul (2002) 'Filtering out terrorists' on the ABCNews.com website http://abcnews.go.com/sections/scitech/DailyNews/cybercafe020415.html <viewed 02.04>

Forman, Chris; Goldfarb, Avi; Greenstein, Shane (2003) 'The Geographic Dispersion of Commercial Internet Use', in *Rethinking Rights and Regulations*, Cranor, L & Wildman, S [eds], MIT Press, Cambridge, Massachusetts, 113-145

Freedman, Michael (2004) personal communication, March 1, 2004

Garmo, Rhonda; Hagar, Bill; Wojtowicz, Meghin (2004) http://www-personal.umd.umich.edu/~rgarmo/ <viewed 02.04>

Gillespie, Thom (n.d.) *The MIME Project*, Department of

Telecommunications at Indiana University www.mime.indiana.edu/ <viewed 02.04>

Griffin, Em (2003) *A First Look at Communication Theory*, McGraw-Hill, Online Learning Centre, http://highered.mcgraw-hill.com/sites/007248392x/student_view0/glossary.html <viewed 24.02.05>

Gruhl, D. & Bender, W. (2000) 'A New Structure for News Editing', *IBM Systems Journal*, vol. 39, Nos 3 and 4,

Hallinan, J. (2003). 'Self-organization leads to hierarchical modularity in an internet Community' in Palade, V., Howlett, R. J. & Jain, L. (eds.) *Proceedings of the 7th International Conference on Knowledge-Based Intelligent Information and Engineering Systems*, Lecture Notes in Artificial Intelligence 2773: 914 - 917.

Henney, Sue (2002) email communications with the author

Hogan, Tom (2005) personal communication, citing Asia-Pacific Broadcasting Union (2005) http://www.abu.org.my/public/compiled/p515.htm#Article1004 <viewed 22.02.05>

Huesca, Robert (2003) 'Participatory Approaches to Communication for Development' in *International and Development Communication*, Mody, Bella [ed], Sage, California

Ifra website www.ifra.com/website/ifra.nsf/ All/69DF55DB2524935EC1256A14005FF9E9/ $FILE/NewsGear_2004_matrix_R2.pdf <viewed 02.04>

Infostradasports.com website (2004) <viewed 02.04>

JCDecaux website (2004a) www.jcdecaux.co.uk/profile/ <viewed 02.04>

JCDecaux (2004b) www.jcdecaux.co.uk/innovate/ specials/category.cfm?SpecialCategoryID=10 <viewed 02.04>

Jupiters website (2003) www.keno.jupiters.com.au/external_frameset.htm <viewed 12.03>

Kielbowicz, Richard Burkett (1984) *News In The Mails, 1690-1863: The Technology, Policy, And Politics Of A Communication Channel*, University of Minnesota, PhD thesis; also published as Kielbowicz, Richard Burkett (1989) *News in the Mail: The Press, Post Office, and Public Information*, Greenwood Press, New York

Macromedia Corporation website http://www.macromedia.com/software/ <viewed 05.04>

Maddox, B. (1972) *Beyond Babel: New Directions in Communications*, London, Andre Deutsch.

Mahler, Peter (2003) *IT Transformation*, released on September 25, 2003, http://www.corporate.colesmyer.com/ <viewed 02.04>

Man, John (2002) *The Gutenberg Revolution*, Review Books, London

McKinnon, Michael (2001) 'Secret plan to kill tax returns', *The Courier-Mail*, October 25

Meadows, Michael (1993) *The Way People Want to Talk: Media Representation and Indigenous Media Responses in Australia and Canada*, University of Queensland, unpublished PhD thesis

Mellor, John (2003, 2004) personal communication May 17, 2003, and April 2004, for details see www.mellor.net/mellor/enews.nsf/aboutus?readform <viewed 02.04>

Meyer, Thomas & Hinchman, Lew (2002) *Media Democracy: How the Media Colonize Politics*, Polity Press, Cambridge

Microsoft website (2003) www.microsoft.com/presspass/press/2003/Jan03/01-09WMDevicesSupportPR.asp <viewed 02.04>

Miller, Jeff (2002) website http://members.aol.com/jeff560/jeff.html <viewed 08.02>; also information from http://www.alpcom.it/hamradio <viewed 08.02>

Nash, Trevor (2002) Personal communication at QTQ9, August 2, 2002

National Office for the Information Economy web site http://www.noie.gov.au/projects/access/Connecting_Communities/Digitaldivide.htm <viewed 04.03>

New York Times website (2004a) www.nytimes.com/membercenter/faq/acrosslite.html <viewed 02.04>

New York Times website (2004b) www.nytimes.com/membercenter/faq/cookies.html <viewed 02.04>

NewsStand Inc (2004) press release, June 16, 2003, http://www.newsstand.com/corporate/release.cfm?PRESS_RELEASE=47 <viewed 02.04>

Northrup, Kerry (2003) 'Growth Market' in *NewsPlex Trend Reports*, No. 3, September 2003, website http://www.newsplex.org/knowledgebase/ntr3.shtml <viewed 04.04>

NUA Internet Surveys, 2004, website http://www.nua.com/surveys/how_many_online/index.html <viewed 23.03.04>

Old Bailey Online, Proceedings of the Old Bailey website, http://www.oldbaileyonline.org/history/london-life/london-life18th.html#Population <viewed 04.04>

Online Journalism Review (2003) website, http://ojr.usc.edu/content/resources/education_programs.cfm <viewed 29.07.03>

Optus website (2004)
www.info2you.com.au/cocoon/mms_news/MmsVideoNews.xml
<viewed 02.04>

OSISoft website (2002)
www.osisoft.com/presentations.aspx?id=525&event=td2002 <viewed 01.04>

Poole, Ross (1989) 'Public Spheres', *Australian Communications and the Public Sphere*, Wilson, Helen (ed) Macmillan, Sydney

Population Reference Bureau website, www.prb.org/Content/ NavigationMenu/PRB/Educators/Human_Population/ Population_Growth/Population_Growth.htm <viewed 04.04>

Ritter, Jonquil (2000) 'The Conversion to Digital Television in Australia', paper presented at the IBC conference, May 2000. Australian Broadcasting Authority, Sydney, www.aba.gov.au <viewed 02.04>

Roberts, Noel (2006) personal communication

Robson, Gary (2001) *Closed Captioning FAQ*,
http://www.robson.org/capfaq/
overview.html#What <viewed 02.04>

Robson, Gary D (2004) 'Closed captioning', *World Book Online Reference Centre*, World Book, Inc. www.worldbookonline.com/wb/ Article?id=ar119630 <viewed 02.04>

Rogers, Everett (1995) *Diffusion of Innovation*, 4th Ed, Free Press, New York

Romano, Angela (2001) 'Inculcating public journalism philosophies into newsroom culture', *Australian Journalism Review*, 24:2, pp43-62

Schramm, Wilbur (1955) 'Information Theory and Mass Communication', in B. Berelson & M. Janowitz (Eds) (1966), *Reader in Public Opinion and Communication*, 2nd edn, New York, Free Press. pp712-732

Seven Network website (2004) www.seven.com.au/sunrise/smstv, <viewed 02.04>

Silverstone, Roger (1998) 'Mediation and Communication', in Calhoun et al [eds] *The International Handbook of Sociology* (in press) Sage, London

Silverstone, Roger (2003) personal communication

Sydney Morning Herald website
www.smh.com.au/contacts/index.html#freexword1 <viewed 04.04>

TEAMtalk (2002) www.teamtalk.com/satellite <viewed 08.02>

Thompson, Erica (2004) 'Amateurs scorch the pros with hotel fire snapshots', *The Courier-Mail*, May 22, 2004, Pg 9.

Three.com website (2004) www.three.com.au/
index.cfm?section=Explore&pid=450&pageid=522&sid=873 <viewed

02.04>

Tickle, Sharon (2002) 'Online journalism capacity-building in East Timor', paper presented at the Journalism Education Association of New Zealand annual conference.

Voxi, Heinrich; S Amavilah (1995) 'The Capitalist World Aggregate Supply and Demand Model for Natural Uranium', *Energy Economics*, Vol. 17, No. 3, July 1995, abstract viewed at the Social Science Research Network http://papers.ssrn.com/sol3/ papers.cfm?abstract_id=308963 <viewed 03.04>

Walsh, Brian (2004) *Channel Vision*, Sunday Mail TV Guide, March 14, 2004

Whelan, Lisa (2004) personal communication, March 4, 2004

Willcox, Peter (2002) 'Journalism training: Is the industry game enough to have fun?' *Australian Journalism Review*, 24(2):75-99.

Williams, Darryl (2004) media release by Carina Tan-Van Baren in Williams' name, website http://www.darylwilliams.dcita.gov.au/ Article/0,,0_7-2_4011-4_117925,00.html

World Airline Entertainment Association website (2003) www.waea.org/events/avion/2003/avionwinners2003.htm <02.04>

Chapter 3

'Neo-firefighters': a new model for international news correspondents in the changing context of world journalism

Rebekah van Druten

Much has changed since 1989, the end of the Cold War, in how international news is gathered and published. An Australian Broadcasting Corporation correspondent in Europe, Michael Brissenden, reflected on the new circumstances: 'Seven years ago we had more than twice the number of correspondents covering Europe ... but demands have increased, so the output has increased ... financially there is no money'. He was alluding to the common trend among Western media organisations: where they can, to de-emphasise foreign news in their products; cut costs by reducing newsgathering operations abroad, and rely on new technology to enable journalists to fill in gaps, by doing more with less time and money. This chapter focuses on the current state of correspondents' work, addressing specific topics like budget cuts, and broad topics like changes in international news reporting caused by social and economic globalisation. It proposes that new ways of doing things are producing a new model for correspondents, called here the 'neo-firefighter': journalists equipped with advanced professional skills and knowledge, able to be highly productive thanks to 21st century communication technology, able to occupy an individual territory, or field of specialist expertise, and able to work autonomously, with or without strong corporate support.

Introduction

Since the Cold War ended, the amount and standard of foreign reporting has been widely studied. Academic observers argue two elements have greatly altered the foreign news landscape: the growing globalisation of nations' economies and politics, and new geo-political realities following the demise of the 'us versus them' orthodoxy of the East-West confrontation. Increasingly countries are facing up to the signs that their interests, and even their survival, tie into those of other nations and the world. For example, the destruction of rainforests in Brazil causes the ozone layer to deteriorate and has an impact on weather patterns in Australia.

One of the biggest challenges foreign correspondents now face is how to report this interrelatedness. Foreign correspondents are having to re-evaluate the way they work and the volume of international stories they produce for their home audience. It has implications for the quality of work as well, because journalists are having to equip themselves mentally to handle more complex issues. Economic pressures – corporate efficiency measures especially – have become another prime cause of change, including recent downsizing of the foreign bureaus of many news organisations. At the same time advances in communication technology have allowed for instant and remote news reporting, as well as very efficient syndication and pooling of news products, meaning again less active demand for the services of correspondents based in bureaus.

The study reported on in this chapter tests these propositions. In general, it is accepted that international journalism has been in retreat, that bureaus are closing, that the number of regular correspondents is being reduced, and that news organisations have been cutting back on their offerings of foreign news. However there are factors that offset or deflect such a movement, like the empowering, higher-productivity effects that new communications technology can have for reporters in the field; so the study seeks to determine how developments overall are affecting the way correspondents work – and it perceives them developing into a new journalistic identity.

While systems, technologies, bean-counters and hour-by-hour needs of the home desk are militating in favour of more standardisation and pooling of products from organisation to organisation; audiences may be relied on to expect more in the way of a good range of news content and perspective, and journalists in the field are prone to oblige them. Here the 'neo firefighter' is described, showing how journalists empowered with present-day reporting technology, with a good base of knowledge, and the standard high-order reporting skills of an international correspondent, can today operate with considerable independence. Able to go into foreign but familiar places, well prepared, such journalists can cover both specialised interests and a wide range of geographical territory. Neo firefighters have started walking a new path, away from the model of 'old-style' news bureaus, set up something like their companies' domestic news rooms; the model of 'old-style' 'hit and run' reporters (firefighters), or 'old-style' locally-based stringers, often semi-amateurs in journalism, frequently wedded to just one spot on the globe.

Research method

This research project was in three parts: a review of relevant literature; a sampling of contemporary international news coverage in leading mass media outlets; and a qualitative study based on interviews with a large group of foreign correspondents. The writer appraised a set of readings on issues in foreign news, to initiate a general empirical study. To test theory or points of analysis uncovered in the literature review, news content was reviewed, by reading and viewing a selection of stories from Western media outlets. These were 'general interest' publications in their approach, selected because they give substantial attention to foreign news coverage, and the review was made in order to obtain an organised account of their treatment of ongoing issues in the news. Finally, a study based on conversational interviews with 25 foreign correspondents was conducted in July 2003 in the European Union, to further test the common themes in the literature and media content review.

Globalisation

A check on the relevant literature shows the notion of globalisation may help define changes taking place in foreign news media. Many references are in the category of 'neo-Marxist theory' (Wallerstein, 1990; Chew and Denemark, 1996; Hirst and Thompson, 1996) where there is strong reliance on globalisation being a product of capitalist drive to expand markets and maximise profits. Other texts focus on sociological and cultural studies (Featherstone, 1995; Hall, 1992; Waters, 1995) emphasising plurality of cultural development, as a result of the anti-colonialism movement. Servaes et al in *The New Communications Landscape* (2000), offer workable definitions for the purpose of this project, such as: 'globalisation refers to a process through which the entire human population is bonded into a single society' and 'the ever closer trade relationships among nation-states, the growing number of transnational corporations, the emergence of global health and environmental issues and the common style of consumption of material and cultural products have all helped to bring about what is described as the globalisation of our world' (Servaes et al. 2000: 2).

Herbert (2001:1) provides an extensive theoretical and methodological consideration of globalisation specific to the production of foreign news. He provides a comparative study of journalism practice worldwide and draws on case studies from Europe, Australia, the Asia Pacific, South Asia, China, Africa and the Americas. Herbert (2001:7) gives a general assessment of the environment in which journalists operate, and 'the global journalism of today, helped and hindered as it is by the digital revolution, by convergence of media onto one communicating platform, by instantaneous distribution of facts and information throughout the world'. He (2001: 6) considers global news coverage is in danger of becoming too simplified because of time and money constraints and asserts that 'globalisation is having the effect of homogenisation on news flow, news content, news style, news presentation'.

Corporatisation

An initial literature review into the business of international news revealed that news is no longer seen as a craft but a manufacturing operation, with the potential to make profit. A common theme (Kimball, 1994; Warren, 1996; Hachten, 1996) is that the advent of advancing technology and the breaking down of cultural barriers in the commercial field has turned the news business, broadcasting in particular, into an international battleground, which has unintentionally changed the nature of news.

Two articles, *Stop Press* (1999) and *Here is the News* (1999), argue that significant corporate structural changes have occurred at the top three American media organisations – ABC, CCN, NBC. *Stop Press* (1999: 17) gives a case study of the corporate restructure of the news production process at NBC.

Look at the quantity of NBC's output: over the past two years, it has gone up from three hours of television news a day to 24 hours a day, plus a constantly updated website. And that is only with a few extra reporters. Like the next factory owner, NBC has thought hard about how to screw more output from its workers ...NBC is an example of what is happening across the industry. Until two years ago, America had three evening news shows, one cable news network and a couple of weekly news-magazine programs. Now it has three evening news programs, ten weekly hour-long news-magazine shows, three cable news networks, two sport news networks and three news websites finished with video' (1999: 17).

This complements a common theme for this chapter, that media organisations are continually increasing the number of news outlets they have but are either cutting back or keeping the same number of staff they had ten years ago. Therefore, domestic and international correspondents are being made to produce more material, for more programs, in a shorter period of time. The article also includes an examination of audience behaviour and demands; the costs of producing foreign news; the amount of foreign news coverage; and the American race to produce 'water cooler' stories or stories that people will gossip about in public. It concludes that 'there is nothing wrong with treating news as a product for sale' but warns employee trust, audience interest in foreign news and self-image of the news organisation may be spoiled if the situation is not handled carefully. A limitation of this study is its concentration on NBC; it does not explore media organisations in the United Kingdom or the Asia Pacific.

Kimball (1994: 27) also evinces a common theme of the chapter that correspondents are reviewing their work practices in order to produce the amount of material their news organisations require. He (1994: 27) argues that drastic budget cuts have forced the three major United States media players to close down or downsize all of their overseas bureaus, acknowledging that 'news organisations are feeling the pinch of global recession and have had to tighten their purse strings and fire all those that are not necessary' (1994: 30).

This text also details some trends for the future of international reporting (1994: 28): firstly, 'multitasking' – where correspondents are expected to work for numerous shows for the one network and act as the producer, camera operator and reporter, and secondly, pooling – the act of getting one network crew to cover a story and share the video pictures / information with domestic journalists for the other networks. Kimball argues (199: 28) these processes may lead to greater errors in the reporting of international news and acknowledges that 'the voice-over spot, where the correspondent talks over the tape from places he or she has never visited, is increasingly in vogue... but some argue this is no worse than the previous practice of flying in network correspondents for a hit-and-run story from countries where they were newly arrived' (1994: 30).

Foreign News Content

A literature exists (White, 1991; Conley, 1997; Dennis, 2001; Tiffen, 1978) that analyses a complex web of factors that determine the international newsgathering, selection and presentation process. Tiffen

(1978: 33) argues that all news stories are selected based on a core set of news values and, whether domestic or international, all stories must be new, interesting, informative and exciting. Hess (1996) expands on this argument, providing an analysis of what news values are, explaining why some countries are covered more regularly in the news, stating 'most of the world's countries are seen rarely, and then only because they host an important event or person, a pope or a president, or because hurricanes happen, or because a producer finds an amusing, sentimental, or ironic story that can end the program on an upbeat note' (1996: 31).

Hess details what various types of international stories get covered including: combat; human rights; diplomacy and foreign affairs; accidents and disasters; crime; and 'offbeat'. He also acknowledges that technological advancement and the demise of the Cold War have changed the amount of foreign news content available to audiences, but says 'the basic governmental character of international news values remains remarkably consistent and unchanging... bloody, bloodier, bloodiest' (1996: 44), concluding:

What gets covered – overwhelmingly the actions of governments, especially those engaged in combat – gets covered because it is news. Every journalist knows that... but as foreign news becomes increasingly violent – even at a time when the world is not more violent – there must be additional explanations. One is technology: the possibilities now of covering violence faster, from more places, more vividly is difficult for journalists to resist. Another is said to be demand. 'You've got to have bang-bang or a massacre to get on the air,' said one network producer from El Salvador in 1982. 'It is what the consumers want'. Certainly consumers want the big story and the stories in which the Americans are involved. (1996: 46).

Culture of correspondents

Many texts explore the socio-professional culture and backgrounds of foreign correspondents (Hess, 1996; Chen, 1995; Furlonger, 1981; Hemmingway, 1970; Hohenberg, 1995; Roy, 1996, Tiffen, 1978), but evidently little so far about how this culture is changing with the advent of advancing technologies and closing of foreign bureaus.

Knight (1995) provides an overview of what Australian foreign correspondents have been doing in South-East Asia. He argues that due to economic constraints news bureaus in the region are closing, foreign correspondents are finding themselves out of a job, and the ones who have remained do not have enough time, money, language skills or cultural understanding to analyse stories in depth – therefore coming under pressure to remodel the way they work. Knight argues that lack of knowledge forces correspondents to rely on a restricted pool of information from non-independent sources, distorting the reader's image and opinion on the story and region. He argues that the future of foreign correspondence lies in the hands of enterprising, local freelancers who have a strong knowledge of the area, are fluent in all local languages and have the luxury of being able to write more in-depth political and socio-economic analyses thanks to the wonders of instant technology. That theory links in with this study's idea that for foreign correspondents to continue working they should remodel their work practices, and that there are signs of it happening.

Professional Autonomy

We have a set of readings that deals with the notion that the newsroom has an underlying structure little different from any other organisation that markets a product (Berkowitz, 1997; Hall, 1978; Wallis and Baran, 1990). Like other organisations, it is argued that news is affected by a myriad of historical, technological, cultural and chance factors that govern possibilities within the organisation. However, there is a difference in that the product will be the creative and intellectual professional output of journalists. As David Berkowitz observed: 'the newsroom rarely works like an assembly line' (Berkowitz, 1997:281).

Berkowitz (1997: 282) argues that journalists acknowledge they have to produce a uniform product in a limited period of time that conforms to certain organisational protocols. Yet even after a period of institutionalisation, Berkowitz argues journalists still live and work by their own professional ethos, stating that journalists feel empathy towards their audience and feel it is their duty to provide them with all the information available (1997:15). Wallis and Baran (1990: 217) expand on this argument, stating 'the journalist is involved in a constant process of balancing the demands of the owners, gatekeepers and stakeholders with the professional principles of journalism.'

In more situated critiques of the nature of journalism professionalism, Tuchman (1978) and Schlesinger (1987) examine the context of journalistic work to see how journalists' particular cultural adaptations to social structures might influence their professional approaches. Tuchman (1978) has undertaken ethnographic work in a number of newsrooms and foreign bureaus to examine how journalists, domestic and international, and their organisations relate to other institutions and how these relationships affect the sorts of accounts that they acknowledge as examples of professionally competent work. Schlesinger (1987) meanwhile concentrates on journalism's professional values as they are exhibited within a news organisation. These studies concede that journalists might still exhibit a relative autonomy allowing exercise of professional judgment. However they do argue that journalists' claims to a professional distance from authorities, for example diplomats, are compromised through their particular work practices, like the pressure of deadlines that can head-off checking or a search for alternative sources.

Media Contents Review

In an effort to confirm or deny conclusions made in this literature, the writer set out to conduct a review of foreign news coverage. From March 17, 2003 to March 23, and again from May 12 to May 18, the nightly news bulletins on SBS, ABC and BBC World were monitored, as were the international news pages in *The Australian* and *Time*. To organise the material, questions asked while monitoring the stories were: Was the story an RVO or package, news brief, news story or feature; did a correspondent or wires service produce the story; did the story give sources; if so, how many and who were they; did the story make use of still or moving pictures; and what subject category did the story fit into?

It is important to note that during the initial monitoring period the second Gulf War began; its dominating coverage had to be included in the review. It is not difficult to surmise that the massive mobilisation of media resources for such an event would distort the normal, everyday patterns of international coverage. Or it would create a second kind of normality, i.e. international coverage at times of war and crisis versus international coverage at other times. For the purpose of this study, the writer categorised the war stories under a separate heading and concluded that by the end of the monitoring period war coverage took up 25 per cent of the international space in the publications or programs under review.

Findings on Media Contents

ABC, BBC and *Time* fared the best in the review in respect of originating their own material and accounts. All three news organisations had correspondents producing a majority of their international stories; they offered a wide variety of international stories from the United States, United Kingdom, the Middle East and South-East Asia; and all three media organisations quoted more than one source in most of their stories, giving them balance.

SBS, while producing a large variety of international stories, relied heavily on wires, pictures and packages produced by bigger news organisations like the BBC. Putnis (2001) notes that due to financial restrictions, SBS was forced to close all overseas bureaus in the late 1990s and now employs a team of writers in Sydney who produce original scripts to match the pictures coming in from the wire services. SBS would also create international packages, with a local focus. For example, on May 12 SBS produced a package about a suicide attack in Israel that also included the reactions of a Middle Eastern community in Sydney.

The Australian scored the lowest points in the review in terms of originating their own material. Although the paper currently boasts that it has a bigger team of permanent correspondents than any other Australian newspaper, they still relied heavily on copy from major news agencies to fill the world pages. The news briefs featured were often out of date. Stories with interesting pictures normally got a better run than stories without any picture, suggesting perhaps a weakening of focus on factual content and analysis of processes in the news.

Overall, there was a tendency for the television news programs to run a minimum of three international reader voiceovers (RVO) per night and one to two packages produced by staff correspondents or sourced from the major United States stations – CNN, ABC or NBC. The BBC was the only news program to run international feature stories. For example, on March 19 they ran a six minute feature on the state of poverty in Angola and the famous English actor Joseph Fiennes narrated the package. The ABC tended to do a lot of background work, covered mostly diplomatic and international affairs and linked their packages to stories which would be aired during the week on their current affairs programs, e.g. *Foreign Correspondent*. SBS on the other hand had an exhaustive coverage of international issues outside of the normal news genre. For example, on March 20 they aired a backgrounding, in-depth report into continuing conflict in East Timor that no other news organisation under review reported on.

The Australian followed the practice of keeping a series of stories running for a period of seven days. For example, from May 12 to May 18 suicide bombings in the Middle East dominated at least 15 per cent of their daily international news coverage, and their resident correspondent would have either a feature or opinion piece published each day to supplement the news copy. Most of *The Australian's* longer international news stories were sourced from the major wire services – AFP, Reuters and AAP – or top selling British newspapers, like *The Times*, giving little originality in the coverage. Feature and essay length background/ investigative pieces affecting American interests, in particular the continuing war on terror, dominated *Time* magazine's international space, though the material was 85 per cent of the time produced by a staff correspondent or stringer.

It was usually possible to divine from the reportage where the stories originated and who the sources were. For example, the BBC correspondent in Jerusalem would usually use two or three official sources in his report, accompanied by some vox pops on what happened. However, *Time* magazine did not always quote sources. In all 80 per cent of all stories for the entire review used disclosed sources. Of that, 30 per cent of the sources were politicians and officials, 25 per cent were experts or academics in the field being discussed, 20 per cent were unnamed and 5 per cent were general bystanders or 'members of the public'. As Hess noted in his 1996 study, any story with vivid moving pictures made it to the evening news bulletins, whether it be a fire in Cuba or bomb blast in Chechnya. This production value limited the coverage ABC, SBS and BBC gave to some stories. For example, they did not match *The Australian* and *Time* in giving extensive news and features coverage to the hunt for Osama bin Laden, or even to the lead-up to the 2003 Oscars. ABC, SBS and BBC did report those but usually using just a 30 second RVO, putting a limit to the commitment of air-time. On the other hand, a bomb blast in Argentina that injured nine, accompanied by lots of moving pictures, received top international billing on the television news during the review but only got a 50 word news brief write-up in *The Australian*, and did not make it into *Time*.

Based on Hess's (1996) model for reviewing international news copy, the writer concluded that there were eight categories under which international news could be organised, in order of prominence in usage:

1. War and Crisis
2. Diplomatic Events and Issues
3. International Relations
4. Business, Finance and Economics
5. Lifestyle, Features and Columns
6. Colour and Humour
7. Culture and Celebrity
8. Other

The main conclusion drawn from the review was that Hess's (1996) proposition that crisis, war and violent stories dominate international news bulletins is correct. The other categories of international stories that featured prominently were diplomatic events and then other issues – including human rights, business, finance and economics and colour and humour. The review made it apparent that editors and reporters often relied on stereotypes when writing and producing international stories. For example, stories about Japan focused around new technologies, business and the environment whereas stories from Britain normally focused on the offbeat or the royal family. The only country that seemed to get a sufficiently diverse array of stories written about it was Iraq, by reason of heavy attention due to the recent fallout of war, with many correspondents working there.

The review of media contents produces a cross-sectional guide to what Australians receive as international news and information, from mass media committed to offering significant levels of overseas coverage. It shows the volumes of space or air-time allocated are not vast or excessive, with television bulletins sometimes confining themselves to only three international reports per evening. On the other hand, there was significant autonomy of coverage across the board, with most media outlets using their own correspondents as prime providers of stories or features. As an alternative, the media outlets would use a variety of outside sources and, as in the case of SBS, would add local treatments. Because news is a business committed to interesting the audience or readership with its offerings, production values rated highly. There was a concentration on vivid moving pictures, country stereotypes emerged, and war, with its powerful impact, tended to dominate coverage during the period in review.

The focus of this study is on the way the foreign correspondents produce this work. While technologies impel media outlets to economise, i.e. by pooling coverage for television, this review made it clear that expertise in understanding, interpreting and representing the news stories is also of high importance. That conclusion can be derived from the way the products appear, for example: SBS uses its own reporters over syndicated images; *The Australian* buys-in international copy but includes additional copy from other syndicated sources within the News Limited organisation; *Time* places a strong focus on investigations and stories of international importance; and the ABC and BBC both commit major expenditure to put their own foreign correspondents in the field.

Interview Analysis

Wanting to confirm or deny conclusions drawn from the literature review and media contents review, the writer obtained extensive, in-depth interviews with 25 foreign correspondents. (The full list of names is given in the appendix to this chapter.) The aim of this process was to get the correspondents to consider change; to personally identify what they thought the issues pertinent to the quality and quantity of international news were; and to comment on the future of foreign correspondence.

The 25 full-time international correspondents were Australian, American, British, German or French, were living and working in the European Union, and were mostly higher degree graduates familiar with or receptive to theories and ideas discussed in this chapter. The writer chose to focus on correspondents in the European Union because the news focus on international affairs is more prominent there than in the United States or South-East Asia.

Although the interviewer did not ask each journalist participant set questions, each interviewee was asked to comment on five broad subject matters: globalisation, corporatisation in the media industry, international news audiences, professional autonomy and the future of foreign correspondence. For the purpose of this chapter information from ten of the correspondents will be directly used: Betrand Benoit, *Financial Times*; Michael Steen, Reuters; Michael Brissenden, ABC; Geoff Hutchinson, ABC; Gaven Morris, CNN; Angus Roxburgh, BBC; Majella Anning, freelancer; Maria Louise Francesco, freelancer; John Litchfield, *The Independent* and James Graff, *Time*. In this analysis the topics are grouped into five broad areas: changes to bureaus, economic factors, technology, productivity and professional autonomy.

Changes to bureaus

As a starting premise it was posited that Western media organisations have reduced their newsgathering operations abroad and reduced their emphasis on foreign news reporting in their coverage since 1989. This is a standard trend identified by Hess (1996), Knight (1995) and Goodman and Pollack (1997). Questions were put to the respondents about the possible influence and impacts this trend has had on the quality of foreign news, and complicity or involvement of the news teams in the making of international news stories. The media panel interviewed for this study unanimously agreed that Western media organisations were being forced to close or downsize their international bureaus and find alternative ways of reporting the news. These changes registered with Bertrand Benoit, Angus Roxburgh and Gaven Morris as an 'inevitable' movement, because of the advances in communication technology making remote foreign reporting much easier and cheaper. But to Michael Brissenden, whose work from Brussels normally focused on finding a European Union story that would interest Australian audiences, international bureaus have been closed because 'there is no money' to sustain them.

Geoff Hutchinson, Benoit and Brissenden claim that as a direct result of these cuts the quality of foreign news has decreased. The three make the point that correspondents are consistently finding themselves under increased pressure from their separate home desks to produce more international copy, even though 'sectors that were once covered by many people are now covered by one... and that is a trend which is continuing,' said Benoit. Benoit, Hutchinson and Brissenden argue the expectation from themselves and the home desk to produce quality work is still paramount; however to produce the quantity of work required they only had time to be reactive and report the headline news stories. They also noted that corporate amalgamations and pressures from shareholders had resulted in 'dumbing down' of international news. Michael Steen of Reuters noted that at his organisation a similar trend was occurring, though if a major bureau was downsized local stringers would be contracted to fill in the gaps: 'The bureau in Kiev ... used to have two international staffers, now they only have local staffers who write in both English and Russian.'

Developing this line of argument, the BBC's Roxburgh claimed budget cuts had forced news organisations to create major bureaus in central locations, and rely on freelancers and stringers in other areas: 'The BBC has tended to go with a system of what we call "hub" bureaus around the world. Washington is the biggest one, Brussels the next, Moscow after that, Middle East, then the Singapore bureau and a kind of half-hearted "hub" in Southern Africa. They have main news correspondents based in all of those places, plus stringers everywhere else.' He had the impression the BBC would never completely rely on freelance correspondents and stringers, even though the vast majority of its 'huge network', 150 correspondents, were freelance: 'They are mainly in areas that don't generate huge amounts of news... we also have super stringers, who are paid a certain amount of money to stay in one area and then get paid by the piece when they produce some kind of news.' Maria Louise Francisco, James Graff and Hutchinson agreed the closure of some bureaus was directly related to the amount of copy generated from that region. All three argued that news stories were always selected based on a core set of news values and, whether domestic or international, all stories had to be new, interesting, informative or exciting; and if a region was not producing enough of that, an editorial decision to close the bureau would be justified. Hutchinson said media organisations needed to be able to reassess the importance of certain bureaus every few years, without backlash from media analysts and foreign correspondents.

Developing this argument, Graff said that closing or restructuring a bureau is not always a negative thing and likened it to refocusing a spotlight on stage. Reflecting on the trend at *Time* he said: 'We haven't closed any bureaus in Europe. We haven't fired x amount of correspondents per city. We had a bureau in Seoul at the time when Korea hosted the Olympics and there was a lot going on. Then we closed that. We have now opened a bureau in Baghdad because that is where news is being generated. That is just how news organisations work.' However, Hutchinson, Francisco and Graff all formed the impression that the quality of international news would suffer greatly if media organisations closed their international bureaus indefinitely. To Hutchinson, 'bureaus are journalistic luxuries we should afford.'

Economic factors

From the interviewees' perspective, the tightening of purse strings and budget cuts commanded the closure of many overseas bureaus. Like Kimball (1994) they concluded the business of news was no longer seen as a craft but a manufacturing operation with potential to make profit. Brissenden, Roxburgh and Hutchinson agreed that the cost of producing foreign news and audience behaviours and demands for international news were constantly under scrutiny by Western media organisations. Roxburgh noticed that full-time foreign correspondents at the BBC were being replaced by a rotating journalist, equipped to fly solo into a region, set up a temporary bureau, report on the major event occurring for the next six months, and then fly home or to their next assignment. Roxburgh observes: 'This seems to be a cost cutting exercise because if you have a full-time correspondent you have to pay for all of their staff expenses, accommodation, school fees, if they have children, but you don't have to if they are just flying in and out.' Roxburgh fears this type of reporting will lead to greater errors in the reporting of international news.

Graff disagreed, thinking quality would not be affected, and considering that international journalism was following a general trend towards contractual employment in the workforce: 'In Italy we used to have a full-time, New York paid correspondent living in Rome. It was just too expensive. We still have a full-time correspondent ... on a contractual basis. He doesn't have the same status and doesn't get the same benefits but still reports on the same stuff.' As part of other cost cutting exercises, Brissenden and Hutchinson of the ABC were being required to produce copy for numerous shows in different media formats: for example if an Australian official disappeared in Rome they might be required to produce 30-second radio updates, one television package for the evening news, possibly a short documentary-style piece once the person was found and backgrounding reports for the *ABC Online* service.

Steen acknowledged that coverage on Reuter's stories could not be fully free from commercial considerations, and decisions to close bureaus in more remote corners of the globe, e.g. Nairobi, were heavily influenced by the fact that most clients were based in the Britain or the United States. He notes: 'This company sells its news, therefore a train crash in Britain which kills 20 people will get far more coverage, and deeper coverage and better quality of coverage than 200 people drowning in a ferry accident in Kenya. Why? Because Reuters has no business interests in Kenya.'

The media panelists interviewed for this study generally agreed economic trends would dictate much of the future of foreign news coverage. All agreed that media organisations since 1989 had felt the pinch of occasional global recession, had tightened purse strings, and had downsized costly overseas operations seen to be not necessary.

Technology and productivity

Today's journalists speed to the world's most current hot spot and then on to the next. Computers and satellites deliver instantaneous reporting. The public gets very brief but intense images of strange places and often violent events. Then the spotlight moves on. (Hess 1996: 28).

Getting into and working in African, South-East Asian, South American and Eastern European countries had generally been difficult prior to 1989, and John Lichfield, an experienced field reporter turned to organising correspondents' work from Paris, saw the breakdown of geopolitical barriers as one of the main signs of basic change in foreign correspondence. That fact, and the aid of new communication technology, enabled the journalists to operate very effectively. While digital technology including satellite phones and the Internet has reduced the cost of producing foreign news, the panel of correspondents interviewed agree there seems to be no indication that news organisations will use these savings to increase the quality and quantity of international coverage.

Graff does argue this communication technology revolution has had positive impacts for international news because foreign correspondents can be more productive. Satellite dishes allow correspondents to receive and file news stories in real time from all over the globe, in turn giving audiences the most up-to-date, fresh and current report. He suggested that these advances have helped improve the quality of foreign news being produced by correspondents: 'Technology has certainly changed, even in the time I have been working as a correspondent. I used to use a telex machine at the public post office in Munich and back in 1997/98 when I was in Bosnia I had to walk from story to story and I had no telephone and I couldn't file. I had a satellite telex but it was really complicated. If my stories ever made it home they were normally out of date. So definitely, the incredible increase in immediacy that has been gained from technological advances has helped correspondents tell the news.'

Benoit also reflected on his past struggles with technology:

Technology makes my work much easier. I remember having to phone in stories from phone boxes that were jotted down on a notebook. Now it's great. It's nothing fancy, just a laptop and mobile satellite phone and it is very slow and it doesn't work very well, but at least I can sit down anywhere and write a story and file it from location. I think I find it much, much easier. And I think the quality of international news has improved from this.

Roxburgh took the same view, that while the BBC has had to decrease the number of foreign bureaus they have in operation, when a big foreign story breaks, e.g. the second Gulf war, correspondents have the ability to be on the air instantaneously telling the audience in real time what is happening. 'The importance of everyday foreign news in the media has been downgraded, but on the other hand when a big foreign news story breaks we have the means to cover it, bigger and better than ever before. We have the technology to get out there en masse, with dozens of correspondents and producers and cameramen and are required to report to 24 hour news outlets, 24 hours a day'.

Hutchinson and Brissenden have a strong critical view of the way new technologies have changed international news practices. Brissenden argues that while cost efficiencies may be proved in tight financial circumstances, depth and perspective can be lost: 'The expectation and demand from the home desk is high and the reality is we cannot be everywhere, all the time. So a lot of the time we are forced to repackage someone else's work and supplement their script with our own.' However he also noticed that new communication technologies had empowered foreign correspondents with the ability to produce more international material: 'We have online coming on, we have correspondents going off and doing digicam trips, where you're shooting stuff yourself and now you're empowered for doing everything.' Hutchinson agreed but feared quality could still suffer: 'I often find I am rewriting wires copy rather than shooting my own stuff because the home desk wants me to provide more copy than I can handle. I just hope that is not where the future of foreign correspondence is headed.'

Working autonomously

It was suggested to the interviewees that news professionals shared common understandings about their work ordinarily summed up as 'news values' to be applied when choosing and constructing their stories. These are practical standards identified with the 'Western liberal' tradition in news media and are spelt out in journalism texts as lists representing 'news values', 'characteristics', 'elements' or points for a news 'checklist' all familiar to practitioners and barely disputed among them. They draw attention to the importance to the journalists' craft, of accuracy; speed; the power of disaster; the high interest value of conflict; proximity; prominence; the unusual or novel, and the need to work under intense pressure and scrutiny (White, 1996: 11). Berkowitz (1997) contributes to the argument that the standard of news values is important, and should be recognised as such, agreeing with the widely accepted view that application of these values is integral to autonomous professional work by journalists. Looking at the values and assumptions of journalists understood in this way, the respondents in this study considered deadlines, high volume, accuracy and prescience, (being able to look ahead, to be at the right place at the right time), to have imposed strongest demands on their performance since 1989.

According to Steen, establishing the facts is the hallmark of Western liberal practices in journalism and the importance is heightened in crisis situations where there is a focus on international journalism abroad. He did acknowledge tighter deadlines, brought about by improved technologies, and a stronger reliance on stringer material had magnified the challenge involved in getting the facts and so getting the story right.

If you have a stringer in 'country x' and you are sitting in 'country y' and the local journalist is feeding you information about the latest crisis, it can become too easy for you to fool yourself into thinking that you are actually getting the story. What foreign correspondents have to remember is that when you're dealing with stringers you are dealing with someone whose English is probably not that great and who maybe hasn't been trained enough to understand what your international audience it is going to want, and too often the stringer's copy gets rewritten, and unfortunately then the person rewriting it will tend to rely on clichés about the country and the subject. So although stringer networks are invaluable and they're cheaper to run, I think the quality and accuracy of reporting suffers if you entirely rely on that. Foreign correspondents of the future have to become better equipped and backgrounded so they can fly in and out of news hot spots, the technology is there so they can do that.

In the journalistic ethos the ability to recognise trends and grasp their importance in advance always has premium value. An aspect of that skill is to be on hand for main events, and, as former ABC correspondent Majella Anning believes, to know potentially what will occur and be thoroughly backgrounded in the situation. To Anning, it is a foreign correspondent's duty to produce a uniform product in a limited period of time that conforms to certain organisational protocols but they must also maintain their own professional standards and make it their duty to provide their audience with all the information available: 'Correspondents have to be adaptable if they want to get their story out to their audience; my problems with the home desk were minimal and mostly they accepted my judgment because I was on the spot.'

Roxburgh recognised the centrality of the time problem, with instant communication very possible, and actually prone to work against discovery:

Somebody, a few years ago, coined the expression dish monkey; we are all dish monkeys now. We just stand beside these satellite dishes, sprouting at the top of every hour when the home desk comes to you for your latest impressions of what is going on, and frankly you've got no idea. You often have had no time to go out and find out what is really going on and you're often in the idiotic position of having people in London telling you, through your ear phone, what the wires are saying and asking you to repeat it on air. I don't know any correspondent that likes being in that situation and I think we have come up with a better system.

Steen concluded that although correspondents still have considerable professional autonomy, technological advances have intensified pressure for performance, which has in turn led to the demise in the quality of international news:

I argue that technology increases the pressure on correspondents to deliver more because they have more opportunity to publish for a variety of outlets – 24-hour rolling television and radio news and the Internet. So if a correspondent is chasing a huge story and everyone is interested, the beauty of modern technology is that more news can be delivered, more quickly, all around the world. But I argue the quality of international journalism has suffered by being able to splatter news everywhere instantly.

Neo-firefighter model

The literature review, the media contents review, and especially the considered projections made by the panel of foreign correspondents, provide evidence to conclude that the profile or model of the international journalist must be expected to adjust to the pressure of changed international conditions. It is posited that two factors have remained stable: news events and processes greatly interesting to audiences are continuing to occur, and journalists of high calibre are engaged as correspondents, in some mode of work, to report on what is happening. Other circumstances are unstable: geo-political circumstances, the wave of globalisation, economic rationalisation on the part of corporations, and new communication technology – to list the leading factors. From all this we derive the possibility of an adjustment by journalists, firstly in accepting that many corporate overseas jobs will go, and that thanks to technology, much worldwide news gathering will be more industrialised – with more syndication of products. Secondly the journalists are able to take up the empowerment offered by their new tools, better communication technology developed mostly in the last few decades; they are able to prepare themselves very effectively to practice in the new international arena, through their education, languages, ability to handle information, skills of writing and presentation; they can travel to work at destinations where they will know the field well; and they can be autonomous in the new world economy, doing business inside or outside the framework of large corporations, supplying services as required by audience demand.

In many ways this new type of foreign correspondent may resemble the so-called 'firefighter' or 'parachute' journalist, who Goodman and Pollack (1995) and Roxburgh describe as an ill-informed international correspondent required to drop into a scene of crisis, report on the situation without having any background knowledge, capable only to record and report instant impressions and half-checked facts. However Roxburgh also foreshadowed a correspondent who would have to be better equipped to provide in-depth, analytical, quality reportage:

> *The parachute model worked for a time, but the correspondent of the future has to go further. They need not only to fly in and report the facts but they need to refocus the spotlight, get the world's attention with a big, well written and researched piece of work. They need to be experts in their field. And now because of advances in technology etcetera correspondents have the ability to achieve this.*

In agreement, Hutchinson, Brissenden and Benoit argue that advances in technology have forced foreign correspondents to change. According to Benoit, laptops, satellite dishes and mobile phones have made the job of a correspondent much easier because 'you can now sit down anywhere and write a story and file it from location; you couldn't do that four or five years ago'. Brissenden acknowledged that the pressure to provide more, using new equipment and drawing on syndicated services and wires copy sometimes can work to the correspondents' advantage if they have a good eye for news. He recalled spotting a small local news item that an Australian-owned mining company was accused of polluting a river in Romania. When followed up aggressively it became a major international story for all.

Steen, Morris and Anning stressed the importance of knowing other languages and having a specialisation in a region. Steen argued that the quality of coverage automatically increases if the correspondent knows the language and can communicate with locals, officials and experts in their native tongue, rather than going through a translator. Lichfield added:

> *I think coverage does benefit from having correspondents that know a lot about the culture and preferably know the language ... but, if coverage quality is to continue to increase we need more bloody good correspondents who are well educated, know other languages and basically are just brilliant at what they do.*

There was a common feeling amongst the interviewees that today's conventional 'firefighter' or 'parachute' correspondents did not provide news stories that were analytical or informed. Reflecting on his personal experience as a 'parachute' correspondent in Afghanistan, Steen criticised the work he produced during his posting. He said not knowing local languages, customs or backgrounding information affected his work and hoped that in the future news organisations would employ correspondents 'equipped to report on issues and make them new, interesting, informative and exciting – not just flash in the pan stuff'.

Steen and Francesco both stressed the important role stringers play in the production of international news. Francesco contended that news organisations will continue to employ stringers even if the role of the foreign correspondent changes because they are an invaluable resource for local information, cheap to employ and often have a good book of local contacts that the roaming correspondent does not always have.

> *Often you go to a place and if there is a stringer that is the first person you contact because he or she can give you all the information, the contacts and even practical information about the country. They often know the language of the country, but we can't rely on them completely because often they can be biased in their telling of local stories.*

According to Roxburgh change is also driven by audience needs and demands:

> *The BBC world service tends to use a lot of stringers for their international reports but studies have shown audiences don't like this. Now the domestic news service is aiming to have a small number of well-known faces on air reporting on international events. They don't want dozens of people popping up ... because the audience doesn't recognise them and doesn't trust them. So now they are really aiming to have a couple of big correspondents who cover the regions and only use the stringers on the day when a big story breaks.*

These are telling reflections to illustrate a point about the changes foreign correspondents are facing in their everyday lives. Based on these observations, a description of the future foreign correspondent was developed. The 'neo firefighter', as such an identity is called here, would still be as mobile but would only be required to travel within a set territory of responsibility, dropping in on events as frequently as he or she felt was necessary. They may have a knowledge 'field', e.g. a business and finance speciality. This so-called 'neo firefighter' would also be equipped with the latest technology, such as a satellite phone, laptop computer with remote Internet connection and digital handheld camera, to be able to file text, audio, moving and still images on location, and have the ability to travel at short notice to the remotest area in their specialised region. These technologies, which have advanced dramatically since the end of the Cold War, would empower the 'neo firefighter' making him or her highly productive.

Ideally, these would be at least bi-media correspondents experienced in reporting news and current affairs for radio, television, print and online service. The 'neo firefighter' must have independent knowledge of political, social, economic and cultural affairs in their region of speciality. He or she would have to be adaptable to change and willing to work elsewhere in the world according to news demands. A 'neo firefighter', like conventional correspondents, must be able to work to tight deadlines and provide both short and long-form stories. In a general portfolio of high-order skills the 'neo firefighter' must also possess management abilities, enthusiasm and energy to take on arduous and/or hazardous assignments, and (in down-time, or at times when the going has been hectic) readiness to take holidays on command (!).

The correspondents interviewed acknowledged that a 'neo firefighter' would most probably be overworked, however as Steen argues the evolution of the correspondent role is inevitable: 'If the quality and quantity of foreign news is to continue in the future, foreign correspondents must learn how to adapt and be willing to take on more responsibilities. Believe me, most correspondents will be willing to do this because they love their job and they have a passion for news'.

Conclusions

There is evidence to conclude that the model of the so-called 'neo firefighter' could be expected to develop as the profile or model of future international journalists, from three sources: The discussion of technological expansion and its impacts, contained in the literature; the variety of sourcing, the opposing factor of more pooling or syndication, and rapid presentation of news, monitored in the review of media contents; and especially the considered projections made by the panel of foreign correspondents in the interview study.

Such correspondents are seen as positioned at a mid-point among conventional bureau reporters, 'firefighters' dropping in on news stories from anywhere and everywhere, and locally-based freelancers who work as stringers for news outlets. They will be recognisable successors to traditional correspondents, in terms of having advanced reporting skills, and ability to work autonomously, identifying news and building the news agenda. They will differ in being more highly productive through use of 21st century communications tools; will need extremely good background and preparation, and so be likely to specialise on one world region or news theatre; and in their organisational setting may be as likely to work as sole traders, or entrepreneurial journalists, as employees of large news corporations.

Appendix – Correspondents Interviewed

Name	Job description / Employer	Date interviewed	Place
Majella Anning	Freelance	09.07.03	Brussels
Bertrand Benoit	*Financial Times*	27.06.03	Frankfurt
Michael Brissenden	*ABC*	07.07.03	Brussels
Jan Dahinten	*Reuters*	28.06.03	Frankfurt
Judy Dempsey	*Financial Times*	07.07.03	Brussels
Peter Ford	*Christian Science Monitor*	10.07.03	Paris
Maria Laura Francesco	Freelance	09.07.03	Brussels
James Graff	*Time*	12.07.03	Paris
Tom Heneghan	*Reuters*	10.07.03	Paris
Jon Henley	*Guardian*	11.07.03	Paris
Jeremy Herron	*International Herald Tribune*	27.06.03	Frankfurt
Geoff Hutchinson	*ABC*	07.07.03	Brussels
John Litchfield	*Independent*	11.07.03	Paris
James MacKenzie	*Reuters*	27.06.03	Frankfurt
Victor Mallet	*Financial Times*	10.07.03	Paris
Jeff Mason	*Reuters*	26.06.03	Amsterdam
Gaven Morris	*CNN*	11.07.03	Paris
Gerrino Mulder	Freelance	04.07.03	Maastricht
Bill Neely	*ITV News*	12.07.03	Paris
Alan Riding	*New York Times*	12.07.03	Paris
Angus Roxburgh	*BBC*	07.07.03	Brussels
Michael Steen	*Reuters*	27.06.03	Frankfurt
John Tagliabue	*New York Times*	11.07.03	Paris
Paul Taylor	*Reuters*	05.07.03	Brussels
Peter van Lier	*One World*	23.06.03	Amsterdam

References

Berkowitz, D. (1997). *Social Meanings of News: A Text Reader*. USA: Sage Publications.

Chen, W. (1995). *A Socio-Professional Portrait of the Washington DC Correspondents*. University of Missouri, Columbia, USA.

Chew, S. C., & Denemark, R. A. (1996). *The Underdevelopment of Development: Essays in Honour of Andre Gunder Frank*. California, USA: Sage Publications.

Conley, D. (1997). *The Daily Miracle: An Introduction to Journalism*. Melbourne, AUST: Oxford University Press.

Dennis, E. E., & Merrill, J. C. (2001). "Deciding What is News". In E. E. Dennis & J. C. Merrill (Eds.), *Media Debates: Issues in Mass Communication*. New York, USA: Longman.

Featherstone, M. (1990). "Global Culture: An Introduction". In M. Featherstone (Ed.), *Global Culture*. London, UK: Sage Publications.

Furlonger, B. (1981). Introduction. In B. Furlonger (Ed.), *Then and Now: ABC Correspondents Abroad*. Sydney: Australian Broadcasting Corporation.

Goodman, A., & Pollack, J. (1997). *The World on a String: How to Become a Freelance Foreign Correspondent*. New York, USA: Henry Holt and Company.

Hachten, W. A. (1996). *The World News Prism: Changing Media of International Communication* (Fourth ed.). USA: Iowa State University Press.

Hall, S. (1992). "The Question of Cultural Identity". In S. Hall, D. Held & T. McGrew (Eds.), *Modernity and its Future*. Cambridge, UK: Polity Press.

Hemmingway, E. (1970). *By-line: Ernest Hemmingway*. London, UK: Penguin Books.

Herbert, J. (2001). *Practising Global Journalism*. Oxford, UK: Focal Press.

Here is the News. (1998). The Economist, 148(3075), 11.

Hess, S. (1996). *International News and Foreign Correspondents*. Washington, USA: The Brookings Institute.

Hirst, P., & Thompson, G. (1996). *Globalisation in Question: The International Economy and Possibilities of Governance*. London, UK: Polity Press.

Hohenberg, J. (1995). *Foreign Correspondence: The Great Reporters and their Times* (Second ed.). USA: Oxford University Press.

Kimball, P. (1994). *Down-sizing the News: Network Cutbacks in the Nation's Capital*. Maryland, USA: The John Hopkins University Press.

Knight, A. (1995). "Re-inventing the Wheel: Australian Foreign Correspondents in Southeast Asia". *Media Asia*, 22(1), 9-15.

Knight, A. (2000). Fact or Friction? The Collision of Journalism Values in Asia. In D. Kingsbury, E. Loo & P. Payne (Eds.), *Foreign Devils and Other Journalists*. Victoria, Monash Asia Institute..

Kingsbury, E. Loo & P. Payne (Eds.), *Foreign Devils and Other Journalists*. Victoria, Monash Asia Institute.

Roy, N. (1996). "So you want to be a Foreign Correspondent?" *Reportage*, Winter, 40-42.

Schlesinger, P. (1987). *Putting Reality Together: BBC News*. London, UK: Metheun.

Servaes, J. (2000). Introduction. In G. Wang, J. Servaes & A. Goonasekera (Eds.), *The New Communications Landscape* (pp. 1-18). London, UK: Routledge.

Stop Press. (1998). The Economist, 148(3075), 17-19.

Tiffen, R. (1978). *The News from Southeast Asia: The Sociology of Newsmaking*. Singapore: Institute of Southeast Asia Studies.

Tiffen, R. (1989). *News and Power*. Sydney, Allen and Unwin.

Tiffen, R. (2000). "New Order Regime and the Australian Media: The Cultural Contributions to Political Conflict". In D. Kingsbury, E. Loo & P. Payne (Eds.), *Foreign Devils and Other Journalists*. Victoria, Monash Asia Institute.

Tuchman, G. (1978). *Making News: A Study in the Construction of Reality*. New York, Free Press.

Wallerstein, I. (1990). "Culture as the Ideological Background of the Modern World-System". In M. Featherstone (Ed.), *Global Culture*. London, UK: Sage Publications.

Wallis, R., & Baran, S. (1990). *The Known World of Broadcast News: International News and the Electronic Media*. London, UK: Routledge.

Warren, A. (Writer) (1996). "The Business of International News [Radio]", *The Media Report*. Sydney, AUST: Australian Broadcasting Corporation.

Waters, M. (1995). *Globalisation*. New York, USA: Routledge.

White, S. A. (1991). *Reporting in Australia*. Melbourne, Macmillan Education Australia.

Chapter 4

Making television current affairs in Australia: are the flagships flagging?

Elaine Ford

There has been much speculation about the destiny of television especially its long-term flagship programs in current affairs. Such speculation registers the impacts of new communication technology; corporate demands for high cost-effectiveness, and social change, which have seen journalists searching for ways to adjust their products and retain audience support. For this study, practitioners responsible for the leading national programs have been consulted, in interviews, to tell their own story; to assess what they think of their methods, their industry and its future. Most demonstrate a strong attachment to conventions of television current affairs production established in the early years of the medium, which built on a long creative tradition in other fields like drama, cinema or photography. While facing competition for audiences from innovative entertainment and lifestyle shows, most indicate they recognise a need to adjust but are reluctant to abandon established program styles or 'serious' editorial practices, beyond the limits of existing formats. This investigation concentrates on production values, meaning the structure and shape of programs rather than their substantive content drawn from news, and it relies on television or film 'genre' theory as its critical language. Informed non-practitioner media observers are quoted, for an additional perspective.

Introduction

Television current affairs is a much talked-about branch of mass media and one that looks to be entering a period of forced change. It has been the centrepiece of network programming strategies for three decades, but has seen some attrition in audience support as new kinds of television, like the 'reality' programs, draw in numbers. The ability to shift information for news and current affairs around the world has been accelerating; television program makers can deploy a wider range of production values and techniques; the economics of television are changing in line with corporate activity everywhere; and in a climate of economic and social change the interests and behaviour of audiences are shifting too. This chapter takes stock of the situation of television current affairs; it treats it as a creative genre under pressure to alter its ways, and makes its study principally from a practitioners' perspective. It notes developments already under way and considers implications for the future.

Method of research

In the research on which this chapter is based, a review of literature was undertaken on genre theory, television production, and general broadcasting issues. It began with the researcher being engaged in production of a pilot metropolitan current affairs program, called MetroView, on the Queensland community television station Briz31, in 2003. Reflection on the exercise raised several questions about current affairs production, to discuss with practitioners on the mainstream television programs. Therefore, nine interviews were conducted with current affairs Executive Producers and senior journalists from four Australian free-to-air, public and commercial networks; supplemented by interviews with two academic media analysts. The interviews were standardised, each respondent being asked a set list of 14 questions in order to facilitate cross-referencing of responses. Transcripts were made and used in a comparative analysis. The readings and personal interviews are integrated in the analysis that follows. The list of interviewees is given as Appendix 1.

Focus on public affairs as a television genre and field of professional work

The research project differs from much previous work in the field of television journalism by focusing on the specific genre of television current affairs rather than considering it just as an affiliate of television news or an aspect of television generally. It identifies trends in production practices, and with respect to the way that programs themselves are constructed and styled, standing conventions. It emphasises programming issues, for example, duration of program, time of broadcast, and production values, like forms of illustration that are used. This chapter is concerned also with ways that journalists are able to represent current affairs topics in programs, and the relevance of that to professional concerns and development of journalism.

Genre studies have been consulted as a theoretical model with practical applications for understanding television current affairs production. Having its focus on production styles and production values – ways that representation is achieved – the project stops short of other main concerns that arise in analyses of broadcast journalism, for example, agenda-setting or news content analysis, third-party considerations including government regulation, or extensive audience research.

Analysis of the findings

The investigation through readings and interviews showed what the practitioners are concerned with. It showed that as might be expected current affairs producers and reporters were preoccupied with 'editorial' issues, such as the contents of news reports and analysis, but that there was also a sharp focus on production values. These production values are to do with the construction and styling of the product, such as, to do with illustration, or with building illusions of time and/or space, in order to compress time when telling about those events, and then relay debates about them. The analysis is broken down into five parts: **audience** – what producers think audiences want and will respond to; **practical concerns** – techniques, time and money; **short/long-form** television current affairs and documentaries; **production conventions** tried over time; and **genre** theory treatment of concepts in television current affairs production

First though, consider the character of conventional current affairs television products and practice. An assumption has been drawn from observations made while working on programs that the overall drive of television journalism is to simulate life as experienced in the natural world. This naturalistic tradition derives from cinema, which in turn looks to have derived in part from the stage. In both cases, the product is made to be seen from a fixed perspective, as from the perspective of a person at the scene. Mostly the images in a sequence will move from distance, giving a summary version of a situation, not emotionally engaged, to close range, where emotions, for instance as seen in faces close up, can be treated – and this process mainly follows a narrative line. That is a key aspect of conventional television practice as known in current affairs broadcasting.

Another conventional understanding of the way that television current affairs functions, derives from an historical treatment, which among other things sees current affairs as a break-out from news broadcasting. Tracing the beginnings of television current affairs, Alysen (2000: 171) states the current affairs program was devised as a response to address the brevity of broadcast news: 'Its purpose was to give background and context to the stories in the news and to offer in-depth analysis of current issues.' Reflecting on the historical development of Australian news and current affairs, Lumby (1999: 43) states the first news broadcasts were 'short, clumsy and inevitably experimental' and in the early years, non-fiction television programming comprised a 'patchwork of overseas documentaries, local [magazine-style] programs, news analyses and studio interviews'. She said: 'it wasn't until the 1970s that Australian networks viewed evening news bulletins as a springboard to winning the evening ratings and began devoting large resources and creative energy to fashioning the prime-time news and current affairs packages we are familiar with today.'

To help define television current affairs as distinct from news bulletins, many media practitioners interviewed for this project said television current affairs was not just about running longer duration packages but about what you actually do with that longer time and the use of strong story-telling techniques. A quality current affairs report should provide much more analysis, but hand-in-hand with good journalism is good story-telling.

Paul Ransley, producer of Nine Network Television's *A Current Affair* office in Brisbane (telephone interview – 12 May 2003) said that 'a story that lends itself to current affairs treatment is a compelling story that speaks to the human condition in some way, and with individuals who are able to tell that story in a compelling kind of way …'

However the trend of television current affairs programs threading into the entertainment arena shows that content of the news is not necessarily driving what current affairs stories are being produced. Jason Sternberg, media communications lecturer at the Queensland University of Technology, (telephone interview – 10 June 2003) considers the main difference between prime-time television news and current affairs such as Seven's *Today Tonight*, Nine's *A Current Affair*, and even ABC Television's *The 7.30 Report* is that television current affairs is very rarely now hooked to the news agenda. 'So what you find is a proliferation of stories that are based around infotainment rather than covering breaking news and covering politics'. This may have widened the scope of the television current affairs genre to allow a broader range of production techniques and conventions to be used in compiling story content, although Alysen (2000: 174) notes that in the field of 'easy-watching' television, they were not to be the leaders: 'one problem for current affairs programs was that the newer lifestyle and infotainment programs had eaten into their traditional subject matter'.

Audience

Whatever the conventional understanding of the origins and present shape of current affairs television programs, what do audiences make of it? Genre theorists argue that audiences recognise and share an understanding of generic norms and conventions of television production with industry professionals and academic analysts (Neale in Creeber 2001: 1). Specifically considering the television news genre, Ward (1995: 84) says, 'television news-as-text will carry a layer of meanings which derive from other television genres. Here the term genre refers to recognisable categories of television program each understood by producers and audiences alike to have a particular narrative sequence and structure.'

Audiences frequently are seen to be not only open to stimulus and change, but also resistant to it. Considering public broadcasting, Fiona Crawford, executive producer of ABC Television's *Stateline Queensland* program (telephone interview – 16 May 2003) assessed the ABC audience as typically older than a lot of commercial audiences and suggested that if producers interfered too much with a current affairs program's look and style, they risked alienating viewers who did not particularly want change. 'There's always talk of changing the format, but at the end of the day there's only so many different ways to invent the wheel.' Crawford's acceptance of the idea of a finite range of possibilities is also indicative of a common view among practitioners, especially on questions of format or presentation/production values. Television current affairs producers are uniformly concerned about not losing the appeal of their programs to audiences they know they have.

Practical Concerns

Issues of time and money strongly influence what is done in television current affairs and how it is produced. According to Peter Hiscock, producer at the Nine Network's *Sunday* program, (telephone interview – 13 June 2003), there have been past instances where managers cut in on the editorial path of a program. As an example, he said in the 1990s a current affairs program called *Witness* by the Seven Network was affected by managerial interference. 'There were some personality differences, which inevitably there is in television. There was a difference in opinion about the way stories were done and what they were doing. So in that sense, the managers were interfering with the editorial direction of the program'. In another example, Hiscock said tight budgets had forced Networks Seven and Ten to share vision. 'They have been forced recently into a pool arrangement, pooling each other's footage, swap it around, that's another bit of compromise. The same at SBS ... The ABC's problems are almost the opposite: too many people'. Producers will often resist this economic reality, said Bruce Belsham, executive producer at ABC Television's *Four Corners*, (telephone interview – 20 May 2003), holding that it should always be content that drives decisions, not cost or technical ability. David Margan, senior reporter at the Nine Network's *A Current Affair* program, (personal interview – 6 June 2003) said:

> *Perhaps it's a reflection of a wider community attitude bred by the wit of 'Frontline', but these days the world of commercial media is full of key company men and women who have no understanding of, and even less respect for, journalists and their role. Imagine the retail equivalent, store managers who loathe one of their key products despite its prime position in the store – they don't respect its function, they openly disparage it and won't even look at it – it's a ready-made marketing disaster.*

Asked whether creativity was being stifled by management imperatives to chase profit and better resource efficiencies, Paul Bongiorno, bureau chief, political editor and executive producer at Network Ten's *Meet the Press* (telephone interview – 4 September 2003), denied it: 'Commercial realities have always, [repeat] have always, determined journalism – unless you own your own outlet and then the commercial realities bite even harder because you won't even exist unless someone buys your product'. Mike Carey, executive producer at SBS Television's *Insight* program (telephone interview – 11 June 2003), averred that a lack of money can force creativity. 'I think sometimes people are loath to change and just complain there's not enough money. You've got to think laterally sometimes to change the look of the program and also be more cost-effective... I believe some people think the way current affairs is done is set in stone'.

John Westacott, executive producer at the Nine Network's *60 Minutes* (telephone interview – 25 August 2003), agreed program makers did not need money to be creative. 'I think that's a very sensible comment. The only time money comes into it is whether you travel from here to there to cover a story that you think will be relevant to Australians... It sounds like an excuse to me.'

Another practical factor is availability of production time and broadcast time, with Ransley pointing out there is often more time than with news, to construct a current affairs story. 'Current affairs television is more a story-telling process, more akin to a feature article in a newspaper and because of that, the extended period of time, because you're not tied down to 90 seconds or 80 seconds, you can use a variety of conventions to convey the information.' Westacott appreciates weekly current affairs programs allow more time to put the program together: 'We're not chucking it all together for that night's news. We have a bit of time to polish it.'

Short and long-form television current affairs, documentaries

Television current affairs as a genre has moved over time, with some intensification of a distinction between short-form and long-form television presentations. Australia's media industry awards, The Walkleys, categorise these two sections as 'current affairs reporting (less than 20 minutes)' – short-form; and 'current affairs, feature, documentary or special (more than 20 minutes)' – long-form. Many industry professionals say long-form current affairs production is closely aligned with documentary-making, and uses many of its story-telling techniques and production conventions. Short-form stays closer to short news formats. The two may have different destinies, judging from the expectations expressed by interviewees.

Ransley said the Nine network's *Sunday* program where he worked for eight years, was current affairs and also a documentary program. 'Most of the stories I did were 40 minutes long, and at that length, they were documentaries although focused on immediate events. Daily current affairs is ... definitely a short form of documentary making, although the documentary format tends to be a lot more lyrical. Sometimes you get a writer in *A Current Affair* and you can get a very lyrical piece.' Belsham also said all long-form television current affairs programs were really documentary making. Crawford defined current affairs television as such, as being more documentary in approach than news: 'It involves a lot more thought about structure and picture opportunities.'

Westacott said his program's current affairs stories were 'telling little stories, mini-documentaries on a topic that could well be a news topic ... and clearly as the program is current, you're doing stories on news events or backgrounding news events or on people who are in the news'. In such views, long-form and documentary making can be seen as an effort to break away from established traditions – stage, cinema, daily television news – to apply techniques specifically to a single program or series, and so begin to create entirely new forms. Seeing an actual blurring of genres between long-form television current affairs and documentary production, Jarvis (1998: 140) states many documentary makers seek to avoid news currency altogether, to 'rebel against the tyranny of the journalistic style and try to make programs without any commentary whatsoever. If television really is primarily a visual medium this ought to be possible.'

Professor Graeme Turner, director, Centre for Critical and Cultural Studies, University of Queensland (telephone interview – July 2003), has followed weakening audience numbers obtained by short-form current affairs, but sees documentary being used differently by audiences, and with a more assured future: 'Good old-fashioned documentary will be in ten years' time a popular form'. He said short-form television current affairs programs saw their survival depending on the perceived authority of the program, but present-day audiences would not be tuning in just to receive a 'bunch of stories', or to take notice even of a most trusted presenter.

In considering how to construct effective documentary programs, Masterton and Patching (1997: 248-249) emphasise the partnering of abundant research with imaginative production and presentation; where length becomes an indicator of quality: 'This scavenging for material and striving for total comprehension usually means that the hardest decisions are those about what must be left out, not what should be left in... '
Moving on to discuss production values, Masterton and Patching (1997: 255) consider use of media in ways appropriate to viewers' receptiveness. They argue that most video editors say pictures have a natural length, which is a key consideration when constructing long-form current affairs and documentary programs. 'In news reporting, a reporter pressed for time might edit pictures to fit a prepared audio track. For documentary work, this is not good enough. The words must be written to fit the pictures. This allows the picture to tell its share of the story.'

Belsham said rhythm tended to be different in terms of interview grabs being used at a greater length in television current affairs programs and documentaries.

The ideal was to, 'illustrate it precisely with what we're looking at. A lot of our effort is in trying to in some way, either through actuality or sometimes through a, not direct, re-creation, [make] a kind of abstract re-creation, on the visual environment, more than television news which is much more factually-based. I guess it is sometimes the fact that the content often goes more to opinion and feeling and emotion, along that scale from news to documentary that affects the shape as well. It affects the kind of pictures that we use, where to cut pictures, sometimes use some music, which is not a news device.'

Conventions in use today

A search for why current affairs is produced and timed in certain ways, and given a certain look, invokes an exploration of production techniques and conventions. Most of the analyses found in publications do not probe deeply. 'Artful' considerations are restricted in theorising about television journalism. The interviews for this project suggest industry professionals do not ruminate at length over why they use certain production techniques over others, or where their assumptions have originated, except to say it is a formula that has proven over time to work effectively, and that audiences also share and understand these assumed conventions.

Jarvis (1998: 1), a director, does go further, identifying a television language – 'a language of pictures but also of words and sounds and music'. He says that for the most part this language derived from cinema, now over a century old, and that cinema grammar was understood by 'practically the whole human race'. Looking back further he said, 'many of the conventions of both television and the cinema derive from photography, which is nearly 200 years old, and the theatre, which is considerably older than that.' Therefore, although Jarvis (1998: 6) says 'breaking the rules, or at least playing fast and loose with conventions can be liberating'; before trying new ways it is important to learn what the old rules are and why they have been so universally adopted: 'Television grammar is rooted in universal human psychology and social responses. We respond to sounds and images less because of conditioning by television itself but because well-made television mirrors the way we constantly interpret the everyday world without the benefit of a camera lens'. Lumby (1999: 130) sees that while television current affairs programs may change and evolve, the programs still draw on known practices, like the 'tools of entertainment programming originally developed in the cinema such as re-enactments, dramatic music, fast-paced editing, and a focus on narrative, emotion and personality.'

The familiar conventions of television current affairs production are persistently used; trusted by all; no matter what new possibilities might be impelled by the arrival of fresh competition, financial pressure, changing habits and interests among the viewing public, or possibilities opened up by new broadcast technology. These are some of the ongoing conventions in use.

Role of television current affairs practitioners

The role of producer in television current affairs production is integral to the process, with many of the personnel drawn from journalism; Masterton and Patching (1997: 241) stating 'sometimes it is the producer or researcher who is the 'real' journalist in the [current affairs] team'. Hiscock says staff deployments determine much; it is important that all reporters, unlike counterparts in news, will have producer backup. 'There's usually two people involved in telling a current affairs story – a producer and reporter. And a producer by and large, is more familiar with the production techniques – what's possible, what's not, whether the machine can do a wipe or a dissolve or whether a graphic sequence would work ... I think their techniques are more honed through experience, what works, what doesn't.'

Jarvis (1998: 61) acknowledges the importance of the directors' art, cautioning that journalists as directors may have a backlog of old habits to overcome, before beginning to innovate: 'With them has come the illusion that the written script takes automatic priority. Working methods that emerged of necessity for one-minute bulletin reports are assumed to be appropriate for hour-long documentary features. This is a delusion ...'. Alysen (2000: 186) gives a leading role in the construction of programs to staff who are not reporters, the producers, often called 'segment producers' who also must find ways to tell stories in television current affairs. 'Producers, many of whom come from a journalistic background, develop stories and devise angles. They do the research... they line up interviews... sometimes conduct the interviews... organise locations for taping pictures... write scripts. Producers can do almost everything connected with a story except for putting their face on it.'

Picture sequences

Ideally, good pictures are essential to effectively tell the story in the predominantly visual medium of television. Current affairs practitioners talk of images as sequences, carefully made, different to their use as simple documentation or verification of facts, as may occur in the news. Carey says, 'You're trying to shoot nice sequences of shots – sequences of images that help tell your story visually'. Crawford agreed sequences of shots for current affairs production are essential and by necessity, the shots can often be fairly long. There is also the goal of adopting a more naturalistic approach to mimic what the eye would see if the person was witnessing part of the situation the story was covering: 'You can't have that staccato type of shots you get in news, without being confronting to the viewer.'

Camera shots and angles

In discussing the choice and duration of shots when constructing television news and current affairs packages, Jarvis (1998: 41), from a director's perspective, stated 'editing means more than chopping out the bits the director does not like. Editing is a creative process and the picture editor needs to be provided with the means to break down and reassemble questions and answers in various different ways... The type of journalist/producer who thinks that the words are all important and the pictures are somebody else's job is arrogant'. Continuing on this theme, he considers selection and sequencing of shots is integral to telling any story.

> *The size of the shot tells the viewer about the geography of the studio set or the location, the gravity of the content, and the intimacy of the subject matter... Seemingly every human language has turns of phrase which refer to looking up to superior beings and looking down at inferior ones... The easiest way to show the dominance of one character over another is to shoot the dominant one looking down towards the lens and the submissive one from a lower position looking up. It is universal and instantly recognised body language.*

Katz (1991: 239) wants to refine such understandings, asserting that by themselves camera angles have no meaning. 'The (by now) reductive analysis that claims that low-angle views of a subject place the subject in a dominant position while high-angle views place the subject in a diminutive position is only valid in certain situations. The value of a shot really depends on the narrative'. Ward (1995: 83) says many of the assumed visual codes are not inherent in communication for the television medium, but directly taken from cinema, such as the shot-reverse shot device or 'noddies', in which successive takes of a character looking say to the left of the screen will be interspersed with shots of another looking to the right. He considers audience members will play their part in sustaining the illusion: 'Television viewers are likely to decode these images not 'simply as one face after another', but 'as two people occupying the same space and in close proximity to one another' (Bonney and Wilson 1983: 168 in Ward 2001). To White (in Ward 2001: 84), the shot-reverse shot device is highly artificial and does not, as other cinematic devices may do, allow viewers to look through the eyes of either speaker. She argues that 'natural' dialogue scenes filmed in this way only appear natural because viewers are familiar with the conventions or codes of representation being used.

Editing

Boyd (2001: 354) provides the standard rule on editing practices along with the standard defence for continuing such practices, passed on from cinema and its antecedents, and developed further yet, many film industry devices being used to aid effective story-telling and meet time constraints:

> *Edited shots should cut from one another smoothly and logically, and follow a train of thought. If this rule is broken, the images that result are likely to be jerky, unrelated and confusing, and detract from the story... Rearrange the sequence of ... shots and you remove the context. Begin with a close-up and you have no idea of the scale of [a riot]; cut then to the long shot and the action appears to be moving backwards. Unless you cut progressively and smoothly – like the human eye – the logic of the sequence will be destroyed. It is easier to follow the action if you bridge the close-ups and long shots with medium shots.*

Sound

Sound is a powerful element when constructing television current affairs packages, once again, in this account from Jarvis (1998: 155), nothing very new:

> *There never was a silent cinema. From the beginning of motion pictures the audience felt uneasy with watching images in silence except for the clatter of a projector. The immediate answer was to have an accompanying pianist and then later a small musical ensemble ... The eve of the talkies was a golden age for the mighty Wurlitzer theatre organ which combined musical scores with a wondrous array of sound effect from horse's hooves to slapsticks, church bells and gun shots.*

In an analysis of prime-time current affairs programming in 1999, Alysen (2000: 177) found that current affairs stories would be driven more by interviews, news stories more by narration; and the most popular production device for current affairs was to start the story with a sound bite.

> *This appeared almost universally on Today Tonight and was common on [A Current Affair and The 7.30 Report]. Those stories that didn't start on a sound bite usually began with natural sound and music before the reporter's voice cut in. Starting a story on a sound bite directs the audience's attention to the interviewees and helps make them more the focus of the story...*

Hiscock believed music was part of an armoury of standard devices available to producers of current affairs, who might make assumptions about how they worked on viewers' perceptions: 'Music brings mood and aids the storytelling process…to make a point more interesting or accentuate the sadness, or accentuate the doom and gloom … I think that most people when they watch current affairs programs respond more to the use of music than perhaps anything else'.

Staging re-enactments

With a policy of bringing in a greater range of techniques to tell a story or make a point, current affairs may go so far as drama; the re-enactment. Alysen (2000: 185-186) says:

> *This is not merely because longer stories would become boring if told using just the narration/sound bite style of news. It's also because these programs often cover subjects that don't easily lend themselves to visualisation. … If they involve 're-enactment', this needs to be made explicit to the audience … Other techniques used in current affairs include rapid editing of images accompanied by music or effects, or the use of slow motion.*

Belsham stated a preference for impressionistic types of re-enactments where necessary, more than strictly literal treatments.

> *… Or for example, [we] very rarely use re-enactments where we have dialogue in them because that's suggesting a level of reality that we can't claim to have. So sometimes we will do things like use the same location, creating a mood through that with a bit of music … But we try to sort of not to suggest that everything you're seeing in that frame is what it was at the time.*

Carey endorsed the idea of creative licence, with some caveats: 'As long as you're being honest, take anything that comes your way. While I hate using them and recommend my team does not go to the trouble, then it can be a technique that is useful on occasion, as long as it's done honestly and not misrepresenting reality'.

Graphic devices

Graphics as conventionally used stay close to strictly representing content (for example location, figures), and are important for station identification. They are another instance of producers doing whatever they can to present a story in an attractive package without distorting elements of the story. Producers will look for the most attractive graphic presentation, time permitting, for such purposes as covering information that cannot readily be portrayed by the voiceovers, the reporter in shot, picture sequences, or interview talent.

Reporter presence

Television current affairs stories may feature a substantial reporter presence, which Hiscock said can get producers 'out of a picture hole', where there is something to be said, but no illustration available. Further than that, Westacott said reporters were featured prominently in Nine's *60 Minutes* stories as a conscious style adopted for that program.

> *[ABC Television's] Four Corners seem to have their reporters as disembodied people... Our program is produced more as a feature report, and the feature report is a subjective report by one of our four reporters... We're happy to have them give professional opinion and if the story requires some comment, then they're there to show why they're commenting... It's 60 Minutes style, the same as someone who would write features in the newspaper ... People like to read not only what they've written, but the way they've written it and I suppose that's what we do here.*

Carey said the SBS *Dateline* program uses video journalism as its production standard. It is obvious the reporter is there in the story because they make it plain they are shooting everything. This is a case of latter-day conventions and styles of representation moving in some new directions:

> *When you're using video journalism techniques it becomes fairly obvious that the reporter is there because it's more intimate ... So to have the actual physical presence of the reporter on camera is less important, I think.*

Genre

This review has shown current affairs television is very eclectic in use of technique, where anything may be brought in to tell a story or make a point. Yet the devices used, while diverse, are standardised, and shared by most practitioners and programs, so it is considered viable here to class them as a genre, providing a framework of common production elements. One writer on genre, applied to films, Butler (1994: 297), points out that stylistic definition of a genre is used little in analysis, though there are a few genres that recognise programs based on how material is presented, such as musicals, westerns, film noir, or horror. He does (1994: 296) give three useful, overlapping categories, for making definitions of a genre: presumed audience response; style, being techniques of sound and/or image; and subject matter – both narrative structure and thematics.

To recapitulate, the above sections list leading generic elements of television current affairs production, indicating the range of approaches, conventions and techniques most used, with a high degree of uniformity from program to program: Most production is by a team consisting of a journalist and producer; vision is shot in logical sequences and attempts are made to make it as naturalistic as the human eye witnessing an event; strong story-telling abilities are considered imperative to drive a clear narrative line; camera angles and matching eyelines in interviews are kept 'neutral' to preserve story objectivity; 'impressionistic' re-enactments, rather than literal re-enactments, can assist in filling vision 'holes', as long as they do not purport to represent an actual event; reporter presence in stories is higher in current affairs production, to promote the program's brand or as a device to fill vision 'holes'; studio interview production techniques are continuing to evolve in the wake of technological advancements such as satellite transmission and web broadcasting; and video journalism is increasingly being utilised as part of the television current affairs genre.

These considerations connect with the 'art' of television production (Masterton and Patching 1997 :203) but are definitely pragmatic. They do not come together as any kind of theoretical statement about how products are made and engage viewers. Questions as to why a certain technique, such as shooting vision in logical sequences, may be employed, will be answered in common sense terms – for example because that is the way things are seen in the everyday world, with the human eye. Over time, a catalogue of agreed devices has been assembled and is widely shared in current affairs television, virtually among all producers and all audiences. Producers may experiment, for instance in the case of Grant Mooney on the *MetroView* pilot, who considered colours and colourisation could be important, opting for a suffusion of blue in the titles for the program, on Brisbane current affairs, to invoke the omnipresence of a river. However such diversions or developments do not have an integrated context, such as a generalised theory or code book on television aesthetics or construction of meaning. Treating television current affairs as a distinctive genre helps with its definition but does not complete our knowledge about the creative elements in the program-making process.

Absence of a generalised theory or handbook on principles underlying work in television may never have mattered to concerned parties; the producers or viewers. Questions about deploying more and different production styles may have been left open indefinitely. It might have continued, except that the television industry is now confronted with new possibilities brought on by social change, and by technology, complicated by pressure for increased business efficiency – new technologies being able to help with productivity, hence cost cutting.

Here some questions arise to do with possibilities brought on by the availability of sophisticated, digital production tools. With the power to show a shuttling back and forth in time, should producers any longer be bound to represent simple chronological narratives? With the power to easily split screens and insert windows, should producers still be committed to representing the scene naturalistically as a full frame, as if being perceived by somebody in that situation? Where producers have the power to easily and – to the eye – convincingly place images of people in situations where they have never been, should such a dramatic device be banned from current affairs, if a way can be found to exploit its impacts without dishonesty towards the viewer?

With handy devices for switching between action and talk, should producers remain committed to the tradition of screening a pre-recorded, outside report and then afterwards, bringing the issue into the studio for commentary; (when instead they might just mix the commentary and action in a fast alternation)? Already, with slippage of audience numbers for current affairs programs, there is room to speculate that the public is expecting more in the way of presentation than current affairs is offering. Taking up new ways may be the response that moves current affairs into a new generation of program styles. It may mean metamorphosis into a new genre form.

Future for television current affairs

The television current affairs genre is facing a period of transition. Along with the pressure of technological and corporate change, there is social evolution: demographic change, new audiences accustomed to new media, willing and able to use media in various ways. Following the advent of new production devices, specifically satellites, videotape, then digitisation across the board, it is simple to imagine the well-tried conventions of television current affairs starting to break down. The overall drive of television journalism in constructing its reports is to simulate nature, but television journalists can now mix media; such as using devices whereby time is manipulated, or showing two parts of vision at once on a split screen, such as the shipwreck and the rescue, at once. Other applications offer the seamless manipulation of images, colours and sound. Complex graphics, and the matching or alternation of live and recorded interviews can be incorporated. The idea of constructing a sit-and-watch television program or report, whether as a broadcast to air, cable service or internet, is itself challenged; the preferred product through any of those channels may come to be a multi-media presentation, delivering the options of vision, audio, text and links to other products. In this advancing new order, the place of reporters is to be reconsidered. Where and how does the storyteller fit, when the means of delivery of stories is transformed?

Current affairs journalists responding to change

Warren (2003) demonstrates an awareness of a transition under way: 'Working in the media right now, it's hard to escape the sense that something big – something really, really big – is happening. [But] it's just that not many of us really understand what it is'. New options are not being embraced too readily. Belsham says 'television current affairs is what you'd call a mature industry, it's been around a long time and certainly is slower in its kind of development changes than it was in say, the 1970s when it first started up and people were experimenting and developing new forms'. Others do see the advance of technology disarming the current affairs industry, removing its main instrument of power, the ability to occupy a limited number of channels of communication – until very recent times, just five or six main free-to-air broadcast frequencies. Bongiorno poses the question of who actually 'owns' the television current affairs concept:

Is the new concept for current affairs an analysis of what is in the news, analysis of what is happening in our world? ... Current affairs from that point of view is sort of an old-fashioned category ... In a sense ways of doing it have moved on and anybody can own it.

Hiscock sees the industry biding its time with potentially a lot more people coming into the audience, but there is uncertainty about future directions. 'There's no new investments in the industry because, I think, of a delay in getting the media laws sorted and the introduction of digital television. Until it's clear which way the industry is developing, no one is going to spend any money'. Turner echoes that view, saying it is hard to tell what could be on the horizon for news and current affairs, due to uncertainties over government policy on digital television. The option of multiple channels could see broadcasters breaking away from their long-standing use of news and current affairs as foundation programs for a general entertainment service, on a single-frequency station.

Once there is provision of news from Channel Nine, Channel 7 and Channel 10 on another channel, on a dedicated channel, they'd be entitled to say we're providing this, it's free, people can access it any time they want, even if it's just a television version of 936 on radio, pretty much like CNN; just roll the bulletin on over and over again. I mean if [the commercial television networks are] doing that, then they don't have to provide news and current affairs programming. They wouldn't have to do that and they would fight that in the court and they would win.

Technologies driving change

The media practitioners consulted for this research agreed one of the biggest changes of all was immediacy of information, though this would not warrant a total change of habits. The speed with which information could be shifted around the globe was a great factor in digital technology, as seen by Westacott:

These days we can travel with a satellite camera and send back the stuff virtually live here. We can email back our voiceovers, satellite back pictures. It allows us to be a lot more immediate and that's probably one of the great advantages that have made the program continue to be relevant. I think as digital technology improves, and digital cameras improve, it'll be more and more immediate, and that's got to be to our advantage.

Hiscock sees technology actually aiding the story-telling process, with more material for producers to choose from.

There's more of a demand for the sound bites to be concise and pointed, if not witty. There's less of a tolerance for boring points of view. There's the production standards, the quality of cameras, and the sound especially is much better than it used to be, and that's given producers a better opportunity to illustrate their stories more imaginatively... [But] the techniques are by and large, the same.

Video journalism

The one-person crew, journalist with digital camera, and probably some kit for transmitting from the field, looks like a catalyst for further radical change. Use of small cameras and transmission packs permits regular and rapid filing of straightforward material not extensively edited. Sound quality will suffer to a degree, with no camera operator or sound recordist to monitor levels and quality. The technology also would suggest a different view of the recording process, with emphasis on action and settings, not crafted expositions of a theme in a film-making style; though editing and packaging in the field, by reporters, is taking place. Crawford predicted many more journalists would be shooting their own material:

> *Purists argue it is going to be detrimental to quality of pictures but advocates say it will give you a much broader scope for collecting news... Digicams are much more simple, easier to rig up to shoot a piece to camera for yourself and that sort of thing ... Current affairs style I suppose has become more modern in its look. Current affairs people follow film trends in a lot of ways. For a while in current affairs you had that Hill St Blues look – you know the motion camera and things like that, they are affected by film and cinema trends. But I think the basic core of current affairs doesn't change and that is to provide the commentary, the analysis, the sort of complex stories that aren't available or don't have space for in the news.*

Bongiorno said the quick amenity of video journalism was winning support: 'Channel Ten uses video journalists in some of its bureaus … Most of the objections are industrial, they've got nothing to do with editorial, they've got nothing to do with quality and look … You don't really care how scratchy the sound is if what you've got is a world exclusive.' Carey said *Dateline* on SBS had already taken up a program style appropriate to video-journalism because it no longer invested heavily in camera crews.

The Internet, web broadcasting, cable television, 24-hour news channels, had brought substantial change. 'News cycles are reduced. So people don't just work on one big story to satellite out for the nightly news, they're doing a lot more than that these days. Sometimes that may dilute the quality of what they're doing.'

Belsham equally saw positive aspects of video journalism; not really seeing a revolution on its way, but acknowledging powerful cost benefits. 'That's an interesting and exciting area and has implications for the way we make television, implications for our capacity to be able to gather longer-term actuality. It's not as expensive to put an individual journalist in the field to cover a story'. Turner on the other hand has reservations about journalists with cameras, and possible impacts on quality.

'The kind of cost-cutting measures that the ABC use, for instance in using their radio journalists to do their TV, I do think that affects the quality of the material on both media. I think [video journalism] enables people to get to places they mightn't be able to get, but it does have an effect on the quality … I think it makes them get in and get the pictures and get out – it actually doesn't encourage people to really hang around and find out what's going on. But that's just not only video journalism. I think the whole culture of news production at the moment is to just have we got enough for a story, let's go back, rather than what is the story, what's going on. I just don't think they have the time anymore to do the kind of thing they would have done 20 years ago.'

Industry habits and change

The practitioners surveyed in this project were reluctant to change main aspects of the television current affairs process, although recognising that new circumstances have arrived. One key response, like that of Westacott and Hiscock, above, talking about adopting new technology, is that new forms may be adopted, enhancing what is already being done, without altering its essential high value. There is a sentiment both among practitioners and observers like Turner, that too much wild gathering and rough packaging would threaten editorial standards, best preserved where the current affairs journalist takes time to form judgments.

Informed observers not inside the news media are usually not so circumspect about change. Of the two directly consulted here, Sternberg considers that new formats like the news-commentary and comedy show, *The Panel*, on Network Ten, have shown audiences can be flexible about some of the conventions, like careful objectivity. '*The Panel* doesn't purport, doesn't pretend to be objective. It is opinionated and that's what people want, people want to hear an opinion, and want to be able to give their opinion back to the television or the person sitting next to them ... It's talk and people thinking through; public discussion of what's going on in the world that's the most important thing. That's what journalism, and particularly current affairs, should be doing and isn't doing enough'. Turner argues that changing work and lifestyle patterns are causing a change in the essential factor of audience availability and audience attitudes, which the producers, however reluctantly, ultimately must come to terms with:

> *Certainly people's work patterns have changed, fewer people are watching television at that time at night the way they were ten years ago, and even though their ratings, the percentage of the audience isn't that bad, the numbers watching have gone down dramatically... I suspect we are looking at such changes in behaviour that hanging onto that ... [6:30pm] flagship time, may actually be a dumb idea... It's just a bunch of industry habits that nobody's got the nerve to break and the consequence of course when you're wrong if you break*

them are pretty disastrous. But then, it's not that long ago that [Network] Ten went to a one-hour 5:00pm news broadcast which many said they were crazy. For the first year or so, it looked like they were. Now, there actually isn't much difference to those who turn on to that time now, then those who turn on at 6:00pm and [Network Ten have] got them for an hour. That's been quite a clever decision.

Resistance can go well beyond a reflexive defence of professional habits, with Hiscock arguing that the 6:30pm commercial television current affairs programs were very nervous about changing their formula, because of advertising revenue that continued to come in. 'That's a key point coming into the evening, in a sense they need to maintain an audience in order to follow through to the evening. There's supposed to be a bit of a science involved; I've never understood it, [but] they're really nervous about changing it'.

The Seven Network director of news and current affairs, Peter Meakin (in O'Regan 2003) saw style trends in general television, with a high entertainment focus, and trends in society, delivering a shorter audience attention span. Circumstances were actually putting pressure on journalists to move away from their conventions, towards simple, not innovative treatments: 'Stories do not speak for themselves, they need to be told, they need to be packaged in such a way that the interesting points and the importance of an issue is highlighted, made digestible, and made appealing – it's what a journalist's job is.' Lowell Bergman, a former producer for *Sixty Minutes* in the United States, portrayed by Al Pacino in the movie *The Insider*, (in O'Regan (2003), has identified a process of positive adaptation.

Quality of information and analysis might be maintained, but for serious television current affairs to address audiences accustomed to clever and sophisticated entertainment media, they would themselves have to be entertaining to hold attention.

It's the form that Sixty Minutes developed for instance, to figure out a way of having the stars tell the story, that allowed people to sit there and in a sense, be entertained if you will, and occasionally actually get some real information ... I'm not so personally opposed to having entertaining news presentations, it doesn't have to all sound like the BBC [British Broadcasting Corporation] and be very serious all the time.

Conclusion

These media professionals value techniques and styles of production that have been in use for a long time. As they indicate, media practitioners are having to adjust to a new wave of change propelled by technology, corporate pressure, and different social relations in the community. Most are cautious about committing to radical change but have shown a process of adaptation is under way. While alert to opportunities offered by new technology, like the economies provided by single-operator 'video journalism', and prepared to adjust the style of programs to accommodate such innovations, they are concerned first and foremost with following the demands of audiences. That is proving to be difficult as audience trends are unsettled, leading the more cautious producers to hold on to established formats in familiar timeslots, at least until the alternatives are clearer and longer-term programming options less uncertain.

Yet, well-established traditions in current affairs are having to change. This investigation has found the industry showing a certain ability to adjust to its changing environment, though reluctantly for much of the time. It has also shown that the conventions followed by program-makers have a long background of development, manifesting historical links with theatre, early cinema, film theory or photography. It has been suggested that this is making it hard for the industry to adjust to new circumstances. There was a successful, historical adjustment in the early years of television, with journalistic practices grafted onto an appropriate version of the new medium, to the accolade of audiences. Television networks could design their brand around the prestigious news and current affairs shows leading their evening schedules. It stood the test of time, but times have changed, and journalists in current affairs now face the prospect of needing to achieve a new historical adjustment. Though uncomfortable with present trends and anxious to retain traditional values, they have the option of consulting alternative genres, where there are increasingly rich possibilities in techniques to be developed, and in design, styling and presentation of programs. It will require hard thinking about the communication goals of current affairs in the 21st century; it will be a test of creativity in a business that has always been a field of creative work.

Appendix – The interviews

Belsham, B. (2003). Executive Producer, *Four Corners* program, Australian Broadcasting Corporation (ABC) TV - telephone interview on 20 May 2003, Sydney, Australia.

Bongiorno, P. (2003). Bureau Chief, Political Editor and Executive Producer, *Meet the Press* program, Ten Network - telephone interview on 4 September 2003, Sydney, Australia.

Carey, M. (2003). Executive Producer, *Insight* program, Special Broadcasting Service (SBS) TV - telephone interview on 11 June 2003, Sydney, Australia.

Carey, M. (2005). Executive Producer, *Dateline* program, Special Broadcasting Service (SBS) TV - telephone interview on 29 April 2005, Sydney, Australia.

Crawford, F. (2003). Executive Producer, *Stateline* Queensland program, Australian Broadcasting Corporation (ABC) TV - telephone interview on 16 May 2003, Brisbane, Australia.

Hiscock, P. (2003). Producer, *Sunday* program, Nine Network - telephone interview on 13 June 2003, Sydney, Australia.

Margan, D. (2003). Senior Reporter, *A Current Affair* program, Nine Network - face-to-face interview on 6 June 2003, Brisbane, Australia.

Mooney, G. (2003). Cameraperson/editor, *MetroView* current affairs program, Queensland University of Technology Educational Television (QUT ETV) - email interview on 12 May 2003, Brisbane, Australia.

Ransley, P. (2003). Producer, *A Current Affair* program, Nine Network - telephone interview on 12 May 2003, Brisbane, Australia.

Sternberg, J. (2003). Media Communications Lecturer, Queensland University of Technology - telephone interview on 10 June 2003, Brisbane, Australia.

Turner, G. (2003). Media Communications Professor, University of Queensland - telephone interview on 21 July 2003, Brisbane, Australia.

Westacott, J. (2003). Executive Producer, *60 Minutes* program, Nine Network - telephone interview on 25 August 2003, Sydney, Australia.

References

Alysen, B. (2000). *The electronic reporter: Broadcast journalism in Australia*. Geelong, Deakin University Press.

Boyd, A. (2001). *Broadcast journalism: Techniques of radio and TV news* (5th ed.). Oxford, Butterworth-Heinemann.

Butler, J. G. (1994). *Television: Critical methods and applications*. California, Wadsworth, Inc.

Creeber, G. (Ed.). (2001). *The Television Genre Book*. London, British Film Institute.

Jarvis, P. (1998). *The Essential TV Director's Handbook*. Oxford, Focal Press.

Katz, S.D. (1991). *Film directing shot by shot: visualising from concept to screen*. USA, Focal Press.

Lumby, C. (1999). *Gotcha: Life in a tabloid world*. Allen & Unwin, St Leonard's

Masterton, M., & Patching, R. (1997). *Now the news in detail* (3rd ed.). Geelong, Deakin University Press.

O'Regan, M. (2003). *The Media Report – Current thinking on current affairs*, Australian Broadcasting Corporation (ABC) Radio National broadcast on 12/6/2003. [Internet]. Transcript available: http://www.abc.net.au/rn/talks/8.30/mediarpt/stories/s879082.htm. [Accessed 7/07/2003].

The Walkley Awards. [Online], 2003. Available: hrrp://www.walkleys.com/categories.html. [Accessed 10/03/03].

Ward, I. (1995). *Politics of the media*. Sth Melbourne, Macmillan Education Australia Pty Ltd.

Warren, C. (2003). 'The media's muddy future'. *Walkley Magazine*, 22, p.4.

Chapter 5

Dot TV: remote Tuvalu adapts media to its ways

Mark (*'Maleko'*) Hayes PhD[1]

The spectacle of tiny Tuvalu, a very remote Pacific community, seemingly sinking under the waves of the Pacific Ocean helped to raise awareness of the threat of global warming around the world. Delivery of reports from journalists located in a flooded environment, indeed demonstrated the potency of satellite technology and other increasingly accessible tools. It demonstrated the 'one world' scenario where news media in even the furthest corner have truly global reach. However in this report Mark Hayes makes some qualifications. It is true that Tuvalu, like many thousands of lonely places, can rapidly communicate its interests abroad, and not to be wholly at the mercy of outside cultural forces, it can operate domestic 'mass' communication services of its own. At the same time, a small and isolated community will remain vulnerable. The very story of the 'sinking' of Tuvalu was much a creation of outside news media leaving gaps in the information and interpretation. Add to that, more conventional and universal problems of finance, and politics, get in the way of a free flow of media services; and then there is the question of cultural adjustments: While the picture of Tuvalu presenting itself to the world is a dramatic sign of global news culture, real culture on the ground imposes some limits. A short anthropological study shows how traditional ways of society influence the way media services can operate, and how far journalists can go. The Tuvalu chapter is based on extensive field work and background investigations, providing a window on the process of linking parts of this Earth, very small and very large, together in common interests.

---

[1] With the assistance of several Tuvaluans

Prologue

Wednesday afternoon, February 9, 2005 – Funafuti Atoll, Tuvalu. The wind and rain were blasting across the usually placid Te Namo[2] from the southwest, with waves crashing on to roads, causing flooding, erosion, and tossing debris around. Silafaga Lalua bent into the howling wind, raised the camera, and took some more pictures of the raging storm. Glancing at her watch, she realised she had to get these pictures away soon. Drenched, she ran down Funafuti Road and into the Government Building. In the Information technology office, (site of the world renowned 'real.TV'), Lomi Paeniu, a young IT worker, was waiting, helping her to download the pictures to a folder containing the record from the day before. Yesterday had been just as bad, with an extreme high tide adding to the flooding around Funafuti Atoll. Lomi had borrowed a digital camera so he could get more pictures and headed out into the howling storm. Meanwhile Silafaga composed herself while the Yahoo mail area loaded in front of her, snail's pace, given the tiny signal coming from a satellite to the north through the small dish out back of the building, itself battered by the terrible weather outside.

Rivers of water cascaded down the windows as Silafaga began to type: 'It's that time of the year again when my tiny island nation gets hit once again by strong winds and high tides....' Attaching the pictures to her e-mail, she reviewed her story, and clicked on 'Send'. In Brisbane, Australia, I was anxiously awaiting Silafaga's e-mail and pictures, as was Brian Cannon in Vancouver, British Columbia, for addition to his Tuvaluislands.com Web Site. At 16.14pm Brisbane time, the world's first story and pictures package of an extreme high tide event prepared by a journalist from one of the world's smallest, most remote, and one of the most threatened countries arrived. Within minutes it had been passed on to centres throughout the region, to New Zealand, Canada, and France[3]. This chapter tells how this occurred and places it in the context of doing journalism in, and about, Tuvalu.

Introduction: *Tuvalu mo te Atua – Tatou ne Tuvalu Katoa*

Tuvalu means 'eight together[4], though I've heard it translated as 'eight islands standing together'. The statement one makes to show

---

[2] *Te Namo* translates as 'the lagoon'.

[3] Ms Lalua's story and pictures, and Mr Paeniu's pictures, can be seen here: http://www.tuvaluislands.com/news/archives/2005/2005-02-22_tmta3.htm (accessed, August 25, 2005)

[4] 'Tu' means 'standing' or 'standing together' or 'us'

respect or affection for the country, 'Tuvalu mo te Atua', means 'Tuvalu for God' or 'the Almighty', and is incorporated into its coat of arms adopted upon independence from Britain in October, 1978. It, and the coat of arms, was first used on October 1, 1975, the day Tuvalu separated from Kiribati. At the time, the southernmost atoll, Niulakita, once owned by a Samoan family when first contacted by missionaries, had been uninhabited for many years, but has now been reinhabited, making Tuvalu a country with nine inhabited atolls.

'Tatou ne Tuvalu Katoa' translates as 'We are all Tuvaluans' and was often said by elders to promote unity. The term is also a powerful slogan used by a French documentary maker, Gilliane Le Gallic, to promote a campaign aimed at assisting Tuvalu to respond to the grave threat it faces from sea level rise caused by global warming; rendered as 'We Are All Tuvalu'[5], though one of my Tuvaluan informants said that the latter translation '... sounds boastful and individualistic'[6], two cultural 'no-nos' in Tuvalu, as will be explained later.

I have been privileged to have visited Tuvalu for a total of six weeks, the first time for three weeks in November, 2002, and then for three weeks in November, 2004[7], both times working closely with journalists employed by the Tuvalu Media Corporation (TMC), which operates Radio Tuvalu, the national broadcaster, and publishes the monthly A4 sized newspaper, *Tuvalu Echoes*.

This chapter draws extensively on first-hand experience of the main atoll of Tuvalu, Funafuti, and of doing journalism in and about this tiny and permanently fascinating country. I have also sought input into this chapter by friends in Tuvalu, as well as from the Tuvaluan Diasporas worldwide, and their comments have been incorporated, and acknowledged, as appropriate. In particular the generous assistance, advice, and guidance of friends and informants in Tuvalu are acknowledged in **Appendix / Notes**.

The basics

'Where the hell is Toovaloo?' is a question often asked by people, usually mispronouncing the name. The correct pronunciation is 'Too-VAH-loo' and never the several other ways the country can be called. Mispronouncing the name of their home offends its people and demonstrates insensitivity. Tuvalu is located about 3500km northeast of

---

[5] See http://www.europeantelevisioncenter.tv/ (accessed, August 14, 2005)
[6] Tito Isala, personal communication, September 1, 2005.
[7] This second visit was part-funded by a Queensland University of Technology Community Service Scheme grant awarded in July, 2005.

Australia, about half way to Hawaii, and about 1200km north of Fiji[8]. You get there by going to Fiji, then to Suva airport, Nausori, and board an Air Fiji long-range twin engine turboprop 35 seat plane for the two and a half hour flight to the tiny airport with the best airline destination code on the planet: FUN. It is also very expensive to fly to Funafuti Atoll, the main atoll in the nine island country, some $AU 900 one-way in 2005. Once on Funafuti, if you want to visit the eight outer islands, you have to travel on one of the country's two cargo boats *Nivaga II* and *Manu Folau*, which make their rounds quite regularly, travelling to Suva as required, though not on a regular schedule except to bring Tuvaluan students home for the long Christmas holidays.

The population of Tuvalu is about 11,500 people 'On Islands', with about 4,500 on Funafuti, which is about 12km long, about 700m wide at its widest, and less then 25m at its narrowest. Tuvalu's one of the world's smallest countries, 190th a bit larger than the Vatican, with a total land area of 26sq.km, and 193rd in terms of population[9]. Its sea area covers some 900,000sq.km and includes a 200km Exclusive Economic Zone. There are also small communities of Tuvaluans scattered all over the world, including on Kioa[10] off eastern Vanua Levu and Veisari in Fiji, in New Zealand, Australia, Kiribati, Hawaii, and elsewhere. Seven Tuvaluan families live on underpopulated Niue and there's talk of more moving there as parts of their home islands become uninhabitable due to global warming and sea level rise. New Zealand already allows 75 Tuvaluans to emigrate annually there under the Pacific Access Category Migration Scheme[11].

The GDP of Tuvalu is about $AU11 million – it uses Australian currency with some local coins – with a per capita GDP of about $AU1,100. National income is derived from foreign aid and loans, remittances from between four to six hundred seafarers crewing cargo boats globally sending money back to their families, fees from the official licensing of fishing rights to Tuvalu's vast exclusive economic zone, interest from the well-managed Tuvalu National Trust Fund, some money

---

[8] The best general atlas on the Pacific is: Quanchi, Max Jacaranda Atlas of the Pacific Islands Milton: John Wiley & Sons Australia, Ltd., 2003, esp. Pp. 48 – 49 for Kiribati and Tuvalu.

[9] The best and most up to date statistical information on Tuvalu can be obtained from relevant Government departments on Funafuti. Failing that, the next best place is the Pacific Regional Information System (PRISM), maintained by the Secretariat for the Pacific Community (SPC) - http://www.spc.int/PRISM/country/tv/tv_index.html (accessed, August 14, 2005)

[10] The island was bought by the people of Vaitupu just after World War II to ease then severe population pressure on their home island.

[11] http://www.immigration.govt.nz/migrant/stream/live/pacificaccess/ (accessed, September 20, 2005)

from philatelic sales, and leasing of the .TV top level internet domain name (about which more soon)[12].

Tuvaluans are a Polynesian[13] people, who settled their islands about two thousand years ago, during the second great wave of Pacific migrations, possibly from Samoa or Tonga. There certainly was occasional contact between parts of Tuvalu and other Polynesian peoples from Samoa and Tonga, these contacts executed by arguably the world's greatest pre-historical seafaring navigators[14]. One of the islands in the group, Nui, has some ties to i-Kiribati, Micronesians from the islands to the north, and also has ties to the southernmost island, Niulakita, to which some Nui people migrated in the late 1940s.

Tuvaluan language bears many similarities to Samoan and even Maori, the linguistic similarities having been traced by anthropologists, as well in part influenced by Samoan Faifeau[15] sent to Tuvalu by the London Missionary Society late in the 19th Century and the early 20th Century, established a feagaiga[16] with their congregation, brought with them Samoan Bibles and preached in Samoan until they better understood Tuvaluan[17]. The Tuvalu Ekalesia[18] is the most important non-government institution, with 98% of Tuvaluans being Christians. Periodic contacts

---

[12] Asian Development Bank, Asian Development Outlook 2005: II. Economic Trends and Prospects in Developing Asia http://www.adb.org/documents/books/ado/2005/tuv.asp (accessed, August 14, 2005); see also, Mellor, C. 'An economic survey of Tuvalu' *Pacific Economic Bulletin, Vol. 18, No. 2, 2003, Pp. 20 – 28.*

[13] Polynesians may originate from the indigenous peoples of countries such as Vietnam or the Philippines, or even from indigenous Taiwanese. Micronesians probably came from Taiwan or southern China.

[14] The best histories of Tuvalu are: Macdonald, B. Cinderellas of Empire *Towards a History of Kiribati and Tuvalu* Suva: Institute of Pacific Studies, University of the South Pacific, 2001; and Faaniu, S. et.al. Tuvalu – A History Suva: Institute of Pacific Studies & Extension Services, University of the South Pacific & Funafuti: Ministry of Social Services, Government of Tuvalu, 1983. The advantage of the latter is that it was written by Tuvaluans, over against Macdonald's rather staid *Palagi* history, though Doug Munro asserts some of the material in Faaniu, et.al, was plagiarized. See, Munro, D. 'On Being a Historian of Tuvalu: Further Thoughts on Methodology and Mindset' *History in Africa* 26 (1999), 219 - 238. A shorter, and rather eulogistic discussion is by Finn, G.A. 'Small is Viable: The Global Ebbs and Flows of a Pacific Atoll Nation' Honolulu, Hawai'i: East-West Centre Working Papers, Pacific Islands Development Series, No. 15, April, 2002.

[15] *Faifeau* translates as pastors or ministers.

[16] *Feagaiga* refers to or describes the covenant relationship between *Faifeau* and congregation.

[17] In addition to Macdonald *ibid.* See also Kofe, L 'Palagi and Pastors' in Faaniu *et.al.* Pp. 102 – 120, and Goldsmith, Michael & Munro, Doug 'Conversion and Church Formation in Tuvalu' *Journal of Pacific History* 27:1 (1992) Pp. 44 – 54; Munro, D. & Thornley, A. (Eds.) Covenant Makers *Islander Missionaries in the Pacific* Suva: Pacific Theological College & Institute of Pacific Studies, USP, 1996, esp. Munro, D 'Samoan Pastors in Tuvalu', Pp. 124 – 157.

[18] Church

between Westerners, or Palagi[19], occurred during the 1800s, including by Peruvian slave raiders between 1862 and 1864, who kidnapped some 400 Islanders from Funafuti and Nukulaelae. These raids prompted the British to make the group, and the major island group to the north, a protectorate and called the lot the Gilbert and Ellis Islands, noticing that the Gilbertese, who call themselves i-Kiribati, were a Micronesian people, quite ethnically, culturally and linguistically different from the southern Polynesian people in the Ellice group. The protectorate became a colony in 1915.

Historian Doug Munro summarises the British and Palagi attitude to Tuvalu (Ellis Islands) thus:

Tuvalu is unmistakably a marginal archipelago. It was, and is, economically unimportant and strategically insignificant. The paucity of exploitable resources, itself a function of an inhospitable environment and smallness of scale, together with an aggregate population of fewer than 3,000, rendered the islands unattractive to trader and labor recruiter, and unsuitable for European settlement and plantation development[20].

During the colonial years, many Tuvaluans relocated to parts of the Gilberts, particularly the western, phosphate rich, island of Banaba[21], and the main atoll of Tarawa, for education and work. Some Tuvaluans married i-Kiribati, learned the language, and Tuvalu still has many cultural ties with their northern neighbour.

The next major Palagi intrusion into Tuvalu was in World War II[22], when, starting in October, 1942, American troops arrived to build the airstrip on Funafuti, set up a communications bunker on Tepuka motu[23] on the Western edge of Te Namo, built other airstrips, now abandoned,

---

[19] Tuvaluan for 'Westerner, outsider'. The Samoan word, *Phalagi*, may come from an old legend which said that the Gods, or God (Burst), would be white and come over the horizon on wings (*lagi*, sky). Westerners are white, came over the horizon, and the sails on their boats looked, sort-of, like wings. Westerners were those 'who burst upon the Samoans from the sky'. The Fijian word is *Vulagi*, in Tongan *Papalagi*, and in i-Kiribati, Westerners or outsiders are called *Im-a-tang*. In Samoan and Tuvaluan, 'g' is pronounced 'n', so *Palagi* is pronounced ' *'pfa-langii'*.

[20] Munro, 'On Being a Historian of Tuvalu', *op.cit.* P. 220.

[21] See, http://www.banaban.com/ (accessed, September 21, 2005) The British name for this island was Ocean Island.

[22] The Allies' Pacific campaign was plotted largely in Brisbane, where General Douglas McArthur set up his HQ after the fall of the Philippines. When showing visiting Tuvaluans around Brisbane, I always show them McArthur Place on the corner of Edward and Queen Streets, and the Forgan Smith Building at the University of Queensland, both sites from whence wartime intrusions into the Ellis Islands were planned.

[23] Motu translates as islet.

on Motulalo motu at Nukufetau atoll, and on Nanumea, and used their bases as forward staging posts for raids against the Japanese, occupying the Gilbert Islands, particularly on Tarawa Atoll. In return, the Japanese occasionally attacked Funafuti and Nanumea. The Seabee engineers cut down many valuable coconut palms, dug several large pits on Funafuti for rock and soil for the airstrip, told the locals that they were 'borrowing' the materials for a good cause, and that the 'loan' would be repaid.

These, now polluted, water and rubbish filled pits are a major feature on Funafuti, and are called the 'Borrow Pits'[24]. The excavations also shattered parts of Funafuti Atoll, allowing seawater to pollute the fresh water lens beneath the atoll[25]. I have tasted salty water on Funafuti, drawn from the polluted water table saturated after major tropical storms have dumped massive fresh water rain on the atoll, and I have seen gardens of Tuvalu's large, slow growing, yam-like tuber, Pulaka[26] damaged by salt water pollution seeping up through the shattered atoll.

After protracted negotiations[27], the Gilbert and Ellis Islands colonies were split in 1975, and on the first of October, 1978, Tuvalu became an independent country.

Global Warming

Tuvalu is best known globally because it is gravely threatened by the effects of global warming caused by greenhouse gas pollution of the world's atmosphere, which has rapidly escalated subsequent to the industrial revolution.

I have stood on the highest point of land on Funafuti, which I called 'Mt Funafuti' much to the amusement of the head of the Tuvalu Meteorological Office[28], Hilia Vavae, who took me there, after showing me her meticulously collected data about the changing climate around Tuvalu and particularly Funafuti over 20 years. 'Mt Funafuti', a nondescript spot in the middle of the atoll, is 3.7 meters above mean high tide. There's a small concrete circle with a steel pipe set in the middle of it, left from scientific drilling actually conducted by the 1897 expedition

---

[24] See, Telavi, M 'War' in Faaniu, S. et.al. Op.cit.140 – 144. A first hand Tuvaluan discussion of the war years is by Frank Pasefika (Pasifika Falani), The Autobiography of Frank Pasefika Funafuti: Tuvalu Extension Centre, & Suva: Institute of Pacific Studies, USP, 1990, esp. Pp. 31 - 39.

[25] See http://www.sms.si.edu/irlspec/Hammock_FWLens.htm (accessed, August 29, 2005) See also, Crocombe, R. The South Pacific Suva: University of the South Pacific, 2001, esp. P. 38.

[26] *Cyrtosperma Chamissonis*

[27] See, Macdonald, B., Cinderellas of Empire, op.cit, 220 -275.

[28] http://tuvalu.pacificweather.org/ (accessed, January 8, 2006)

led by Professor T.W. Edgeworth David[29] from New South Wales colony which drilled some 340 meters into Funafuti Atoll and largely confirmed Charles Darwin's theory, proposed some 50 years earlier, that coral atolls often form on top of ancient, extinct volcanoes. Locals still call this spot 'David's Drill'.

The threat of global warming and sea level rise concentrates the mind of every Tuvaluan on their and their children's future. The ferocious political debates about global warming have coupled with responsible journalism to cause a practice dilemma to do with balanced reporting. When reporting some global warming story, journalists feel obligated to seek 'pro' and 'con' scientific comment, suggesting to general audiences that scientific opinion is finely balanced 'pro' and 'con' the phenomenon. Rigorously peer reviewed scientific literature suggests it isn't[30]. As hard science steadily and strongly firms up, scientists arguing the 'con' case become lonelier, yet insist that their opinions be heard in the interests of 'balance'[31]. These opinions are seized upon, mostly, by governments holding out against the Kyoto environmental accord, and their business supporters, to cast doubt upon the scientific veracity of global warming research findings[32].

Setting to one side the fearsome fights about global warming and its effects, on the basis of what I have seen and what I have been told about the environmental effects of global warming and sea level rise in Tuvalu, and specifically on and around Funafuti Atoll – it's real, it's happening, and it's damaging Tuvalu.

---

[29] See, the fascinating book by his wife, Mrs David, Funafuti or Three Months on a Remote Coral Island: an unscientific account of a scientific expedition London: John Murray, 1899; See also, http://en.wikipedia.org/wiki/Edgeworth_David (accessed, December 22, 2005); Branagan, David F. T.W. Edgeworth David: a life: *geologist, adventurer, soldier and 'Knight in the old brown hat'* (edited by Paul Cliff) Canberra: National Library of Australia, 2005.

[30] In addition to the rigorously peer reviewed scientific literature, usually arcanely technical and accessed only by specialists, the best science on global warming can be found at the Intergovernmental Panel on Climate Change (IPCC): http://www.ipcc.ch/ (accessed, August 14, 2005). Another authoritative source is RealClimate: http://www.realclimate.org/index.php?p=1 (accessed, August 14, 2005) which is maintained by climate scientists. A good Pacific perspective on global warming and its effects is maintained by the Pacific Regional Environment Programme (SPREP): http://www.sprep.org.ws/sprep/about.htm (accessed, August 14, 2005)

[31] Realclimate.org has a specific discussion of 'The False Objectivity of 'Balance' http://www.realclimate.org/index.php?p=218 (accessed, December 23, 2005).

[32] Though not representative of the stronger global warming deniers, John Connell does argue that Tuvalu, with the assistance of some elements of the (gullible, sensationalist) media, and some environmental NGOs, has exaggerated its vulnerability. See, Connell, J. 'Losing Ground? Tuvalu, the greenhouse effect and the garbage can' *Asia Pacific Viewpoint* Vol. 44 No. 2, August, 2004, Pp. 89 – 107.

Successive Tuvaluan Prime Ministers have described the threat to their country and people as 'creeping terrorism' and have threatened to sue developed world Kyoto Protocol holdout governments for the damage being done to them[33].

Recent research on what's causing severer hurricanes, typhoons, and cyclones, such as Hurricanes Katrina and then Rita in September, 2005, strongly points to global warming amplifying these phenomena due to increased sea temperatures adding energy to tropical low pressure systems and otherwise weaker hurricanes. Luckily, Tuvalu is located outside 'cyclone alley' in the South Western Pacific, where many cyclones which sweep south and west are formed. Knowing that Funafuti is so low, with effectively nothing between it and a raging blow, and allowing that Tuvalu and particularly Funafuti do have disaster plans in place, nevertheless contemplating what could happen there if the country's ever hit by a Katrina-intensity monster is the stuff of nightmares[34].

The continuing story about Tuvalu and global warming attracts overseas journalists like bees to a honey pot, yet a lot of what they report infuriates Tuvaluan journalists. The general impression many of these reports convey is that the locals huddle in permanent dread, terrified every time the tides rise, and that, when the tides rise extra high, all nine atolls are flooded from end to end[35].

Opening *The Courier-Mail* or the *Sydney Morning Herald* on Saturday February 21, 2004, Australia-based Tuvaluans saw headlines like 'King Tide Gives Atoll Dwellers a Sinking Feeling' (SMH) with pictures of the Van Camp[36] wreck on the central western, lagoon, side of Funafuti at low tide, and locals tossing plant rubbish off a truck on to a dump at the end of Funafuti Road; and 'King Tide Threatens to Cover Atoll Nation' (CM), with an aerial picture of Funafala motu just to the south of Funafuti, lifted from Tuvaluislands.com, and children thigh deep in a flooded borrow pit near their house. Both stories were by the AFP's

---

[33] I have collected links to some of the recent statements by Tuvaluan leaders on global warming and the threat it poses to Tuvalu here:
http://www.tuvaluislands.com/news/archives/2005/2005-02-22_tmta2.htm (accessed, August 17, 2005); Some original stories on the legal action threat are here:
http://www.planetark.com/dailynewsstory.cfm/newsid/17514/story.htm,
http://www.planetark.com/dailynewsstory.cfm?newsid=14869&newsdate=06-Mar-2002,
and http://www.planetark.com/dailynewsstory.cfm?newsid=17512&newsdate=30-Aug-2002 (accessed, August 17, 2005).
[34] The worst cyclone to hit Tuvalu and Funafuti in recent times was Bebe on October 21, 1972. On its effects, see, Maragos, J.E. *et.al.*, 'Tropical Cyclone Bebe Creates a New Land Formation on Funafuti Atoll' *Science*, Vol. 181, 21 September, 1973, Pp. 1161 - 1164.
[35] This also infuriates scholars like John Connell *op.cit.*
[36] *Van Camp* was the mother ship of a three vessel fishing fleet wrecked on the shore of *Te Namo* in 1972 by Cyclone Bebe.

then Auckland-based Pacific correspondent, Michael Field. He, TV NZ's Pacific correspondent, Barbara Dreaver[37], and a few other reporters, were on Funafuti for the February, 2004, king tides[38].

Carol Farbotko specifically analysed 'Tuvalu and Climate Change: Constructions of Environmental Displacement in the *Sydney Morning Herald* and concluded:

> *The emphasis on island vulnerabilities in Western news media in the context of climate change-induced sea-level rise can superficially be welcomed as an awareness-raising function to what is undeniably a very frightening phenomenon. However, the construction of Tuvaluans as 'tragic victims' through a hierarchical island/mainland alterity is problematic in the way it presents a particular perspective of Tuvalu, through a lens of vulnerability[39].*

Radio Tuvalu's News Editor, Yvette Isaac, sums up how Tuvaluans regard so much of this as nonsense:

> *Sometimes those reports really exaggerate (sic.). In some of the reports I have read, I gather that the writers just want to give a bad image of Tuvalu to the outside world. While at the same time imbedding fear in every Tuvaluan who read the story. Not only that, some of the reports are inaccurate in the sense that they used such words as flooding for normal king tides or spring tides, and Tuvalu will be underwater. As a Tuvaluan reporter it is awful. They have to see the situation themselves and fully understand Tuvalu to make accurate reports. Sometimes the informations (sic.) are inaccurate because these writers do not receive them from first-hand sources[40].*

Palagi reporter's stories lurk in On Line databases like ticking time bombs, and surfaced again in wire service or agency stories published

---

[37] TV NZ News 'Tuvalu seeks aid on submerging' TX Feb 28, 2004, Online, with video, at: http://onenews.nzoom.com/onenews_detail/0,1227,258464-1-7,00.html (accessed, August 17, 2005). Barbara Dreaver's story was considerably more restrained than those by Mike Field.

[38] Mike Field's Web Site has other stories on Tuvalu, including one on the February, 2004, king tides, see http://203.97.34.63/tuvalu8.htm (Accessed, August 17, 2005)

[39] Farbotko, C. 'Tuvalu and Climate Change: Constructions of Environmental Displacement in the *Sydney Morning Herald*' *Geogr.Ann.*, 87 B (4): 279 – 293 at 289. I had access to an earlier version of this MSS prior to publication. She does not specifically discuss the February, 2004, stories, but they fit squarely into her assessment of many *SMH* stories emphasising Tuvalu's powerlessness and victimhood.

[40] Isaac, Y. E-Mail interview. I've also had many conversations with Yvette and her colleagues on Funafuti where they have strongly put the same views.

when the February, 2005, king tides occurred, this time coinciding with a solar and lunar 18 year perihelion. Tuvaluans are a polite people, not given to strong language, but ask local journalists like Yvette Isaac what they think of reporting on their country they feel is hyped, and a sense of anger rises like the tides: 'I feel as a Tuvaluan and local journalist, that my fellow colleagues in overseas countries should consider our feelings as Tuvaluans in their reports. ... We get disappointed too when we hear our country being broadcasted (sic.), talked (about) in a way that hurts us.'[41]

Global warming's effects on Tuvalu are not usually spectacular. The effects are creeping, insidious, eroding, infrequent, and steadily escalating. Entirely normal, periodic, predictable events, like the annual king tides around late January and into February, coupled with awful local weather, cause concern and damage across the region, and have done for as long as people have lived on the islands. But when protective reefs have been weakened by coral bleaching caused by sustained warmer sea temperatures, dazzling coral sand beaches around motu out on the edges of lagoons are eroded, dense tropical vegetation caps on the motu damaged, and so on, sea level rise caused by global warming is amplified; and the damage that extreme high tides, awful weather, or larger and more dangerous cyclones cause is all the more severe[42].

It was this combination of effects which wracked Tuvalu, and Funafuti, in February, 2005, and upon which Silafaga Lalua, and Lomi Paeniu, reported.

Some people are also surprised to learn that, when there's a severe El Niño[43] gripping the Pacific, and Australia's being sucked bone dry in drought, Tuvalu, too, is drought stricken, fresh water's rationed, and the expensive desalination plant on Funafuti drones 24/7 to provide some water to drink.

On Funafuti, when the necessary conditions coincide, sea water seeps up through the shattered atoll and polluted water table to flood swathes of land around the airstrip, and flows out of the already full borrow pits to flood nearby homes, fales[44], pig pens, gardens, and roads. A king tide with a stiff wind pushing the sea against the atoll is what's needed for this kind of flooding to occur. It's this periodic flooding that attracts

[41] *Ibid.*
[42] As I discussed in my feature on Tuvaluislands.com:
http://www.tuvaluislands.com/news/archives/2005/2005-02-22_tmta.htm (accessed, August 25, 2005).
[43] http://en.wikipedia.org/wiki/El_Nino (accessed, January 8, 2006)
[44] A *Fale* can be a family's fenced or unfenced yard around their house, or more usually a small, open sided, thatch roofed hut with a raised platform in the yard often used for sleeping, domestic chores, or just as a cooler, breezy, place to sit and yarn.

'parachute journalists' to Funafuti. Tuvaluan journalists are on the spot and better equipped to report accurately, in their own words and with their own pictures, which is what reporter Silafaga Lalua and 'citizen journalist' Lomi Paeniu did on February 9, 2005.

On Tepuka motu, 18km west of Funafuti across the usually placid Te Namo, local ecologist, Semese Alefaio, shows visitors the many large coconut and pandanus palms lying on the beach, brought down by severe erosion as we tread carefully over eroded, rocky, areas where the once thick coral sands beach has gone[45], and we look over at the battered, brown rock that used to be Tepuka sa Vili Vili, once a pretty little motu with dazzling beach and dense tropical vegetation cap which locals visited for fishing and play until Cyclone Meli[46] in early September, 1994, ripped the cap away and the insatiable, indefatigable, and slowly rising Pacific Ocean finished the job. Semese Alefaio has also told me about interruptions to traditional island customs, such as when expected fish migrations, or fish catches, fail, which affects traditional agreements and practices to do with family or island rights to those species, and sharing of particular catches. Going out on to the rocky, barren, and ferociously hot Pacific Ocean, Eastern, shore of the atoll, the feeling can be spooky. I've sort-of sensed that the brooding ocean's out to get the atoll, battering it, nibbling at it, sneaking under it, and into it through fissures and holes to pollute the ground water lens. Locals don't go out there much.

I sat in his house on Funafuti Road listening to Tuvalu's first Prime Minister, and a former Governor General, Hon. Toaripi Lauti, explain why growing Pulaka was getting harder because of salt water contamination of the pits in which the tubers traditionally were grown[47].

When you have seen the effects of global warming, first hand, listened to highly informed locals like the Prime Minister himself, to Semese Alefaio, and meteorologist, Hilia Vavae, looked at their data, pressed them with all the nay-saying arguments, listened to local elders like Hon. Toaripi Lauti, and researched the hard science; reporting back to the world is a vivid journalistic experience.

---

[45] See, http://www.tuvaluislands.com/news/archives/2005/2005-02-22_tmta2.htm (accessed, September 21, 2005); a more recent mini-documentary was shown on PBS television in the USA in December, 2005, see:
http://www.pbs.org/frontlineworld/rough/2005/12/tuvalu_that_sin_1.html (accessed, December 23, 2005).

[46] http://www.prh.noaa.gov/cphc/summaries/1994.php (accessed, January 8, 2006)

[47] See my InterWorld Radio feature:
http://www.interworldradio.net/audio/audio_programme_details.asp?id=1192

Dot TV

The other thing for which Tuvalu is known globally is 'the Dot TV caper'. Tuvalu does not have its own local television service (though plans to bring local television to, at least, Funafuti, were in train late in 2005). The irony of 'Dot TV Land' having no local TV was not lost on anybody.

There is only one Web Site on this planet actually based or hosted in Tuvalu, on Funafuti, so we can call that the 'Real Dot TV'[48]. Their office is located in the new Taiwanese funded three-story two-wing Government Building, which dominates the Funafuti skyline across the small Vaiaku village square from the airport and a Maneapa[49] which also serves as Tuvalu's Fale Palamene, the Parliament[50]. (It takes about 30 seconds to amble from the airport and the Maneapa, across the Vaikau square to the entrance to the Government Building, though much longer if you meet somebody you know and pause for a chat. Tuvalu's like that, frustrating for 'speedy' Palagi who fail to adjust.)

Before the .TV story started, however, in the 1990s, Tuvalu was involved in a deal to lease out its international telephone routing code – 688 – to New Zealand telephone sex firms, a deal which earned the country about $US 2 million a year, a figure which grew to about ten percent of the national budget. But when Ekelesia leaders learned of this, despite assurances that Tuvaluans could not access the 'service', and coupled with transparency issues to do with company calling records, Tuvalu got out of this exercise[51].

Tracing the 'Dot TV' story is tricky, with outsider Palagi reports hyping the vast amounts of money Tuvalu would allegedly get from the deal. 'To Internet incubator idealab!, Pacific island Tuvalu is a potential cash machine' wrote Robert McNatt in *Business Week* for May 1, 2000[52].

---

[48] http://www.tuvalu.tv

[49] A Maneapa is a larger open sided, often thatch roofed, concrete floored meeting house. The word can also describe a more formal meeting of village residents. But the term is from i-Kiribati, so is being discouraged in Tuvaluan. The preferred term is Falekaupule.

[50] Tuvalu's Parliament House, which is also used for all sorts of meetings, *Faatele* (celebrations), and religious meetings by other faiths not accommodated in Funafuti's churches.

[51] Finin, *op.cit.* P. 21.

[52] See, news stories from 1997 – 2005 on Tuvaluislands.com (accessed, August 27, 2005), and,
McNatt, R. 'Cough It up for Dot.TV' *Business Week* New York, May 1, 2000, Iss. 3679, Pg. 12. See also, Raskin, A. 'Buy This Domain' *Wired* San Francisco, September, 1998, Vol. 6 Iss. 9, P. 106; Gruenwedel, E. 'Masters of their domain' *Adweek* (Eastern edition) New York: May 15, 2000, Vol. 41 Iss. 20 P. 100; 'Tuvalu reaps rewards from .tv suffix' *Telecomworldwire* Coventry, Dec 15, 2000, P. 1; Banks, B. 'The Deal's divine' *Canadian Business* Toronto, September 11, 1998, Vol. 71 Iss. 14, P. 85; Pritchard, C. 'Tiny island

But even before idealab! got into the act, one Andrew Rubin, communication manager for WebTV, simply asked for, and received, control of the .TV Top Level Domain (TLD) from one of the major Internet Name companies, Network Solutions. Rubin was offering registration control for $US 10,000 per name. When they found out they didn't 'own' .TV, the Tuvaluan Government asked the Internet Assigned Numbers Authority (IANA)[53] to get it back, and then auctioned the TLD[54]. .TV was bought by a Canadian company, for $US 50 million, but it went bankrupt, and idealab! bought the rights. Then the Dot Com bubble burst and idealab! relinquished the .TV contract[55] Eventually, the .TV Corporation was bought by the US Corporation, Verisign, best known for its security certification systems for e-commerce[56].

All the other .TV web addresses in the world are leased through Verisign, and most of the .TV sites would upset the deeply religious and very conservative Tuvaluans, even allowing that .TV brings in about $US4 million a year of revenue, paved the roads on Funafuti Atoll[57], and paid for other important works. Given the uses made of .TV by several unsavoury outlets, as Ekalesia leaders and their flocks realise what their Cyberspace code is being used for, coupled with better Net access On Islands allowing locals to also access .TV sourced material, further controversy can be expected over this deal too.

On Funafuti, if you want access to the Internet, you'd have to know your way around the atoll, and visit one of a couple of local Internet Cafes, one south down Tuvalu Road near the old Customs warehouse in a shed with the totally unexpected (sic.), tatty, sign nailed above the door – 'Coconet Wireless'[58] – another one hidden on the ground floor in the old Government Building behind the police compound – you'd never know it was there unless somebody actually took you there – at the Telecom Tuvalu kiosk next to the police compound around the corner from the

---

lands big Web Bucks' *Marketing Magazine* Toronto, March 5, 2001, Vol. 106 Iss. 9, P. 6; and Mike Field 'Tiny Tuvalu's unique Dot TV sparking corporate battles around the world' October 4, 2000, http://203.97.34.63/tuvalu3.htm (accessed, August 17, 2005)

[53] IANA - http://www.iana.org/ (accessed, August 17, 2005)

[54] Part of this part of the story is described by Watson, M.I. 'Location, location, location: the geography of the dot com problem' *Environment and Planning B: Planning and Design 2001* Vol. 28 Pp. 59 – 71 esp. 68 – 69.

[55] Transparency International Australia and the Asia Pacific School of Economics and Government at the Australian National University's National Integrity Systems Transparency International Country Study Report Tuvalu 2004 at Page 8 also traces the development of the .TV lease story and concerns about that process from their point of view.

[56] See: http://www.tv/ (accessed, August 17, 2005). Part of the deal is for a Tuvaluan IT worker to spend time with Verisign in New Hampshire, and 'the chosen one' from mid-2005 – 6 was Lomi Paeniu.

[57] A major exercise, with needed roadbed material being shipped from Fiji on barges.

[58] A reference to WiFi Net access installed by the IT office on Funafuti during 2005.

'hidden ISP', or be well connected to Radio Tuvalu or the folks at the Real .TV. All public net access is expensive. According to a report by Silafaga Lalua and Diana Semi in *Tuvalu Echoes* posted on Lomi Paeniu's Online Maneapa in mid-September, 2005, a fourth InterNet Café has been opened in the centre of Funafuti:

> *Situated on the first floor of Nukuvalu building, above its own store and behind the Western Union office, Hapai is at the centre of the second biggest central business district on the island, where the hospital, primary school, retail stores and University of the South Pacific centre are located. It is proving to be very convenient for USP students especially during the busy days, as well as teachers, primary school students and hospital staff.*

Mrs Lita Pita, Nukuvalu's managing director told *Tuvalu Echoes* that she had wanted to cater for the needs of all who need the Internet on the island, when she thought of establishing this Internet outlet.'[59]

Since the middle of 2004, the Government IT Centre – 'Real .TV' – has leased a satellite link from the lagoon side of their office through NewStar 5 to the Noumea-based Pacific ISP, and have steadily increased their bandwidth, 128k up and 512k down[60]. Together with the fit-out of the new Government IT Centre came a roll-out of WiFi capacity, initially to the south of the building as far as the Coconet Wireless, with plans, now completed according to a Pacific Nius story in late August, 2005[61], to extend the signal north up Funafuti Road to cover the Vaiaku Lagi Hotel – Tuvalu's only hotel[62] – and the police, and navy[63] compounds, and the Tuvalu Media Corporation. A kilometre or so further down the road is Fongafale Village, and beyond that, the Funafuti Port Complex. Just off the northern tip of the atoll is Amatuku motu, site of the Tuvalu Maritime Training Institute (TMTI). All the foregoing would amply benefit from good Internet access.

---

[59] http://maneapa.mywebhut.com/news.php (accessed, September 21, 2005)
[60] So the manager of the Government IT office, Opetaia Simati, told me during our first Skype VoIP conversation on December 23, 2005.
[61] 'Tuvalu to get Wireless Internet Coverage' PNS http://www.pacificislands.cc/pina/pinadefault2.php?urlpinaid=16555 (accessed, August 25, 2005) and 'Tuvalu: Government to provide Universal Internet Access' Radio Australia Pacific Beat http://www.abc.net.au/ra/pacbeat/stories/s1445948.htm (accessed, August 25, 2005)
[62] Though there are a few guest houses. Tourism information for Tuvalu can be found at http://www.timelesstuvalu.com/ (accessed, January 8, 2006)
[63] Tuvalu's 'navy' consists of one Australian-provided patrol boat, with assistance from two Australian navy personnel stationed on Funafuti. Occasional New Zealand surveillance flights also assist Tuvalu to keep some sort of watch over its vast EEZ.

Uneven electricity supplies from the aging power station on Funafuti do not help maintaining a 'bullet proof' net access system either. However, Japanese aid, possibly in gratitude for Tuvalu's support at the International Whaling Commission in mid-2005[64], refurbished Tuvalu's major medical facility, the Princess Margaret Hospital, in 2003-4, and is also upgrading the power station.

A further complication occurred on January 15, 2005, when INTELSAT 804 disappeared from its assigned geosynchronous orbit some 30,000km above the Pacific. Despite the temptation to think of the opening sequence of the science fiction movie *Independence Day*, the loss of the uninsured, $US170 million 804 was, according to investigation reports, attributed to a design fault[65]. Telecommunications, data feeds, and direct satellite broadcasting channels ceased across the region until INTELSAT 701 was awakened from redundancy, ground stations retuned, sometimes large dishes realigned, this work in some places requiring charter flights, or special boat trips to remoter islands[66].

Tuvalu literally disappeared off the phone and data maps until Telecom Tuvalu realigned and retuned their gear back to 701. Net access was maintained through the Government ISP using NewStar 5 and the Noumea-based Pacific ISP. In late November and early December, 2005, Tuvalu again disappeared from the global telephone system, this time apparently due to a serious technical failure in Telecom Tuvalu[67].

Doing Journalism in Tuvalu

Tuvalu did not have its own, even modest, local broadcast television service in early 2006. A couple of small businesses, and a few private homes, have satellite dishes, imported at huge expense from Fiji, and do receive several services such as the Australian Broadcasting

---

[64] I pressed the Prime Minister, Hon. Maatia Toafa, about this in November, 2004, and he strongly denied the hospital and power station refurbishments, and other Japanese aid funded assistance was 'encouragement' and 'reward' for Tuvalu's support at the IWC, saying that data on sustainable whaling provided by Japan showed its quotas could be increased. Tuvalu was prepared to review its support if contrary whale population data became available.

[65] 'US' Lockheed satellite failure due to design problem – report'
http://www.forbes.com/business/feeds/afx/2005/08/11/afx2178586.html (accessed, August 27, 2005).

[66] 'REGION: Satellite Outage Cripples Pacific Island Communications'
http://www.pacificislands.cc/pina/pinadefault2.php?urlpinaid=14120 (accessed, August 25, 2005).

[67] 'Tuvalu Incommunicado' http://www.telecomweb.com/news/1134672195.htm (accessed, December 23, 2005); 'Tuvalu: Telecommunications Down for Two Weeks'
http://www.pacificislands.cc/pina/pinadefault2.php?urlpinaid=18924 (accessed, December 23, 2005).

Corporation's Asia Pacific Television[68], BBC World, and US-origin Pentecostal direct broadcast outlets. Fiji TV's Regional pay TV satellite service, Sky Pacific[69], is encrypted. Some dish-owning Tuvaluans on Funafuti record events such as rugby matches and charge a modest fee to show them later in a Maneapa, such gatherings being always well patronised. A really fun night on Funafuti can include watching often pirated VHS or DVD movies folks have already watched many times but turning on the 'JapLish' or 'ChinLish' sub-titles and sound effects for the laughs.

With the Tuvaluan Government wanting a local television capacity by the end of 2005[70], I suggested to well-placed Tuvaluans, that the Australian community television model could serve Tuvalu well[71]. A few Funafuti locals use digital video cameras to shoot community, school, or family events, and use computers to make and sell DVDs, earning them modest extra income. Tuvalu also has the monthly, A4 sized, newspaper, *Tuvalu Echoes*, published in Tuvaluan and English editions, but its limited print run is beset with technical problems to do with reliable inks and paper supplies and maintenance issues with the printing equipment. Newspapers, mostly from Fiji and brought by visitors or returning Tuvaluans on the thrice-weekly[72] Air Fiji flights are pounced upon and read very widely indeed.

On the surface, journalists working for the Tuvalu Media Corporation (TMC) and filing news reports for Radio Tuvalu operate in much the same way as Western journalists do in Australia and New Zealand. Their reports are sometimes also syndicated to the Pacific Nius service operated by the Pacific Islands News Association (PINA)[73] out of Suva, and to Niu FM[74], a radio station in Auckland with a large Tuvaluan audience because it broadcasts in Tuvaluan several hours a week[75].

---

[68] http://abcasiapacific.com/ (Accessed, August 29, 2005)

[69] http://www.fijitv.com.fj/ (Accessed, August 29, 2005)

[70] Though this had not eventuated by mid-January, 2006.

[71] See, Hayes, M. 'Rural community television news: obstacles to innovation' *Australian Studies in Journalism* Number 13, 2004, Pp. 113 – 138. One of the unlikely salvages of this pyrrhic experiment in Rural Australian community television news production is that the professionally written news theme suite for this experiment is now used as the news themes for Radio Tuvalu News.

[72] According to their published schedules. In practice, Air Fiji's flights to Funafuti are notoriously unreliable, despite the fact that the Tuvalu government is a major shareholder in Air Fiji.

[73] Pacific Islands News Association - http://www.pinanius.com/ (accessed, September 21, 2005); For PNS and PINA Nius stories, start here: http://www.pacificislands.cc/

[74] http://www.niufm.com/default.aspx (accessed, August 27, 2005)

[75] Passing mention of Radio Tuvalu and the Tuvaluan media environment is made in Seward, R. Radio Happy Isles *Media and Politics at Play in the Pacific* Honolulu: University of Hawai'i Press, 1999, and Molnar H. & Meadows, M. Songlines to Satellites

Helen Molnar, commenting on Radio Tuvalu's financial difficulties even in the early 1990s, writes that '... Tuvalu is like a remote Aboriginal community...'[76]. I would rather describe Radio Tuvalu as being comparable to a small, rural, Australian community radio station[77], though lacking reasonable access to the kinds of telecommunications, and professional as well as technical support, that a rural radio station in Australia would take for granted. The nearest Dick Smith, Tandy, or Radio Shack-type outlet, for example, is an expensive 1,200 kilometre flight to the south in Suva, Fiji. If the satellite receiver for the BBC World Service fails, it has to be shipped, airfreight and pre-paid, to Radio Australia's technical workshop in Melbourne. In my first visit to Funafuti it was somewhat stunning to hear Radio Australia News being received via short-wave, and broadcast, with its scratchy, fading, sound, at 7.00am and 8.00pm on Radio Tuvalu, a sensation repeated two years later. Radio Tuvalu could not afford to buy the needed, off the shelf, gear to receive RA via satellite when this is now routine and entirely taken for granted elsewhere in the Pacific. Radio Australia might like to provide a satellite reception kit for Radio Tuvalu but the dish and its supporting structures would have to withstand potentially fierce cyclonic winds. I was quoted a figure of $AU 40,000 for such an even modest installation.

Of course, journalist's reports are broadcast in Tuvaluan as well as English, and the Tuvaluan versions must exactly match the English, which limits the use of Palagi technical or legal terms. One informant explained:

> *An example is the translation by Radio Tuvalu of something like this, as it sometimes appears in the news: 'Both Wellington and Canberra have agreed to the request from the Pacific Forum Secretariat that... Radio Tuvalu would usually translate Wellington and Canberra into Tuvaluan as Wellington and Canberra (just as cities). The meaning of the story in Tuvaluan is lost by such translation. The correct translation into Tuvaluan of the reference to Wellington and Canberra (the seats of government in NZ and Oz) should be 'te maalo o Niusila mo te maalo o Aosetalia' (that is, without mentioning Wellington and Canberra at all). Translated back into English this little bit of Tuvaluan would read 'the governments of NZ and Australia' which in fact is actually meant by the reference to Wellington and Canberra.[78]*

Indigenous Communication in Australia, the South Pacific and Canada Sydney: Pluto Press Australia & Wellington: Huia Publishers, 2001. On Pacific journalism practice generally, see Robie, D. (Ed.) The Pacific Journalist *A Practical Guide* Suva: Journalism Programme, University of the South Pacific & USP Bookshop, 2001.
[76] Molnar, in Molnar & Meadows, *Op.Cit.* P. 86.
[77] See, Forde, S., Meadows, M. & Foxwell, K. Culture, Commitment *Community* The Australian Community Radio Sector Brisbane: Griffith University, 2002; and Community Broadcasting Association of Australia, http://www.cbaa.org.au/ (accessed, August 28, 2005)
[78] Tito Isala, personal communication.

Because major sources of news, such as the Government, public service, most non-government organizations (NGOs) including the church, the Tuvalu Maritime Training Institute (TMTI), the Meteorological Office, and the airport are based on Funafuti, specifically the central atoll village of Vaiaku, the northern village of Fongafale, and Amatuku motu, most Tuvaluan journalism focuses on Funafuti. But Funafuti is certainly not Tuvalu in its entirety, or even an accurately reliable snapshot of the country. Tuvalu NGOs also operate on komiti lines, with every NGO, and branches of NGOs, as well as schools, churches, and even the cooperatively owned small supermarkets, Fusi, having a committee, at which proposals are usually, exhaustively, discussed with decisions arrived in consensus-fashion.

The Government almost never issues media releases, not so much because they're secretive but because they don't see much need to. Senior public servants double as media officers, and they are routinely, and personally, approached by Tuvaluan journalists doing their rounds. Occasionally, a Government spokesperson might ring Radio Tuvalu with a statement, or fax one over, and a journalist would walk to their office to do an interview or ask further questions. Radio Tuvalu, located on Funafuti Road diagonally north across the street from the hotel, and next door to the navy and then the police compounds – each the size of a small suburban block of land – is only a minute or two amble north of the new Government Building, and it's usually too hot to walk much faster than an amble anyway. Compared with journalists in other places, Tuvaluan journalists have very few crime stories to report, and what few crimes occur usually have an alcohol component to them, such as when somebody was killed in the middle of 2003 while they slept on the Funafuti airstrip – as many families do because it's cooler and there are so few planes – by a drunk driver. There are very few assaults or other serious violent crimes, almost no thefts or burglaries[79]. The only major Tuvaluan institution not on Funafuti is the Motufoua Secondary School, on the southern end of Vaitupu Atoll, to the north west of Funafuti, which celebrated its centenary in July, 2005[80].

Motufoua Secondary School was also the site of Tuvalu's worst tragedy, a dormitory fire late on Thursday night, March 8, 2000, in which

---

[79] To be sure, Tuvaluan police can and do operate in identical ways to their counterparts elsewhere, as do the courts, and the small number of offenders who are jailed are kept in a small, lightly fenced, compound and *Fale* on Funafuti to serve their sentences. Every morning, except on Sundays, they can be seen around Vaiaku and the Government precinct, sweeping up leaves and litter, under the very benign supervision of a very bored police officer. The point being that jailable crime is exceptionally rare in Tuvalu.

[80] See, Laupepa, L 'Vaitupu' in Faaniu, S *et.al.*, *op.cit.* Pp. 83 – 85; Isala, T. 'Motulu, A Very Short History of Motufoua Secondary School' MSS privately circulated, July 31, 2005.

18 female students and their matron were killed. A New Zealand specialist psychologist in trauma and disaster recovery, Emeritus Professor Antony J.W. Taylor, summed up the impact of this terrible event: 'Its traumatic effects on the total Tuvalu population of about 10,000 was widespread, and said to be in proportion to the immediate loss of either 8,000 New Zealanders or 25,000 Australians in any one calamity in their respective countries'.[81] Nobody in Tuvalu, and the Diasporic Tuvaluan global community, was untouched.

This points to the first of two major issues in the doing of journalism in Tuvalu: the place is very small geographically as well as in terms of population, and everybody seems to know everybody else, and/or seems to be related, one way or another, to everybody else. Colin Mellor's explanation for what he reported as Tuvalu's surprisingly good socio-economic indicators, particularly for one of the world's smallest, most remote, and poorest countries, also points to why doing journalism in Tuvalu is tricky: '...the recognisably high sense of family and community obligations felt by its citizens, in addition to strong respect for moral and democratic behaviour'[82]. 'Urban drift' from the outer islands to Funafuti is causing the 'population explosion' there, and concomitant service delivery, housing, and waste disposal issues. The unsightly rubbish dumps at both ends of Funafuti Road are ample evidence of this urban drift, with population, and thence additional environmental, pressure, as well as the rising living standards of Tuvaluans. Shifts from traditional diets to more Western diets, with greater access to processed foods, coupled with difficulties in growing sufficient green roughage food plants such as pulaka are contributing to significant adult onset diabetes among Tuvaluans. As in small rural towns in Australia, journalists have to live there, and if a story is published which offends somebody, the offence being real or more likely imagined or feigned, the journalist will certainly hear about it, even if only through some words exchanged at one of many routine social gatherings.

Tuvaluan Te Fenua – Really Understanding Tuvalu

There are strong traditional currents infusing Pacific journalism which Palagi could miss entirely unless we strive to become sensitive to

---

[81] http://www.massey.ac.nz/~trauma/issues/2000-2/taylor.htm (accessed, August 14, 2005); see also, Taylor, A.J.W. 'Cross-cultural interaction in the appraisal of disaster trauma in three Pacific Island countries' *Asia Pacific Viewpoint* Vol. 44 No. 2, August 2003, Pp. 177 – 193, esp. Pp. 185 – 198. The Auckland-based Tokelauan-Tuvaluan and leading Pacific band, *Te Vaka* (The Canoe), has a very moving tribute to the Motufoua victims, 'Loimata e Maligi (Let The Tears Fall Down) on their third CD, 'Nukukehe' (A New {or Different} Land'. More information at http://www.tevaka.com/

[82] Mellor, *Op. cit*. P. 28.

how things really work. What follows I have compiled with the assistance of several participants in a thread I started on the main Tuvaluan discussion group on Yahoo.com, Tuvalu2, in mid-2005, particularly the retired former Deputy Registrar of the University of the South Pacific, Tito Isala, Brian Cannon, the maintainer of Tuvaluislands.com, whose wife is a Tuvaluan who 'looks'[83] to Funafuti atoll, Unite Samasoni, a former Tuvaluan senior civil servant now living in Brisbane who 'looks' to Nukufetau and his wife, Suluvia, who 'looks' to Funafuti; and from the only indigenously compiled history of Tuvalu[84].

This was supplemented by a discussion with the Australian Broadcasting Corporation's Brisbane-based Pacific correspondent, Sean Dorney[85], who, asked to identify Tuvalu's major journalistic issue, simply said, 'Size'.

More generally, Mr Dorney explained:

There are limits in Polynesian society about how they approach people which are based on their cultural hierarchy system which you don't tend to have in Melanesian societies. But when you look at it, there've been heaps, and heaps, and heaps of good journalism in Polynesia. It's there, and it's something people are conscious of. When I have these workshops around things like the Forum Economic Ministers meetings (the 2005 Meeting being held on Funafuti Atoll), we always have a session on 'How do you do the job in the Pacific'. So these issues get kicked around. But it's the journalists themselves who say that it's something that we live with and we've got to get around it. It's certainly a constraint, there's no doubt about it. Because everyone knows everyone, it's treading on eggshells, almost. I think the biggest problem journalists have in the Pacific is actually not so much being pilloried for exposing things but it's getting the little things wrong that opens you up to criticism about what you're doing. The biggest problem I think for journalism in the Pacific is accuracy rather than huge retribution for exposure. In Polynesia there's actually a fair regard for the truth, and that getting things wrong is probably a much bigger crime than actually embarrassing somebody.

When discussing specifically Tuvaluan journalism, Dorney said: 'You're talking about a population of about four and a half thousand in the capital, and what, six to eight people working in the news media there who everyone knows. There's a huge concentration there on covering

---

[83] I'll explain the crucial significance of using the word 'looks' below.

[84] Allowing for Doug Munro's plagiarism claims, *Op. Cit.*

[85] Personal interview, 19 September, 2005.

sport (laughter). And it's difficult in those situations to report on things that are going to be personally embarrassing to somebody who's going to be closely related to you,' he said.

'I'm in the process of developing a correspondent in Tuvalu and I'm in no rush to suggest that (this person[86]) try and start digging around unearthing scandals because there's no surer way to end your relationship or to kill off a stringer correspondent than to have them unable to live in their own community any more.

'I've just got this abiding respect for journalists in the region, and the way they go about their job. Often they go much further than we would go if we lived in a community of 4,000 people and we had to be concerned about being shunned. And our kids had to go to school. I actually think they do a better job than we would do in a similar situation. But there are constraints and there are difficulties in reporting contentious matters in small societies.

'There's also a subtly sometimes, I think, in the way some of the media in the region go about reporting things that is lost on us very bland outsiders. And they can actually expose things where we don't think they've gone far enough,' Dorney said.

I also asked Brian Cannon why Tuvaluan journalists seemed so reluctant to send stories to outlets such as his web site, Tuvaluislands.com, or through myself for editing or polishing prior to sending onwards. It's a problem that's beset him since establishing Tuvaluislands.com in 1995.

Our analysis takes full account of issues such as the poor and expensive Internet connections, the permanent budget crisis afflicting the Tuvalu Media Corporation (TMC), the half dozen local journalists having many demands on their scarce time, and their comparative lack of training and even knowledge about what kinds of Tuvaluan stories overseas audiences would want to receive[87], and how best to package such stories for overseas consumption.

Mr Cannon, with input from his Tuvaluan wife, responded thus:

Tuvaluans as a society for hundreds of years relied on word of mouth to spread news, pass information, etc. And being such a small compact close knit society, there was no reason to develop a written language. It took only hours for stories to go from one end of the

---

[86] Who is a good friend of mine and editor of *Tuvalu Echoes*.

[87] Though this can be overcome by running their stories past somebody like me, acting as a 'remote editor' with them. As I have repeatedly told Tuvaluan journalists, and as they should amply know, advice or assistance is always only an e-mail away.

island to the other.... and still does today of course. Their history is in verbal legends and songs or fatele.

Now modern Tuvalu is still just as small, so news that happens is known by all within hours, even without the radio or internet. So why show any urgency to write stories, take pictures, etc they way we do in Canada, Australia, U.S., etc. The western press has millions of people to feed the news to over thousands of square miles, and plenty of competition.

When the President of Taiwan arrives, everyone knows about it, so there is no urgency to write up a report the locals won't read anyway. And why rush to tell the rest of the world? After all, most news stories in the larger nations are geared for the local national audience, especially in the United States. (Watching the American news stations here in Vancouver just a few miles from the US border, you would think Canada does not even exist!).

Anyway that is the wife's thinking, and well, I have to say she may be right, and to tell you the truth, she has told it to me many times over when I sometimes pull what is left of my hair out in anguish!

This is an entirely plausible explanation for Tuvaluan journalists' reluctance to send news overseas, but, as I will show, there are deeper cultural issues in play as well. Disaggregating a complex and evolving culture, whether or not it is one's own, cannot be comprehensive. It helps to make the effort, based on fore-knowledge, for example, to politely ask a Tuvaluan to which island do they 'look', because, no matter how long they have been away, a Tuvaluan will always 'look', or deeply identify with, their family's home island[88].

---

[88] Tuvaluan island traditions are discussed in Part II of Faaniu, *op.cit.*Pp. 48 – 100. Just how intricate these traditions are even for one atoll is shown by Anne Chambers in Atoll Economy: Social Change in Kiribati and Tuvalu – Nanumea Canberra: Australian National University, 1984, for Nukulaelae as described by Niko Besnier, 'Authority and Egalitarianism: Discourses of Leadership on Nukulaelae Atoll (Pp. 93 – 128), and by Barbara Lüem, 'A New King for Nanumaga: Changing Demands for Leadership and Authority in a Polynesian Atoll Society' (Pp. 129 – 141) in Feinberg, R. & Watson-Gegeo, K.A. (Eds.) Leadership and Change in the Western Pacific *Essays Presented to Sir Raymond Firth on the Occasion of His Ninetieth Birthday* London & Atlantic Highlands, N.J. London School of Economics Monographs on Social Anthropology No 66, 1996. As Besnier, *inter alia*, demonstrate, the translation of Tuvaluan, and Samoan-influenced Tuvaluan, terms, varies from island to island. I am following translations and meanings of words as explained to me by Tuvaluan informants.

The Tuvalu Media Corporation, which runs Radio Tuvalu, does not have an Ethics Code, unlike Media Councils in Fiji[89], Samoa[90], Tonga[91], or Papua New Guinea and Solomon Islands[92]. The TMC's Charter[93] sets out general terms for its operations, and thence provides a skeleton for a possible Ethics Code. I pressed Tuvaluan journalists to propose anything specifically Tuvaluan which should be explicitly set out in a code of their own and the major idea was to include acknowledgement of the conservatism of the outer islands compared to Funafuti's rapidly changing social fabric[94].

Putting it extremely simply, the centre of Tuvaluan life is (Te) Fenua[95], which describes and indeed is The Island – the land, the surrounding sea, and the people. This is what I mean when I write of a Tuvaluan 'looking' to a particular atoll, island, or even a village on an island or inhabited motu like Funafala. A Tuvaluan's Te Fenua is absolutely essential to and completely descriptive of their identity.

All Tuvaluan families are extended families, and, traditionally, some extended families would specialise in a particular activity essential to the family, village, and even atoll society's survival. Respect for elders within the family, and the village or even Atoll leaders, called Ulualiki, was and remains central to Tuvaluan life[96]. The Ulualiki can be roughly described as 'island royalty'. Island affairs are also governed by each Island's Kau pule or Island council (literally, 'group of elders'), made up of elected representatives. Typically, 'family' business, which has no

---

[89] http://www.fijimediacouncil.com/code-of-ethics.html (accessed, August 28, 2005)

[90] The delightfully named Journalist's Association of Western Samoa (JAWS) does not have a Web presence, so I had the Secretary e-mail me a scanned copy of their Ethics Code.

[91] http://www.matangitonga.to/home/ads/media-council/ngo2.html (accessed, August 28, 2005)

[92] http://www.png-simediacouncil.org/page.php?id=210 (accessed, August 28. 2005)

[93] Tuvalu Media Corporation Act 1999, Section 6 Charter of the Corporation http://www.paclii.org/tv/legis/num_act/tmca1999272/ (accessed, August 28, 2005)

[94] Following the 2005 Pacific Islands News Association (PINA) Convention in Tonga in November, 2005, a newly elected TMC Board member, Mrs Pulafagu Toafa, told me she was working on a TMC Ethics and Practice Code with TMC staff.

[95] When my informant said that word, and proceeded to explain what it means, I was instantly and forcefully struck by its linguistic and cultural similarities to the Fijian word and profound cultural significance of *Vanua*. In almost every respect, Tuvaluan *Fenua* and Fijian *Vanua* appear to describe the same phenomena, though Tuvaluans would rarely defend their *Fenua* as fiercely or violently as not a few Fijians would their *Vanua*. See, Tuwere, I. Vanua *Towards a Fijian Theology of Place* Suva: Institute of Pacific Studies, USP & Auckland: College of St John the Evangelist, 2002.

[96] This reverence for elders and ancestors includes locating their graves above-ground in what amounts to a family's front yard, or very close by if there's no room on the property. The grave I described in my Tuvaluislands.com feature was across Funafuti Road from the family home – See, http://www.tuvaluislands.com/news/archives/2005/2005-02-22_tmta3.htm (accessed, 21 September, 2005)

input from and is of no interest to the 'formal' government sphere is presided over by the Kaigaliki or the 'ruling family', 'leading family', or 'family of chiefs'. The leading regional educator, Professor Konai Helu Thaman, a Tongan, writes that:

> *In my culture, for example, the ideal citizen is one who is poto – one who knows what to do and does it well. Poto is achieved through the appropriate and beneficial use of 'ilo – defined by Tongans as knowledge, skills, understanding and values that a person acquires through the process of ako or learning.... these important values include: 'ofa (compassion), faka'apa'apa (respect), feveikotai'aki (reciprocity), tauhivaha'a (nurturing inter-personal relations), and fakama'uma'u (restraint). The achievement of poto continues to be measured against such values through people's performance and behavior in different social contexts.*[97]

In quite specific terms, the same can be said of Tuvaluan societies.

Traditional Tuvaluan life was also steeped in oral traditions, carefully kept, passed on through the generations, and learned by all at appropriate times in the life cycle. This is common in all pre-literate and even post-literate societies. In the latter, like Tuvalu, where dual literacy in Tuvaluan and English is virtually universal, poly-lingualism is common[98], and some form of modern mass media exists and is extremely widely and regularly accessed, even if only morning, afternoon, and early evening local radio, and then BBC radio, no television, and occasional newspapers.

The roles and malu[99] of Faifeau[100], religious pastors, have to be fully considered as well because the more modern, Western, conception of the Tuvaluan Faifeau, admittedly with strong Samoan influences, who is, among other things, a professional speaker or orator, as well as a teacher and educator, was, and remains, carefully insinuated into, overlaid upon, and operates centrally within societies in which traditional practices still figure highly[101]. In Tuvalu, the Faifeau often acts as a reference person,

---

[97] Thaman, K.H. 'Whose Values and What Responsibility? Cultural and Cognitive Democracy in Education' Keynote address, Pacific Circle Consortium Conference, April 21 – 23, 2004, Pp. 7 & 8.

[98] Many Tuvaluans I know also speak i-Kiribati (probably a Tarawa dialect), passable Fijian, and adequate Samoan.

[99] *Malu* is Tuvaluan for 'status', and means the same thing as *Mana*. A person with *malu* is also accorded *Faka*, which means 'to be treated with respect'.

[100] Pastors or ministers of religion.

[101] Throughout the region, missionaries of all faiths were, and remain, extremely adept at insinuating themselves, and their doctrines, into traditional beliefs and practices, as any

when Biblical, or religiously informed, moral or ethical, guidance is sought on some issue. The Faifeau also acts as counsellor.

Like other, fairly similar (and the differences are crucial) Pacific societies, such as in Tonga, Fiji, or Samoa, each village's, island's, or atoll's important stories, tales about things which really matter, which we can call discourses[102] were kept safe, and told, only by 'authorised people', whose malu or mana was acknowledged and accepted by all. These stories can revolve around, say, when particular species of fish, which can only be caught by particular families, can be expected to migrate past a particular motu or village on an atoll, how the catch should be distributed, and what other families or villages are expected to provide in return for the catch; or whose pandanus palms should be used when as sources of what raw materials for tapa[103] mats, building or canoe materials, or the fermented drink made from coconut sap, kaleve, kao or kamagii[104].

A way to frame this process is to consider something like 'who is authorised to speak, when, about what, on behalf of whom, and how they can, and do, speak about it' within a particular society[105].

The Fijian name for these orators or heralds, who were, and are, considered members of the Bete[106] is 'Matanivanua' (eye or face of the land, speaker for or on behalf of the land)[107]. In fa'aka Tonga, they are

---

reliable study of Pacific missionary activity will amply discuss, See, Macdonald *op.cit.*, Kofe, L 'Palagi and Pastors' in Faaniu *et.al. op.cit.*, & Goldsmith & Munro, *op. cit.*

[102] *C.f.* Besnier, *Op. Cit.*, P. 94.

[103] One Tuvaluan informant told me that *papa* mats are used for sitting upon, *mekei* are used for sleeping upon, and *takafi* mats are used for formal occasions, gift giving, and for sleeping too. A working mat, made of coconut fronds, often found in Tuvaluan houses, is called *pakau* in the Southern islands, and *kapau* in the four Northern islands.

[104] One Tuvaluan informant was uncertain whether or not this 'division of labour' was an accurate description, while others told me that families might specialise in ocean or *Te Namo* fishing, canoe building, or be warriors, specialising in *Te Lima* (fighting). See also, Taafaki, P. 'The Old Order' in Faaniu S *et.al.* Tuvalu – A History *op. cit.* Pp. 19 – 28.

[105] The intricate complexities of this are illustrated, for *fa'aka Tonga*, in 'I.F. Helu's discussion of the different kinds of kava ceremonies in Tonga, Helu, 'I.F. 'Identity and Change in Tongan Society since European Contact' in Critical Essays *Cultural Perspectives from the South Seas* Canberra: The Journal of Pacific History, 1999, esp. Pp. 18 – 31. The formal seating arrangements are similar to formal *Kau pule* I have attended in Tuvalu.

[106] Priestly clans.

[107] A former President of the Fiji Methodist Church, Rev Dr Ilaitia Tuwere, brilliantly locates and describes the *matanivanua* in Fijian society in Vanua *Towards a Fijian Theology of Place* Suva: Institute of Pacific Studies, USP & Auckland: College of St John the Evangelist, 2002; some of the modern implications of a recovered, and applied, understanding of *matanivanua* practice are discussed by Huffer, E. & Qalo, R. 'Have We Been Thinking Upside Down? The Contemporary Emergence of Pacific Theoretical Thought' *The Contemporary Pacific* Vol. 16, Number 1, Spring 2004, Pp. 87 – 116, esp. P. 95 *ff.*

called 'Matapule', and in fa'a Samoa or, more precisely, fa'a Matai[108], 'Tulafale', who is a herald or speaker for the Fale Matai or, if only telling stories, 'Tusitala' (not to be confused with The Tusitala, Robert Louis Stevenson, who is still revered in Samoa, and not just because his house, Vailima, and grave, high on Mt Vaea, with a spectacular view over Apia Harbour, are 'must see' tourist attractions). A fa'a Matai Tulafale is a very impressive man, with his traditional symbols, pe'a[109], to'oto'o[110] and fue[111], standing at the head of the fale fono[112] meeting house, loudly speaking his message in rhythmic, measured, Samoan cadences, while all others are seated cross legged on tapa mats, listening closely and respectfully, occasionally expressing agreement. In Tuvalu these 'authorised speakers', story keepers and tellers, were, and still are, always men, and are called Tukumuna, who also can speak on behalf of or for the Ulualiki. A lesser malu individual may be delegated or appointed to be a Avefekau, which, informants told me, is a messenger, akin to a town crier.

The speaker, orator, herald, or story teller may be of a chiefly clan, the title and role may be assigned to them through hereditary lineage (which begs the question of what do they do if a hereditary speaker can't tell stories to save their life, or has a poor memory), or they may be authorised speakers, 'speaking chiefs' who speak for a senior Matai, Ratu[113], or senior nobility in Tonga. The Fijian Matanivanua, Rev Dr Tuwere writes, describes a man:

> *...who's standing in the social hierarchy places him in the bete (priestly clan) and close to the turaga (chief). The texture of this role is much broader and deeper than what he ordinarily does, that is, as a spokesperson or herald. In an important sense, a matanivanua is a go-between or a mediator. As such, he sets in motion the principle of 'relationship' or relatedness. He relates people to the god, chief to people and vice versa. In many cases, he is the orator. He speaks and listens, represents, reconciles, mends broken relationships, negotiates, introduces, announces, and so on. Because of this rather alarming list, a matanivanua must know his vanua inside out[114].*

---

[108] The shifting and contested differences between *fa'a Samoa* and *fa'a Matai* are discussed in the essays collected in Huffer, E. & So'o A. (Eds.) Governance in Samoa *Pulega I Samoa* Canberra: Asia Pacific Press, ANU & Suva: Institute of Pacific Studies, USP, 2000.

[109] tattoos

[110] carved staff, indicating their chiefly authority

[111] fly whisk, indicating their wisdom

[112] Open sided meeting house, a Samoan *maneapa*.

[113] A Fijian chief, literally, 'Lord', of which there are several degrees of *mana*.

[114] Tuwere, *Op.Cit.* P 72. In talking with Fijian journalists, one of whom is a *matanivanua* in his *vanua* in the Lau group to the east of the main Fijian islands, we agreed that, as

So too must journalists, certainly with respect to knowing their Fenua, certainly with respect to knowing one's society 'inside out' as well as recording and transmitting current stories of relevance or interest to their audience. In this sense, and probably only in this nevertheless important sense given the crucial role the journalistic media plays in any good governance regime or system, Pacific journalists like those in Tuvalu can be reframed or reinterpreted as modern Tukumuna and certainly as Avefekau.

A respondent to my Tuvalu2 request for suggestions as to why it seemed so difficult to get stories from Tuvalu out to the world wrote,

> *...an (sic.) only other major social issue that I could see hindering stories from making a speedy dash out of Tuvalu is Tuvaluans' sense of group mentality. What I mean is, expressing one's sense of individuality by airing his/her views on any stories or reports could be like committing 'Kamikaze' on one's reputation or family. In other words, nobody would really want to be seen as the first to tell, or have the audacity to speak up and circulate their stories internationally, let alone nationally or locally.*

This, and several other Tuvalu2 thread respondents, in addition to my other informants, were all very aware of the differences between a fair, balanced, approaching 'objective' journalistic report on routine to controversial issues, and a journalist as citizen or family member entitled to express their private opinions on those same issues. In the Radio Tuvalu newsroom, and elsewhere, my journalist friends always demonstrated their clear professional understanding of and practical adherence to this all but universal journalistic standard. Language aside, the Radio Tuvalu newsroom reminds me of offices of small Australian community radio stations, replete with gossip, work focused discussions, and so on.

These kinds of everyday chit chats are called, in Tuvaluan, faipatiiga, and in Samoan, talanoa, in radical contrast to the strict norms and protocols which adhere to a Fijian talanoa[115], as opposed to a friendly

---

journalists, informed by the Fiji Media Council Code of Ethics, a journalist cannot perform or undertake several of the interventionist or advocacy roles a traditional *matanivanua* would be expected to undertake. A Fijian *matanivanua* only has *mana* within their own *vanua* anyway. *Mana* is non-transferable, so to speak.

[115] *Talanoa*, in Fijian, translates as 'stories' but it also describes a process, a particular form of often ritualised, formal discussion about 'things which really matter' which has been unsuccessfully deployed to steer a path through Fiji's recent political and social traumas, See: http://pidp.eastwestcenter.org/pidp/talanoa.htm (accessed, August 29, 2005), and, with respect to a Tongan *talanoa*, see, 'Talanoa: Talking from the heart',

yangona[116] drinking session. The same more serious, ritualised, norms and protocols inform a Tongan talanoa as described by Dr Sitiveni Halapua[117].

However, shame or ostracism can be heaped on someone who violates the accepted protocols or norms of a Maneapa meeting, Kau pule, or talanoa, and speaks out of turn, and that shame also can adhere to their family. The most severe cultural Tuvaluan sanction, deployed against persistent miscreants, is to be filasse[118], and excluded from the community, a kind of social house arrest.

Being, or being seen to be patipole/osopole, so my informants told me, also carries meanings of being enthusiastic, speaking in ways which connote a lack of respect, of putting one's self forward. This may help explain the incessant apologising in which some Tuvaluan friends engage, even, as in one case, when they have been chosen to participate in a major conference in Australia.

A Tuvaluan journalist would be free to attend and report upon a Kau pule at which the Ulualiki would speak through their Tukumuna provided they adhered to the protocols attending and informing such a formal meeting, and would show respect by politely asking permission to be there and to report beforehand. They would report on proceedings at a Kau pule, the Fale Palamene, or Fale Kaupule in ways familiar to a City or Shire Council or Parliamentary reporter in Australia or New Zealand. The Tuvaluan journalist is being a Avefekau. Difficulties would arise, however, when a Tuvaluan journalist was also Kaigaliki, from an eminent class, or if they had a conflict of interest between their Fenua and a Maneapa the proceedings of which they were reporting. Asking not to be assigned to report one's Kau pule meeting due to an actual or perceived conflict of interest might be difficult because there are so few Tuvaluan journalists.

Tuvaluans are also acutely aware of the smallness of their beloved country, and its enormous vulnerability in every respect, and the

---

http://www.matangitonga.to/article/features/interviews/DrSitiveniHalapua221205.shtml (accessed, January, 2006). I would tentatively retheorise '*Talanoa*' as something approaching a Habermassian 'communicatively competent civil society space'.

[116] Yangona is Fijian for kava, also called 'ava in Samoa and Tonga, and is made from the pulverised roots of *Piper methysticum*. Polynesian 'ava is usually far weaker than the diabolical brew in Vanuatu, called tu dai. A bilu (half coconut shell) of tu dai is reputed to effectively knock the drinker out for two days such is the local brew's soporific potency. Kava drinking in Tuvalu is not all that common though it is growing in popularity, in part due to disapproval of public drunkenness, the cost of imported alcohol, and more Fijian kava being brought home by Tuvaluan students and workers.

[117] Dr Halapua is also the main facilitator of the Fijian talanoa process seeking to map a way through the country's post 2000 coups political impasses. See above, Note 106.

[118] Shunned or ostracised, excluded from the community.

temptation is high not to publish or distribute stories which describe their country unfavourably[119]. As a sympathetic visitor I would be reluctant to talk much about Funafuti's serious solid waste problems, or drunkenness seen there, because this would show Tuvalu in a poor light. Another respondent to the Tuvalu2 post wrote:

If we dwell on the claim that the govt (sic.) plays a part in retaining the stories within Tuvalu's shores we have to question the extent to which the govt goes should the 'taboo stories' break out. It cannot do a thing and the journalists should know better. I have heard stories about Tuvalu as far as from England ('Tuvalu: Rags to Riches' as headlines when Tuvalu made it to the .tv deal). That brings me to say that the journos CHOOSE only the 'good' stories out of Tuvalu and leave the more sensitive ones to be buried at home. Typical!!. I dare to say that even the journalists themselves contribute greatly to holding back stories which should be aired at the international level. After all they are Tuvaluans – born and bred the Tuvaluan way thus instilled in them (like most of us Tuvaluans) this sense of 'patriotism'. But it is sad as this prevents them to fulfill the outmost part of their profession. This sense of patriotism am talking about here is the fact that none of us Tuvaluans (journos or not) is willing to taint the image of our tiny nation to the world...(that's our mentality).

As you may have encountered back in Tuvalu, our culture is a major source of our life: it dictates mostly the way we think and the way we are. Therefore put us in the 'modest' mode any human can go for. If something good has been done and someone asks who the initiator is, the real initiator will never say a word, others will say on his/her behalf. WHY?? Because it's culturally bad if you praise yourself! Same thing happen if you say something bad about someone else, if people find out, you and your family will be disgraced either verbally or physically. It is all to do with our culture...

The same applies everywhere one goes, be it at work or at home. The journalists in Tuvalu sure know how to do their work, no doubt, but reporting stories out of Tuvalu especially sensitive ones could be a mission. None of them could ever dream of shouldering the blame (from the whole nation) if ever 'taboo stories' which may taint the image of Tuvalu escape their shores.

---

[119] This can be also seen by reference to Tuvaluan journalist, Yvette Isaac's, critical comments about how Tuvalu is reported overseas. See above, Notes 39 & 40.

From the foregoing glimpse, it can clearly be seen that Tuvaluan journalists are caught between the modern understanding and practice of journalists, particularly in Anglophone media environments from whence Tuvaluan journalism derives, and traditional roles and behaviours, coupled with the expectation that, unless they are properly, traditionally, authorised to do so, they risk shame, or worse, by being patipole/osopole, by being seen or heard to be speaking out of turn, putting themselves forward. Demonstrate respect, ask permission, and do your work well, and you should have few problems seems to be the Standard Operating Procedure for Tuvaluan journalists.

The same phenomenon adheres to the regularly invoked 'Pacific Way', originally described and all but codified by Fiji's Regional colossus, the late Ratu Sir Kamisese Mara, in 1972. In an obituary of Ratu Mara, the leading Fijian sociologist, Dr Steven Ratuva wrote:

> *To Mara ... the Pacific Way of doing things referred to dialogue, consensus and mutual understanding. The politics of confrontation and contradiction, a common characteristic of western liberal democracy, was to be shunned in favour of collective consensual engagement.... Critics of the concept argue that the term Pacific Way as used by some leaders is too elitist and anti-democratic and tends to provide the ideological justification for the status quo. For instance those who question their leaders are regarded as 'un-Pacific' and in some instances, as in Tonga, this becomes an excuse for suppression of free speech. There are those who argue that the concept has been misused as an excuse for everything 'negative' we do. If we are late or lazy we say that it is the Pacific Way of doing things. I doubt Mara had coined the term to justify lateness and laziness.*[120]

The assertion has been made on the part of several of my informants on Tuvalu2, and repeated in the AusAID funded Pacific Media and Communications Facility (PMCF) Tuvalu Situation Analysis and Needs Assessment Study,[121] from August, 2004, by Opposition politicians

---

[120] Ratuva, S. 'Mara's 'Pacific Way' Legacy – Remembering the Pacific's Dominant Leader' *Pacific Magazine* June, 2004,
http://www.pacificislands.cc/pm62004/pmdefault.php?urlarticleid=0005 (accessed, September 21, 2005)

[121] This document mysteriously came my way at Radio Tuvalu and equally mysteriously got put through a photocopier. On the Pacific Media and Communications Facility generally, see: http://pmcf.muprivate.edu.au/ (accessed, August 28, 2005) The final PMCF Report, Informing Citizens: *Opportunities for Media and Communications in the Pacific* Canberra: AusAID, 2005, Pp. 363 – 375 does not repeat these censorship allegations.

interviewed for the report, that the Government actively censors Radio Tuvalu news stories. The consistency of these censorship allegations, heard sometimes first-hand from people who assert it's been done, has been a cause for concern. The Transparency International 2004 report on Tuvalu forcefully states that, despite the legislative protections in the relevant Act (see below), that in reality, 'the government ruthlessly censors media news'[122].

However, during the total of six weeks over four years I have spent working closely with Radio Tuvalu's journalists, tracking and helping develop dozens of stories, some of which the Government would not be entirely pleased to have broadcast, I never saw or heard of any instance of direct or indirect Government interference or censorship. By no means are Tuvaluan sources averse to playing the same games as Australian politicians, such as making themselves scarce or impossible to find for comment, then suddenly reappearing, threatening dire retribution, or attacking a journalist after a negative story has been broadcast. A practical issue, however, is that due to weak communications systems, it can be impossible to obtain a needed comment to achieve acceptable balance in a given story – even across the life of an issue in the news. As communication links, including mobile phones, improve on and to the outer islands, with roving, global, mobile phone access, this practical problem could, in physical terms at least, decline. Costs have been slowly declining, but Tuvalu remains one of the world's most remote countries, and thence also has among the world's highest telecommunications charges. Voice Over Internet Protocol (VoIP) technology might assist in reducing these charges. The Government IT office is well aware of VoIP[123], and routinely officers use Internet Relay Chat to interact with their colleagues in the Pacific Islands Chapter of the Internet Society (PICISOC). The challenge must be to ingeniously wring every electron of value out of available technologies.

Given Tuvaluan officials are all well educated, have extensive overseas travel experience, and routinely interact with overseas journalists from Radio New Zealand International, Radio Australia, the Pacific Islands News Association, and so on, there's no 'special pleading' allowed from Ministers, politicians, or senior and not-so-senior

---

While Tuvaluan journalists might be reluctant to hustle for leaks, this *Palagi* journalist has no such inhibitions. Late in my first visit to Tuvalu in November, 2002, I sat on the lounge room floor of a senior Government politician's house reading the soon to be tabled 2003 budget, thoughtfully passed my way by high level sources.

[122] Transparency International, *Op.Cit.* P. 22

[123] From early January, 2006, I was in regular VoIP contact with the Tuvalu Information Technology Office on Funafuti, though the quality of the connection was rather uneven due to the 128k up and 512 k down bandwidth available, always very congested during weekdays.

bureaucrats, who perhaps despite some protestations, do know how Anglophone, 'Western' journalism is done. Notwithstanding the relevant legislation stating '...It is hereby declared that the Corporation is not to be regarded as the servant or agent of the Government...' and '...the Corporation and its Board are not subject to direction by or on behalf of the Government or any Minister thereof'[124] ; there is a clear impression that the Government, whoever is leading it, will exercise control by way of malicious neglect. Or, as Helen Molnar suggests, when discussing a 1991 incident when Radio Tuvalu was attacked for playing too much Western music, (and then the Government refused to properly fund it, so royalties could go towards playing local music), 'the real issue was one of government priorities'[125]. This general situation still obtains, even more so once the TMC became a corporation in 1999. Transparency International further explained its case, that, 'TMC receives its major source of funding from the Government and the Secretary to Government chairs the Board and it would be impossible for the TMC to be critical of the hand that feeds it'[126].

I have raised the allegations of censorship and Radio Tuvalu with the Tuvaluan Prime Minister, Maatia Toafa, his wife Pulafagu, now Secretary to the key NGO, the National Council of Women, and more recently elected to the Board of the TMC[127], and at least one most senior public servant, and all have rather convincingly denied any interest in such practices. Journalists and broadcasters well known to me have supported what they say.

The Prime Minister responded to these allegations:

Honestly, this government and I believe the same for the previous one under the leadership of my predecessor, Hon Saufatu Sopoaga, there is no such business of censoring news by the Secretary to Government or any other authority within the government circle. TMC has the freedom and is responsible to keep the public informed of the information/news they deserve from the government. For media ethics, the source has the right to check about the accuracy of the news before it is publicised or aired. I am a very open and simple character who allows freedom of speech, and if required as a leader I am prepared to go on air to clarify any issue which may require an explanation for public information[128].

---

[124] Tuvalu Media Corporation Act *Op.Cit.* Section 6.3 & 6.4

[125] Molnar in Molnar & Meadows, *Op.Cit.* P. 86.

[126] Transparency International, *Op.Cit.* P. 22

[127] Personal communication, December, 2005.

[128] Hon. Maatia Toafa, Prime Minister of Tuvalu, personal communication by e-mail, 29 September, 2005.

Prime Minister Toafa further stressed his position on the censorship allegations.

I am 100% sure that there had never been any censoring in its real meaning on any news by TMC ever carried out by this government and also the past governments. It is the practice that for any government press release it is the duty of the officer responsible to just check with TMC authority on the accuracy of the story before it is aired. This is due to some carelessness on the side of TMC when re-writing the story and incidentally changed its meaning, hence disseminate wrong and misleading information. I fully support the primary role of the media of keeping the public abreast with what is happening as well as raising issues of concerns emanating from actions by the government or any other authorities. It is my conviction as a leader to accept criticisms for any of my actions but also stand ready to counter them by giving the public my side of the story and allow them to freely form their opinions[129].

Here is the other, parallel, key to why Tuvaluan journalists seem very reluctant to send stories overseas to supportive contacts such as Brian Cannon's Tuvaluislands.com, or myself, post them to the Wiki on the Government's Tuvalu ISP Site[130], or post them on a recent addition to the Tuvaluan Cyberspace presence, an Online Maneapa[131] set up by Tuvaluan IT worker, Lomi Paeniu: Jobs are scarce in Tuvalu, even allowing for the all but enforced[132] downsizing, rationalising, and outsourcing of formerly Government operated services and operations during the 1990s, including the reduction of government information services to form a consolidated TMC. Tuvaluan journalists' incomes are in the $AU5,800 to $AU7,800

---

[129] Hon. Maatia Toafa, prime Minister of Tuvalu, personal communication by e-mail, 11 October, 2005.

[130] Though this appears to be improving. Silafaga Lalua went to Expo 2005 in Japan in August, 2005, as a reporter with the Tuvalu delegation, and posted several short pieces to the Tuvalu ISP's Site.

[131] http://maneapa.mywebhut.com/ (accessed, August 28. 2005)

[132] A recent, and excellent, discussion of the powerful competing currents impacting on Pacific Island's development and futures, is Van Fossen, A. South Pacific Futures *Oceania Toward 2005* Brisbane: Foundation for Development Cooperation, 2005. See also, Island of Hope *A Pacific Alternative to Economic Globalisation* Report of the Churches' Conference on Economic Globalisation – Island of Hope, Nadi, Fiji, August 2001, World Council of Churches. I use the word 'enforced' because it became a requirement of obtaining loans from major sources such as the Asian Development Bank that Governments, even in tiny countries like Tuvalu, to corporatise, privatise, or downsize their public sectors. Helen Molnar also notes the effects of this process on Radio Tuvalu, Molnar & Meadows, *Op.Cit.*, P. 78.

range, with the TMC Manager on about $AU 13,000, and the TMC pays a housing or rent allowance as well. No observer of any Government would be naive enough to assume that subtle and not so subtle pressures or encouragements are deployed on the media to have journalists 'report correctly' from their point of view.

Journalists also lack resources, and background in research or professional practice, to carry out investigations for many more complex stories[133]. For example, the Tuvalu Government is the majority shareholder in Air Fiji and it is no secret that they are dissatisfied with a decidedly unreliable service provided to Funafuti[134]. Yet interrogating the publicly available accounts, and the responsible ministers, is beyond the Radio Tuvalu operation. The same would apply to another highly specialised and difficult exercise; a thorough treatment of the tabling of and debate about the national budget. The same constraints applied to pursuing allegations, current in 2004, of serious Customs fraud.

The resources dilemma does not look like evaporating. The Government heavily subsidises the TMC to a high local limit, about $AU100,000 annually, as well as paying for broadcast time when the Fale Palamene is sitting, and any Community Service-type announcements it requires. Other users of Radio Tuvalu buy time on a sliding fee scale according to their means. That is still rather little. If the Government really wants the TMC to become largely self-financing, as seems evident from some of its behaviour, the station nevertheless is devoid of commercial advertising at this time. The prime reason for this is simply that the country is so small there is no pressure on potential advertisers to seek air time. The 'coconut wireless' can spread word of a sale or soon-to-arrive shipment almost as fast as the real wireless.

Conclusion

It fits well enough with Church-going Tuvalu to end with a biblical reference, in this case the 'Jesus judges the nations' discourse in Matthew, Chapter 25:31-46, where he who was hungry, thirsty, without a home, naked, sick, or in jail would be aided by the righteous, who are then welcomed into paradise come the day of judgment. The damned did not help the least powerful, or affluent, because they did not see Jesus

---

[133] A point made repeatedly by various Government sources in the PMCF Report, *Op. Cit.*

[134] I was a victim of this poor service when I was trapped on Funafuti for five days longer than I planned to be there in early December, 2004, because Air Fiji's long-range plane had a recalcitrantly leaking fuel tank. A large Air Vanuatu plane was finally chartered to evacuate the back load of passengers, along with the finally airborne Air Fiji plane. Stranded passengers on Funafuti amused ourselves by calculating how much the problems were costing Air Fiji in lost revenue and accommodation costs on Funafuti and in Suva and our rough figures approached $AU 200,000.

standing among them. When Tuvaluan Faifeau preach on that passage, they and their flock could well identify themselves among the needy, (and perhaps the saved), whom the author of the Gospel text metaphorically had in mind. It is a community of proud and resilient people who, apart from money, are possessed of riches – of a cultural and spiritual kind. Reporting the plight of this country is not to invoke some warped kind of 'victimhood'; it is to show just one part of the global mosaic as it is; and how 'home grown' journalists, with their tools of this new century, bring together their command of both local and global culture to carry out their work.

Note on acknowledgments

This chapter could not have been written without the beyond generous assistance, advice, and guidance – so typically Tuvaluan – of my friends in Tuvalu, Hon. Maatia Toafa, Prime Minister of Tuvalu, Melali Taape, Yvette Isaac, and Silafaga Lalua at the Tuvalu Media Corporation, Lomi Paeniu (currently working for Verisign in New Hampshire, USA), and Tito Isala. In Brisbane, Rev Theo Ioane put me in touch with Unite and Suluvia Samasoni whose patience as I groped ever deeper into Tuvaluan Te Fenua was extraordinary, and whose assistance was invaluable. Luanna-Marie Latasi in Melbourne was also of enormous assistance, her un-typical Tuvaluan forthrightness guiding me still further. Several Tuvaluan commentators on the Tuvalu2 list on Yahoo offered useful information and one also commented on a draft. Brian and Helena Cannon in Vancouver, Canada, also offered comments even as they prepared to return to Funafuti and Funafala for a long postponed visit[135]. Dr Max Quanchi complicated matters in the best possible way by prodding me to investigate i-Kiribati society and to explore Fijian, Tongan, and Samoan traditions and practices along lines discussed here with respect to Tuvalu. *Fakafeti lasi lasi* to all.

---

[135] Some pictures here - http://www.tuvaluislands.com/2005/index.html

Chapter 6

Podcasting: giving control 'back to the masses'

Bill Harper

*Podcasting is a way of producing and delivering highly-portable
media services which might soon come to match conventional radio
for ease of use and popularity with large audiences. It is one other
multi-media format, which carries <u>audio</u> services particularly well,
and has the advantage of allowing users to customise listening to
their favourite programs, 'on demand'. This chapter makes a check
on how far podcasting has developed, to assess how useful it might
be from the point of view both of journalists and others wanting to
initiate their own services, and members of potential audiences.
Advantages and problems are considered, including questions about
the production and computing skills required, likely demand for
specialist or general services, interactivity, and business economics
for prospective podcasters. Podcasting, as one more form of service
proposed by innovation in communication technology, is still looking
at a few technological solutions to its main need – giving the
program makers and audience members very free access to one
another. It is a field where skills of journalists and broadcasters once
again stand to be very applicable.*

Introduction

In May 2001, when blogging was in its heyday, J.D. Lasica wrote an article for the *Online Journalism Review*, titled 'Blogging as a Form of Journalism'. It discussed how web logs could 'sow the seeds for new forms of journalism, public discourse, interactivity and online community'. [1] However, Lasica also believed that blogging would be the first step towards what he called 'the personal Webcasting revolution':

> *Weblogging will drive a powerful new form of amateur journalism as millions of Net users — young people especially — take on the role of columnist, reporter, analyst and publisher while fashioning their own personal broadcasting networks. It won't happen overnight, and we're now seeing only version 1.0, but just wait a few years when broadband and multimedia arrive in a big way.*

Thanks to the Internet, broadband, and a technology known as 'podcasting', the webcasting revolution Lasica predicted is now here. People all over the world are producing their own radio shows and making them freely available for download. No longer are you forced to listen to whatever Top 20 song your local radio station is playing. Instead you have access to tens of thousands of programs (known as 'podcasts') covering just about every subject imaginable, from technology to philosophy. What's more, thanks to Apple's iPod and other portable media devices, you can listen to them wherever and whenever you want. Could this be the end of radio as we know it?

What is a 'podcast'?

Essentially, a podcast is nothing more than an MP3 recording made on a digital device (usually a computer) that is put up on the Internet for people to download. These files are usually spoken-word audio files, though some podcasts feature commercial music and even video. Of course, this is nothing new. People have been downloading audio and video from the Internet for years. But what makes a podcast different from a traditional download is the way it finds its way onto your machine.

In early 2000, when broadband Internet started becoming available to consumers, former US MTV video jockey Adam Curry thought about how it could be used to distribute content. What he didn't want to do was get into real-time audio streaming. In an interview with Doug Kaye for *IT Conversations*, he explained that 'with streaming, unlike centralised broadcasting on radio or television, every additional customer that you have, every viewer or listener, costs you more when you're streaming because you have to push out more bits'. [2] Instead, Curry decided to take advantage of another feature of broadband Internet connections: the fact that they were always on. He entered a collaboration with Dave Winer, a software developer who had already developed a way of letting people distribute content from their web site to other web sites, known as RSS (Really Simple Syndication). As Curry explains:

I said [to Dave Winer], 'Why don't we play a trick on everyone, and we'll build an application that will bring in overnight, or when your computer is idle or when you don't know about it, will bring in stuff, but not until it's completely on your machine will we tell you about it'.' [3]

Winer came up with a way to deliver video or audio the same way they delivered web content – an 'enclosure' that pointed to where the media files were stored, so other web sites or programs could find the new content and download it automatically. Of course, depending on the size of the audio file and the speed of the Internet connection this could take some time, but as Curry says, 'there's hardly any content that has to be so timely that you have to stream it immediately'. [4] Later, when the Apple iPod first came out, Curry began working on a program to download the MP3 files to it. 'I knew that the iPods were here, and I just wanted something easy, for myself really, just wanted to subscribe to a couple of feeds, and if there's an MP3 in there, put it on my iPod.' [5]

The result was iPodder (now called Juice), an open-source program that could let someone subscribe to a podcast and download the episodes automatically. The idea was simple.

Take a file that you can subscribe to, download whatever's in there, you know, manage that, and then put it on the player. And then tell me about it. I don't want to know what you're downloading now, don't tell me that. Just tell me when it's ready. I shouldn't notice it at all.' [6]

And this is what gives podcasts their power. Instead of visiting a web site over and over to see if a new episode is available for download, you simply use a program like iPodder or iTunes to subscribe to the show's RSS feed. Then, as each episode of the show becomes available, the software starts downloading the new episode in the background. Once the download is complete you can listen to it on your computer or transfer it to your portable media device. These days there are a dozen or more

139

programs that let you subscribe to podcasts. But it was not until Apple introduced support for podcast subscriptions in their popular iTunes program in June 2005 that podcasts suddenly had a potential audience of millions of people already using the program to download music for their iPod.

What kinds of podcasts are available?

On December 23, 2005, Podcast.net listed the following podcast numbers in their directory:

Category	Number of podcasts
Entertainment (Music, Celebrities, Comedy...)	4529
Business & Money (Career, Investment, Marketing...)	583
Arts (Poetry, Storytelling...)	1285
Computers & Internet (Hardware, Software, Podcasting...)	1342
Science & Nature (Technology, Animals, Environment...)	590
Home & Lifestyle (Relationships, Health, Pets...)	750
Hobbies & Recreation (Games, Autos, Travel...)	704
Learning & Instruction (Biographies, How To, Education...)	866
News & Media (World News, Newspapers...)	1150
Politics & Government (Crime & Law, World Politics...)	743
Religion & Philosophy (Ethics, Christianity, Philosophy...)	1145
Society & Culture (History, Fashion, Parties...)	1393
Sports (Basketball, Olympics, Tennis...)	508
Soliloquies (Rants, Personal Journals...)	490
Local & Regional (Africa, Canada...)	1201
Shopping & Commercial (Companies, Classifieds...)	54
International Podcasts (Italian, French, German, Other...)	781
Kids & Teens (School, Hobbies...)	294

As you can see, out of the 18,000-odd podcasts available at the time, nearly 25 percent of them focused on entertainment (which some would say merely parallels mainstream media). However, there are podcasts covering other subjects that you would never get to listen to on the radio. Under Learning & Instruction you will find several podcasts on knitting. Under Computers & Internet you can subscribe to This Week in Tech, where a group of 'tech' journalists discuss the latest trends in digital technology. There are also close to 800 podcasts in other languages including French, Japanese and Portuguese, proving that podcasting can give everyone a voice, regardless of their nationality.

Why are people listening to podcasts?

According to research company GfK, more than half a million digital music players were sold in Australia between January and June of 2005, with that figure expected to more than double by the end of the year. [7] Just as TiVo and other Personal Video Recorders changed the way people would watch television, these portable devices are changing the way people listen to content. As Leo Laporte said in a keynote address on November 11 at the 2005 Portable Media Expo, at the Ontario Convention Center, California: 'They want to listen to whatever they want, wherever and whenever they want it, with no restrictions.' That is something conventional radio simply cannot do.

Laporte has been doing talk radio for almost 30 years and podcasts almost since their inception, and while he doesn't believe podcasts will ever surpass radio as the everyday person's listening choice, he thinks they are definitely here to stay.

For many people music and talk on an iPod is a very viable alternative to radio. In fact, that's one of the reasons podcasting is so successful. It exists in a niche where there's very little competition. When you're driving (or commuting, exercising, or working in the garden) your only entertainment choices are recorded media, radio, and the driver in the car next to you.

Curry agrees. 'They're using it when they're bored of the radio, or during drivetime, in the morning and the afternoon when they're driving to work, jogging, exercising, you know, hanging out. There's a time when people make a very conscious choice to tune out and tune in.' [8]

Laporte also believes radio itself is partly to blame FOR losing their audience to new formats. 'Radio has gone down that corporate path. Radio is killing itself.' [9] (Interestingly, some commercial radio stations, including Brisbane's B105 and Triple M, are now offering podcasts containing highlights of their daily programs.) There is also a much greater listening choice in the podcast arena. While it is difficult to know the exact number of podcasts available, PodNova, one of the many podcast directories available, has more than 20,000 podcasts in its directory. And there are podcasts on just about every subject imaginable – technology, agriculture, knitting – which you would never get to hear on commercial radio. What's more, they are usually done by everyday people, rather than the 'blow-dried guys' you hear on commercial networks. 'People crave authenticity,' Laporte says. Curry can also see the appeal. 'Now you're hearing regular people talking like regular people. And it's really refreshing.' [10] In most cases, podcasts have none of the commercials and other advertising intrusions that you have to listen to on the commercial networks. While this is for the most part because the podcasts aren't popular enough to attract advertisers, some podcasters like Laporte refuse to have paid advertising on their podcasts. At the 2005 Portable Media Expo he urged all podcasters in the audience to 'keep in mind as a podcaster [that] if somebody gives you money, you owe them something. And I think the joy of podcasting for me, and I think maybe for some of you, is we don't want to owe anybody anything. We want to do what we love. We only owe our listeners an experience.' [11] Laporte says that 'podcasting is a breakthrough because it's cheap and easy to do, and anybody who has something to say can say it', [12] and with today's computing power, that is certainly true.

Roger Gonzalez, who co-hosts BrisPodLive (http://www.rxrmedia.com/brispodlive/), uses nothing more than the built-in microphone on his Apple iBook. 'We had been using mics, but the convenience and secrecy of the inbuilt mic was better, although the sound quality was less... In the end we wanted the audience to know we were outside!' This isn't to say that all podcasts are recorded on bare bones equipment. America's Grape Radio podcast (graperadio.com) is recorded using a custom-built studio that cost US$20,000 to set up. In an interview with Michael Geoghegan for Podcast Solutions (podcastsolutions.com), host Leigh Older said they looked at it as a radio production. 'We wanted the best, highest quality produced product out there for what we're doing.' [13] (Mind you, producer Jay Selman is the first to admit that to them it's more than just a hobby. 'You don't drop roughly twenty thousand dollars on a studio without hoping to get a return on that investment.') [14]

For most podcasters, particularly those just starting out, it is just as much a hobby as building model aeroplanes. They either pay for their expenses out of their own pockets, ask for donations through services such as PayPal, or try to generate revenue by placing advertisements from Google and other providers on their web site.

Why people are making podcasts

Laporte believes it is the medium itself that is the drawcard. 'You have a relationship with your audience that is unique,' he told his audience at the Portable Media Expo. 'It's unlike anything else. It's not like TV... The relationship you have with TV is very distant. You're an audience. You're standing back here and watching the TV. Web is the same, newspaper is the same, it's arms length. In radio [and podcasting], you're talking in people's ears, you're their friend, you're in their head. You're as intimate as you can get with somebody. You're whispering into their ears, especially with podcasting because many of them listen to podcasts with headphones.' [15] There is also the thrill of talking to a potential audience of billions of people. As Laporte says, 'Howard Stern broadcasts to the United States. I broadcast to the world.' [16]

The downside of podcasts

With the number of podcasts growing almost explosively, and the technology becoming smaller, faster and cheaper, it may seem as if it's only a matter of time before podcasting conquers radio completely. However, it still has a number of issues that need to be sorted out before it can be considered a true contender to take over as radio in a new form.

For the listener

If you aren't already connected to the Internet, then those free podcasts are going to cost you quite a bit of money to begin with. While you can pick up a portable radio for just a few dollars, a computer will cost you hundreds of dollars. On top of that you would need a broadband Internet connection (assuming it's available in your area), costing you at least $10 a month. Then, if you want to listen to your podcast wherever you are, you'll need to buy a portable MP3 player, which will set you back another $50 or so.

And while listening to your favourite radio program is as simple as turning on your radio at the right time and tuning in, listening to podcasts is a little more difficult, not to mention time-consuming. To listen to a podcast you have to turn on your computer, connect to the Internet, find the podcast you want, subscribe to the podcast, wait for it to download, transfer it to a portable device (if you want to listen on the move) and finally listen to it. Of course, once you have the subscription in place, this will mostly happen automatically. But it is still a lot of setting up, and for some people it is simply too much trouble. This is a real shame. There's a whole generation of people who grew up on radio shows, and would probably appreciate podcasts the most. Yet because of this complexity, these people are the ones least likely to hear them. 'Podcasts have to be easier to find and download,' says Laporte. 'Right now it's mostly the technologically sophisticated that can figure out how to get podcasts. [Apple's] iTunes helped bring podcasting to a larger audience, but more can be done to make it even easier.'

Even if you're relatively comfortable with the technology, you may still have trouble finding the podcast you're looking for. Unlike radio shows, which are heavily promoted by the station both on the air and in supporting advertising media, podcasts are usually promoted by the creators themselves, who rarely have a budget for the show itself let alone advertising. So, while there may be a web page with a link to the podcast, with millions of web pages out there it can be like finding the needle in the proverbial haystack. (Thankfully, this problem is reduced, as you can now access a number of podcast directories, such as odeo.com and Apple's iTunes, which list podcasts by genre to make the search a little simpler.)

Another big problem with podcasts is that the quality can vary enormously from one to another, not just in terms of sound but also content and even talent. Unfortunately, there's no real way to determine the quality of a podcast until you've already finished downloading it. Doug Kaye, creator of IT Conversations, talked about a possible solution to this problem on *This Week in Tech*. 'On the news thing we're building we have three ratings for podcasts. It's the audio quality, the content quality, and the geekiness, which is no matter what the topic is, how deep is it.' [17]

Finally, in the list of comparative disadvantages, while radio is immediate, podcasts can be hours old, even days old by the time they're available. For news and sporting events, radio is really the only option at this time.

For the creator

If you're thinking of doing your own podcast, then you have an entirely different set of hurdles to overcome. Recording your podcast is probably the one thing you don't have to worry about. Once you have the computer and broadband Internet connection, about the only other expense you'll have is for a microphone. And while you can spend as much on a microphone as you did on your computer, a cheap one from Tandy will do the trick. Your first major hurdle will be uploading your MP3 to the Internet, and then creating the code that people use to subscribe to your podcast – the RSS feed. You may have created your own web page at one time or another, but creating the RSS code needed to syndicate your podcast is much more difficult. Fortunately there are web sites like My RSS Creator (myrsscreator.com) that can generate the RSS code for you just by filling out a few fields on a form. While they generally aren't free, they usually offer a free trial period so you can try the software out and see what the code will look like for your podcast. And who knows? Once you've created a few RSS feeds and looked at the code (which is a normal text file), you may feel confident enough to hand-code your feed. If you want to make sure the code is right, go to Feed Validator (feedvalidator.org) and enter the address of your feed. Additionally, if you already have a blog, either on a site such as Blogger (blogger.com) or with dedicated software such as WordPress

(wordpress.org), there's probably an option to create the RSS feed automatically. Look at the help files to see if it can do the hard work for you. One of the biggest problems you'll face is getting people to listen to your podcast in the first place. 'Finding an audience can be difficult in a 10,000 podcast universe,' Laporte says. And while there are now podcast directories available, he says they aren't the best way to be discovered. On his KFI radio show he said that 'if you're on iTunes, nobody knows you're on iTunes unless you show on the front page'. (The front page of iTunes shows the top 20 podcasts in order of popularity). The chances of you being seen there are very slim if you're only listing your podcast in the directories. 'The top 20 podcasts tend to stay the top 20, and I include myself in this, because everyone can see us,' he says. [18]

So how do you find that audience to begin with?

'The best advice for publicizing a podcast is the same as for publicizing a web site,' Leo Laporte says.

> *Get other quality sites to link to you. Promote your podcast in places where potential listeners congregate: message boards, clubs, chat rooms. Don't forget 'real world' venues: user groups, meetings, mainstream media. And make sure to include an iTunes button on your web site. Getting into the top tier ranks at iTunes is the brass ring and it won't happen unless people subscribe to your podcast on iTunes. [19]*

Remember to also publicise your podcast while you're recording your podcast. Tell your listeners how they can contact you (an email address is best), and where they can go to subscribe to your podcast. This is something they do all the time on radio, giving their listeners the station call-sign, place on the band, main format, phone numbers to call in on. With that kind of constant promotional practice, if your listener gets the MP3 file from somewhere else, they know where to find the rest of your shows.

If your show does become popular, then you'll face the same problem that every other successful podcast faces – bandwidth. At a radio station, the transmitter sends the same signal to everyone's radio. It costs no more to send the signal to ten thousand radios than it would to a hundred. Yet every time someone downloads your podcast, you are sending them more data. When you set up a web site, you are usually given a certain amount of disk space to host your files. What you may not know is that you are also given a certain amount of bandwidth each month, which is the amount of data people can download from your site in that month. If your podcast becomes popular, you may find hundreds of people downloading a file that, even using the latest compression techniques, can be several megabytes (or several hundred megabytes if you're doing a video podcast). Needless to say it won't take too many downloads before you reach your limit and possibly face a hefty charge for the excess bandwidth used. (The other possibility is that your web host will stop anyone accessing your web site until the end of the month.)

As an example, in December 2005 a site hosted by Telstra Bigpond with 100MB of disk space and 1000MB of bandwidth cost around $40 per month. Let's say you have a 10-minute audio podcast, which is around 5MB. It will only take 200 downloads that month before you run out of free bandwidth. If you become popular, and end up with 2000 listeners that month, then you will be charged for 9000MB of excess bandwidth at 8 cents per megabyte, or around $720.

How to beat the bandwidth blues

One solution is to host your podcast on a dedicated podcast hosting site, such as mypodcasts.net or podlot.com. You'll have to pay a monthly fee (the amount depending on how much space you need for your podcast files), but you won't have to pay for the bandwidth.

Another solution is to distribute your podcast over the bittorrent network instead of having people download it from your web site. Bittorrent shares files by breaking them up into small pieces, which can be downloaded individually. Once someone has a piece, other people can start downloading that piece from them, effectively sharing the download across different people. You need a lot of people sharing the file for it to work effectively, but it's a great way of distributing large files over the Internet. Alex Lindsay, a regular on *This Week In Tech's* podcast, says that, 'by the time you downloaded [a file], you uploaded 60% of what you had downloaded'. [20] However, even with such options technically available, it still doesn't look like you can have low bandwidth and high profile, at least for now. 'Unfortunately iTunes and Yahoo don't support BitTorrent, so peer-to-peer solutions, while eliminating bandwidth costs, pose other distribution problems,' LaPorte says.

The final option is to find a way of generating income to pay for your podcast through either of two main avenues, donations or advertising. Fortunately podcasts are the ideal place for people to advertise, because the niche audience is already there. As Kevin Rose says, 'if you can bring the niche advertisers to go along with that, that pay the high dollar rates for that niche audience, then you can turn a profit'. [21] That's exactly what some podcasters are doing. Companies such as podtrac.com are, to quote the blurb on Podtrac's own web site, 'precisely matching audience demographics and interests with the appropriate advertising for those listeners and viewers'. Dawn Miceli and Drew Domkus, creators of The

Dawn and Drew Show podcast, have recently signed up with Podshow (podshow.com), a startup company founded by Ron Bloom and Adam Curry. The company, which is backed by 'prominent Silicon Valley venture capitalists', has deals with companies including Absolut Vodka, Logitech, EarthLink and America Online. According to an article by Michael Bazeley for *The Mercury News*, the deal has 'allowed Domkus to quit his day job so he can concentrate full-time on podcasting'. [22] Unfortunately, you probably won't be able to attract advertisers until you're already so popular that the bandwidth is costing you large amounts. 'It's a Catch-22,' Laporte says. 'Podcasts can't get big without bandwidth, they can't afford bandwidth unless they're big enough to attract advertising or donations.'

The future

If there's one thing you can count on in the technology field, it's change. While these obstacles may be stopping people from listening to and creating podcasts now, chances are people are already working on ways to overcome them. Podcast directories will make podcasts easier to find, subscribe and listen to. And soon you might not even need a computer, with the podcast being downloaded directly from the Internet to your portable media player. As Todd Cochrane says in his book *Podcasting*:

> *I hope that retailers realize that they need to have all their devices WiFi-capable and smart enough to know what podcasts the user subscribes to, so that any time the device is synced up with a WiFi hotspot, it loads the latest podcast for the user. That way, people on the go, like me, can stay synchronized with the latest shows throughout the day, as opposed to being synchronized only when they can physically plug into the Net. [23]*

For the creators, podcasts will be even easier to create and upload, with RSS feeds being created automatically. And bandwidth will become so cheap that distribution will be a trivial matter.

But are podcasts the final result? Or are they another point on an evolutionary path, just as weblogs are today? Phil Leigh, president of Inside Digital Media, believes the podcasting model will become more and more mainstream. 'What we'll find is that ultimately entertainment media is (sic) going to be delivered over the Internet,' he told Erin Allday in an interview for *The Press Democrat*. 'Whether it's ten years from now or 20 years from now, people will think it's odd we waited for a particular broadcast to watch it. All of this is really what podcasting is a prototype of. This is where it's all heading.' [24] Of course, this will only further illustrate the difference between podcasting and traditional broadcasting. Most podcasts are free, even being released under Creative Commons licenses (creativecommons.org) to allow as much distribution as possible. Broadcasters, on the other hand, are going the other way, installing as many restrictions (technical and legal) as they can to stop their intellectual property from being shared.

So what is the future for podcasting? Will it topple radio, and maybe even television? Will it die out as quickly as it appeared? Or will they all merge to become one massive on-demand media empire. While technology will play a big part in its future, the deciding factor may well be whether traditional media are willing to give us content the way we want it delivered, rather than the way they want to deliver it.

References

[1] 'Blogging as a Form of Journalism' by J.D. Lasica – Online Journalism Review [http://www.ojr.org/ojr/workplace/1017958873.php] (last accessed 20/12/2005)

[2] [3] [4] [5] [6] [8] [10] 'Adam Curry - Behind the mic' – IT Conversations
http://www.itconversations.com/audio/download/ITConversations-225.mp3 (last accessed 20/12/2005)

[7] 'Hit the right note' by Simon Tsang – The Age
http://www.theage.com.au/news/icon/hit-the-right-note/2005/09/14/1126377359118.html (last accessed 20/12/2005)

[9] [24] 'Podcasts catching on' by Erin Allday – The Press Democrat
http://www1.pressdemocrat.com/apps/pbcs.dll/article?AID=/20050828/NEWS/508280385/1036/BUSINESS (last accessed 20/12/2005)

[11] [12] [15] [16] Leo Laporte – Keynote address at Portable Media Expo 2005
http://tnc.vo.llnwd.net/o2/Keynote2_Laporte.mp3 (last accessed 20/12/2005)

[13] [14] 'Interview – Grape Radio' by Michael Geoghegan
http://podcastsolutions.com/podcast/PS-2005-06-13.mp3 (last accessed 20/12/2005)

[17] [20] [21] This Week in Tech (episode 23) – This Week in Tech
http://aolradio.podcast.aol.com/twit/TWiT0023H.mp3 (last accessed 20/12/2005)

[18] KFI's Tech Guy – show 194' by Leo Laporte
http://podcast.dslextreme.com/kfi/KFI20051106-194-2.mp3 (last accessed 20/12/2005)

[19] 'Radio Leo shownotes – show 194' by Leo Laporte
http://www.leoville.tv/radio/ShowNotes/Show194#toc10 (last accessed 20/12/2005)

[22] 'Some amateur net radio shows have hit the advertising jackpot' by Michael Bazeley – The Mercury News
http://www.mercurynews.com/mld/mercurynews/business/13273539.htm
(last accessed 20/12/2005)

[23] 'Podcasting' by Todd Cochrane. Wiley Publishing, Inc. (p. 266)

Chapter 7

Trends in freelancing: a difficult road might now lead to success

Elaine Ford and Kasey Glazebrook

Some 3500 journalists are registered in Australia as freelance workers, and the number is growing. Such strength of numbers suggested to the authors of this chapter that today's freelancers, and those who elect to join their ranks, may become leaders in changing the structure of journalism. Certainly new communication technology and the new media it creates have enhanced the scope for independent writers and producers. Freelancers may publish in their own right; they have ready access to very sophisticated tools for research, communication, business management and publication; they can pursue global markets, and can address increasingly diversified audiences, who use a new variety of media. Accordingly a study of the current freelance scene was made for this chapter, to observe what new trends might be emerging. Change was in the air, but also extreme caution. Development of the corporate sector, with the mainstream newspapers and other outlets, was moving towards more syndication and standardization of contents, with opportunities for well rewarded freelance work actually contracting. In the conclusion, the writers recognise the continuing difficulties of independent journalists, but propose also that the creative drive of an individual writer stands to become a prime resource when it is time for innovation to take place.

Introduction

The road to freelancing utopia seems a very attractive option for many who want to write and tell stories in the hope of being handsomely paid for it. With the dream of being your own boss, limited editorial constraints, and naming your price, it seems the best way to go is through freelancing. Rapid technological advances have made it possible to 'tout' your journalistic wares, to be a sole trader with autonomous editorial freedom and control. Pick and choose what you write, who you write it for and when, where, why and how you write it; and those five journalistic essentials, the five Ws and the H, sound easy. Yet, as always, it can be a precarious illusion with devastating financial consequences if you don't research well, before jumping into the deep end in the quest for freelancing freedom.

Method

The study reported on here is the product of a search by the authors of currently available information about the prevalence of freelancing in Australian journalism; the experience of practitioners in that field, and indications for the future. This was backgrounded by selections from general literature on journalism work practices, freelancing in particular. Most of the information however was culled from records of three recent annual Freelance Conventions organised by the Media Entertainment and Arts Alliance (MEAA) – the union and professional association for journalists. These conventions are the central location for information on freelancing and the scene of a concerted effort to keep journalists informed on developments and possibilities, and help them mobilise their resources. All interested parties are represented – freelance journalists, photographers, artists, television producers and other practitioners, media companies, academic researchers and union representatives. Participants deliver prepared papers and provide documents and references. There is information across a broad range, for instance on new products and online facilities, current issues including the state of negotiations on payments with different media outlets, or advice on business and finance.

Access to this concentration of information was obtained through observation. Detailed notes were made and circulated together with collected documents, from two of the conventions, by Journalism academics from the Queensland University of Technology (QUT), who attended: Lee Duffield in 2002, at Brisbane; Sharon Tickle in 2003, at Sydney. In 2004 one of the present writers, Kasey Glazebrook, attended the convention at Melbourne (Cokley 2004), again making notes on speeches and proceedings and compiling documents. She conducted three interviews with participants, referred to in this chapter, **(See Appendix: list of interviews).**

An expanding field

The growth in freelancing and freelance numbers is a worldwide trend. Schroeder in Nies and Pedersini (2003: 2) found that in several Central and Eastern European countries, freelancing was the major work form in journalism. Meehan (2001: 99-100) says that in Australia freelance numbers have also sharply increased over 20 years, with in 2001 the MEAA estimating that 30 per cent of its journalist members were freelancers. That's 3,500 people, and those numbers continue to rise. This growth is strongly influencing how the news media operates, with Nies and Pedersini (2003:3) highlighting impacts on employment relationships, as well as implications for trade union representation and collective bargaining. The stability of work relations is affected, and they say, the 'stability of the employment relationship, together with the related economic stability, will contribute significantly to the effectiveness of independence and autonomy in the exercise of the journalism profession'.

Old problems

While the wherewithal to practice independently may be more available, with accessible journalistic tools and a developed entrepreneurial culture evident in present-day economics, a discussion of freelance journalism still has to begin with cautionary words about costs and other impediments. The daunting challenge of establishing a strong journalistic reputation and marketable byline must be added to the great difficulty of starting up any small business.

Meehan (2001: 99-101) found Australian survey results are consistent with European studies of freelancers, where working conditions have remained poor, or have worsened, despite expansion of media services, and so growth in the profession: 'The freelancer's lot brings financial instability, long working hours, and no protection from a competitive and overcrowded marketplace.' She says (2001: 107) respondents in Australian and European surveys raised similar issues to one another: 'poor work conditions, isolation, slippery contractual arrangements, and inconsistent rates of pay.' These trends don't seem to be changing but that is not curbing the influx of new freelancers, as 'more and more trained and untrained journalists flood to freelancing as their ticket to a new career' (2001: 99). Despite the attraction and unique position of freelancers that is 'advantageous in terms of independence and control over ideas', freelancers lack the secure structure of media organisation staff writers offered more regular assignments, holidays, training and remuneration. Despite this, Meehan (2001:100) found there remains a general, if rather unsound belief perpetuated by do-it-yourself writing guides, that as long as freelancers 'perform' correctly, they will automatically have their work published.

Guy Rundle, an Australian freelance journalist and editor (interview – April 2004) says that, predictably enough, an explosion of freelance numbers has been making it difficult for many to get work in a small media market. In addition, newspapers have become increasingly reliant on material from overseas agencies, and although in reverse there is potentially a huge market overseas for Australian freelancers to tap into, this can impede them getting a byline on the home market: 'There are corporations supplying copy which starving newspapers take up rather than buying an actual piece by anybody.' Structural changes, away from the model of companies maintaining large career workforces, have also weakened a base of support for freelancers who in the past might enjoy associate relationships with a few major outlets – principal 'strings' that would pay the rent. It used to be that journalism was a profession fairly rigorously policed by its unions, and freelancers being few and far between could benefit from that protection. Syndication was not so well established, so that, apart from freelance contributions, what was published in newspapers was mostly written by fully-employed journalists. Rundle found that system had come under a lot of pressure, so production from the freelance sector was exceeding demand, and with more people wanting to write, there was more supply for a weaker market.

To Nies and Pedersini (2003: 13), freelancers, in principle, should have a higher income than employees, in order to balance the higher costs and the risks involved in carrying out an entrepreneurial activity. In practice, given the endless pressure of the financial constraints and extremely competitive markets that media organisations operate under, it is a 'buyer's market' with editors able to pick and choose who they want to use and how much (or how little) to pay. Dick (2003: 5) says newspapers now employ freelancers rather than more staff writers in a bid to cut costs, and it doesn't necessarily translate into being well paid (or paid at all). So how do you stand out in the massive freelancing crowd – and make it pay?

Marketing yourself is a key component to success, with Cohen (2003) pointing out 'of the three skills of a journalist: writing, inquiry and the ability to sell yourself - the latter is the most important'. Duffield (2002) is mindful that freelancing can be particularly difficult for 'new players' and more suited to 'experienced journalists with a developed eye

154

for story prospects and a book of contacts including industry contacts'. Meehan (2001: 103-104) echoes that view, finding a study by the British National Union of Journalists showed established journalists had more success at freelancing than beginner journalists entering the profession by going solo. Meehan (2001: 107) found that anecdotally, freelancers from other industries such as information technology, appeared to retain excellent working conditions because their skills were in high demand. For journalists, 'there are too many people bidding for a small amount of work, which results in the need for individuals to undercut their opposition (and themselves) by accepting sub-standard conditions'. Rundle (interview – 2004) says building relationships with publications and editors is important: 'there's got to be a relationship of trust, between each company and the actual journalist'.

Duffield (2002) identifies collaboration with other journalists, operating partnerships, as an emerging a trend, and adds that the phenomenon of globalisation has provided new options, opening new opportunities to go with the risks: 'Freelancers today need to work on a worldwide basis, using the Internet for research and for advertising and marketing their products. This development was seen as a breakthrough enhancing the position of freelance operators.' Dick (2003:26) agrees, and suggests that beginners in the field can find a way, both though persistence, and also through approaching more experienced writers for advice. As everyone has started as a 'raw beginner, knowing nothing', more senior operators might be so good as to act as mentors.

New modes of operation

Technology provides the positive aspect of the freelance field as we find it at this time. It is plainly vital for media workers to keep up with the pace and uptake of communications technology. With technological advances and media convergence offering easy access to the Internet, digital photography, video and audio options, it is easy for freelancers to self-publish as a showcase of their work. Journalism and technology go hand-in-hand, with Herbert (2000: 7) pointing out technology has been at the 'forefront of journalism development', as always; the profession has 'grown up alongside the telegraph, telephones, satellites and newsagencies'. Ewart (2003: 72-75) states in a survey of US journalists, more than 98 per cent of them used the Internet daily for newsgathering and communication. The survey revealed that journalists had 'an overwhelmingly positive attitude' towards the Internet as a newsgathering and research tool, although they admitted initially being hesitant to use it after its introduction to the work environment in the late 1990s.

How to provide a product that is noticed and is published with payment? Duffield (2002) emphasises there is a need for some business planning and strategic investment. He says it is essential to have good communications equipment and facilities, and to find advance money for the costs of story development. Being able to make good use of computer based facilities goes together with good business sense. Herbert (2000: 3) avers that a basic research tool is email and home pages of journalists, who are themselves good sources – and, 'everyone is a journalist in the digital age'. Tickle and Keshvani (2000: 69) say that over a period of five years, technology (in particular digitisation and equipment and transmission interconnectivity) created an 'intrepid new breed of broadcast warrior', the 'jedder' – electronic journalist, editor, producer.

Another huge challenge for freelancers, but also a field of opportunity: how to negotiate with editors. Meehan (2001: 101) states marketing and dealing with editors is a key concern of freelancing, and under-addressed by do-it-yourself guides. So knowing your target publication inside out is vital. If you have a special writing interest, target corporate and trade publications as avenues for paid work. For any publication you bid for, be it the main media players or the corporates, look for what they want. Look at what stories they do actually publish, the topics and angles they focus on, images they use, other features that are common to that publication. If you offer up work that looks like it fits with the publication, in content and style, you are in a stronger position to make a credible offer likely to be taken up and paid for.

On collaboration and partnerships, Bob Burton, a freelance journalist (interview – April 2004), says collaborating can work, especially sharing contacts, which are crucially important, as successful freelancers often have worked previously in major outlets:

> *They've got all the personal contacts, editors, and people who used to be their colleagues become editors, so it's a lot easier to be commissioned. Coming from the opposite direction, it's a lot harder because you don't have those personal contacts so you've got to establish your bona fides with people at times when editors are under a huge amount of pressure to get the work done ... So you've got to break into that, overcome that problem somehow and for me working collaboratively is one way of doing it.*

Burton (2002) suggests considering joint projects with other freelancers for pooling expenses, sharing sources or research. Shaw (2002) also suggests freelancers could help each other by investing in equipment and 'operating as bureaux', though collaborations have to be based on clear understandings about how material is to be used. Rundle (interview – April 2004) sees the individual and creative character of the work putting limits on co-operation. Although it could be a good idea to set up with other freelancers as a group, it will not happen too much, since 'people who want to be journalists sort of want to write, but it's a very individual sort of idea. I think it would be good if people did, but I think it's unlikely to become a major practice.'

Media carriers and formats are now easily accessible for those wanting to present their wares, or publish independently. Student journalists who want practical publishing experience can set up their own outlets on the web to publish and learn to manage a business. It also provides experience for working to larger online operations and more traditional versions run by existing print or broadcast media; a key difference from the past in modes of publishing. Weblogs are among the latest forms of web publishing and their growth across the world is explosive. They are defined as a kind of online diary with short articles often complemented with photographs, website links and other audio-visual features, running in date order. Bugg (2002) says weblogs are 'outlets and sources of information – news information on weblogs can get to the public much quicker than traditional media'. Weblogs are another cheap option to set up and publish to many audiences.

Such systems are global. The capacity to sell work internationally is virtually endless, and so the volume of potential markets for journalists has multiplied many times over. It is a door wide open with possibilities – no borders, no time zones. Furthermore there is now easy access, to be able to research publication possibilities and story ideas on the Internet; to use emails for making submissions to key editors, or building international networks with colleagues and sources; and to exercise the potential to sell work and publish – independently on the web, or with local or regional-based print or broadcast publishers. Tickle and Keshvani (2000: 68) see the productivity aspects of this very important for sole traders in particular: 'These technologies enable single operators to gather, produce and transmit an electronic news product globally in a matter of minutes.'

Dick (2003: 55) likewise identifies the importance of affordable systems. Freelancers must 'study the markets, do your research, write well to sell your work … and are solely responsible for finding ideas, writing, selling your work, getting paid, and every other aspect of the job'. In this situation, setting up their own webpage is a must: 'Your own webpage is akin to writing your CV online so that everyone and anyone who cares to access it can see it … Setting up your own website is itself likely to generate income if you make a good job of it' (Dick 2003: 134-135). Alison Aprhys, freelance writer and photojournalist (interview – April 2004) adds that having a website has become a highly effective way to sell photographs: 'The website is a perfect medium to have your photographs up to show people what you're capable of.'

Experience of freelancers

This study consulted several writers who work in the freelance field, registering some of their combined experience, attitudes and wisdom. For instance they are highly aware of the need for networking, whether among contacts made in the editorial ranks of media organizations during previous careers, or colleagues with whom they might form a partnership. They are cautious, being blasé about ever making a large fortune, worrying whether efforts to form alliances will succeed, given the individual character of their work; and not being notably eager to work in different countries or push their products too far afield. There is however clear adaptability shown by freelancers in taking up communication technology, such as their use of commercial databases for research, or bulletin boards set up for showcasing products.

Like Meehan (2001: 99) most see an idealised picture of working from home, 'an unharried and easy life', rudely contradicted by 'a grim picture of work outside established employment structures'. The negative scenario is a life with long working hours, under- or over-employment, few breaks and holidays, lack of income protection against illness or retirement and inability to undertake further training. Most report their main job as being a freelancer writer or journalist, but it's common to find them supplementing income with other employment in unrelated fields. For instance, Meehan (2001: 102) found in the results of a survey of 19 Australian freelancers in 1999, where more than half of the respondents freelanced fewer than 30 hours per week, the majority supplementing their income with other work. Respondents to a study by the British National Union of Journalists, quoted in Meehan (2001: 104) reported contract negotiations with editors that generally were fraught with problems. In Australia, Day (2004: 25) refers to an MEAA survey of freelance members that found pay rates were not keeping pace with general norms, superannuation was not getting paid and freelancers were not being informed of copyright entitlements and re-use fees. About half of the respondents said their freelance earnings were not their primary income – delivering less than $20,000 per annum. The other half rely on freelance income for over 80 per cent of their income, with most earning a sum over $40,000 per annum, though often with difficulty. At rates that can be as low as ten cents per word, earning $40,000 per year must become a serious challenge. While top earners were obtaining over $1 per word, most major employers were paying between 50-60¢ per word. The survey respondents said it was rare for employers to cover more than token expenses. As examples of the payments dilemma for freelance journalists, one of the writers of this chapter, Elaine Ford, has recorded early experiences negotiating with editors, with some 'hits and misses'. When one prominent national magazine contacted Ford to publish an article that had been submitted for publication, the editor feigned total surprise when the issue of being paid was brought up, saying only staff writers were paid. Negotiations progressed; the editor offered a byline and free subscription to the magazine – only worth about $40 at that time. The article was 1,000 words and the result of about one week's work, so a byline and $40 was not considered a fair price, and that particular magazine did not get to publish the work. In a more successful example, for another state-wide flagship newspaper published in Australia, the editor was close to settling arrangements to publish, but again balked at a request for a byline and payment; once more a case of someone feigning surprise. Negotiations for payment continued for some weeks *via* email and telephone. An agreement on the amount to pay for the 1,000 word feature article was made, but at little more than half of the market rate quoted by the MEAA of 60 cents per word. The article was finally published with a byline and the agreed payment only received after repeated follow-up contacts, over about two months. Research and other anecdotal evidence across the world supports the impression that these are not uncommon freelancing experiences.

This discussion brings up the question of correct and effective strategies for freelance writers to follow, in their contacts with corporate publishers. Day (2005:26) makes the common observation: 'They report it's a buyer's market, with most employers saying you can take their rate or take a hike'. Some consensus exists among journalists contacted for this study, and it is that nobody should work free of charge. Giving away products for the sake of publicising a favoured cause, building up a portfolio and public recognition, or the thrill of obtaining bylines is common enough, but is considered bad psychology by professionals looking to make a living. Ample free material is available to media outlets already, provided by the public relations industry and proponents of causes or special interests, which can be most valid. For writers contributing directly to publications, the key policy option is to seek to ensure that a payment of some kind is always made. 'Writing for peanuts' is unpopular but the adage in reply is that 'we've got to start somewhere'.

The survey research that has been quoted in this chapter on freelance experience shows that commissioning editors tend to be intractable on payment rates, and difficult getting around to making the actual payments. The rates published by journalist unions like the MEAA are generally not honoured, except for a distinguished elite of high earners in good demand – a few of whom may in fact command much more. The

MEAA and sister organisations like Britain's National Union of Journalists (NUJ) engage staff to pursue payments that have been agreed on; they have significant rates of success, keep a log of cases and can render shrewd advice. Engagement of third parties such as union representatives, in some cases an agent, or billing through a partnership company, makes it less of a lonely battle.

There are moves to try and change the rules and practices. Nies and Pedersini (2003: 5) call for a guaranteed regulatory framework in Europe, granting all journalists, including freelancers, a set of basic rights and protections. They observe that the diffusion of syndicated news and freelance work in journalism makes the existing regulatory framework unsuitable to guarantee independence, autonomy, decent living and appropriate levels of protection for journalists. They provide advice (2003:20-21), freelancers being urged to work together to get minimum conditions set out, fair contractual terms, social security, and union participation to ensure the possibility of collective bargaining. That drive for change has to be considered against the more traditional view of 'reality' expressed by Meehan (2001:106), in which the advocacy of devices such as standard work contracts can prove useless to freelancers, who will continue to work 'in an environment dominated by isolation', with colleagues 'potentially their competitors' and their 'employment status often unclear'.

Conclusion

This study has given an account of the current state of freelance journalism. It notes the enduring problems of freelancers as sole traders in a corporate dominated world. It notes also the fact of changes in the economy, where more entrepreneurialism can produce a crowding of markets, but also opportunities for selling a bigger diversity of products through more diversified outlets. It refers to the new contexts for media produced by developments in communication technology, especially options that have been created for independent publishing and global operations. In this respect the future looks more positive for independents: the technology to easily produce quality work is available to them, and with the public using diversified, additional services, like weblogs, iPod transmissions and emagazines, they can anticipate growing demand.

Are freelancers as they are now known, apt to become revolutionaries? Are they the people to lead the way through a prospective transition towards a more pluralised and maybe democratised media world? At a pragmatic level they have been representing themselves, for instance in surveys conducted by their unions, as rather pessimistic and unadventurous. They might collaborate in projects to obtain more standardised contracts or systems of payments – to get paid a bit better and a bit more often. Looking ahead, it is imaginable that they may do better for themselves than that; that the cadre of independents may yet become very influential, on one main impetus: the creative drive. For one thing their numbers have been growing and stand to grow further as additional people, and types of people, realise on the accessibility of media work to all. In a word, bloggers or *info-tech* enthusiasts can well look for avenues to themselves become semi-professional, and then professional; to be sole traders in journalism and so augment the numbers, and the variety, of personal or professional aptitudes in freelancing. This would be not only a bigger cadre of practitioners but an even more highly skilled and enabled one.

All might then share the necessary personal and professional core motivation in any creative field: to make an original product. As observed by Meehan (2001: 107): 'Freelance writing is a popular profession and shows all signs of continuing to be so as greater numbers of highly trained and skilled people seek more challenging alternatives for their working lives.' Dick (2003: 171) supports the idea of a personal quest at the heart of the enterprise: 'Every published writer began as a raw beginner but real writers have learned to keep professionalism, persistence and productivity firmly in mind.' Cookes (2003) offers a last word, advocating self-confidence, matching the deeper motivations of a creative worker with skills and attitudes useful for the practicalities of business and professional life: 'Be pushy; there is no such thing as luck; it's where preparation meets opportunity.'

Appendix - Interviews

Alison Aprhys, interview with Kasey Glazebrook, Sunday 4 April 2004, at the MEAA Annual Freelance Convention, Melbourne. Alison Aprhys is a prominent surfing writer and photojournalist based in Sydney, who will 'travel anywhere for a good wave'; www.shewrites.com

Bob Burton, interview with Kasey Glazebrook, Sunday 4 April 2004, at the MEAA Annual Freelance Convention, Melbourne. Bob Burton is a Canberra-based freelancer who has written for several leading outlets in Australia and abroad. He currently contributes to the *British Medical Journal*, the US-based non-profit media group PR Watch, and *Inter-Press*.

Guy Rundle, interview with Kasey Glazebrook, Saturday 3 April 2004, at the MEAA Annual Freelance Convention, Melbourne. Guy Rundle is a frequent freelance contributor to several newspapers, a writer-producer for television (e.g. Max Gillies' *Your Dreaming*, and Seven Network's *Andy and Hamish*), and co-editor of *Arena* magazine.

References

Alison Aprhys. (2004). Freelance writer and photojournalist - interview on April 4, 2004, Melbourne, Australia.

Bugg, B. (2002). 'Getting the unusual story', Media Entertainment and Arts Alliance (MEAA) 5th Annual Freelance Convention. April 12-14 2002, Brisbane, Australia.

Burton, B. (2004). Freelance journalist - interview on April 4, 2004, Melbourne, Australia.

Burton, B. (2002). 'Changing Tracks', Media Entertainment and Arts Alliance (MEAA) 5th Annual Freelance Convention. April 12-14 2002, Brisbane, Australia.

Cohen, D. (2003). Media Entertainment and Arts Alliance (MEAA) Annual Freelance Convention. April 5-6 2003, Sydney, Australia.

Cokley, John (2004) Personal communication, March 26, 2004

Cookes, T. (2003). Freelance journalist and documentary maker, Media Entertainment and Arts Alliance (MEAA) Annual Freelance Convention. April 5-6 2003, Sydney, Australia.

Day, G. (2004). 'Freedom to feel secure', *The Walkley Magazine*, 26, 25.

Dick, J. (2003). *Freelance writing for newspapers*, 3rd Ed. London: A&C Black Publishers.

Duffield, L. (2002). (MEAA) 5th Annual Freelance Convention (notes). April 12-14 2002, Brisbane, Australia.

Ewart, J. (2003). 'Studying the Net: A study of Internet search techniques used by some Australian Journalists', *Australian Journalism Review*, 25(1), 71-83.

Glazebrook K. (2004). (MEAA) 7th Annual Freelance Convention (notes). April 3-4 2004, Melbourne, Australia.

Herbert, J. (2000). *Journalism in the Digital Age: Theory and Practice for Broadcast, Print and Online Media*. Oxford, Focal Press.

Meehan, K. (2001). 'It's the hard life for freelancers', *Australian Journalism Review*, 23(1), 99-109.

Nies, G & Pedersini, R. (2003). 'Freelance journalists in the European media industry'. European Federation of Journalists (EFJ), October, 2003.

Rundle, G. (2004). Freelance journalist – interview on April 3, 2004, Melbourne, Australia.

Shaw, R. (2002). 'Business essentials: technology, networking and marketing', Media Entertainment and Arts Alliance (MEAA) 5th Annual Freelance Convention. April 12-14 2002, Brisbane, Australia.

Tickle, S. & Keshvani, N. (2000). 'Electronic news futures', *Australian Journalism Review*, 22(1), 68-80.

Tickle S. (2003). (MEAA) Freelance Journalists, Photographers and Cartoonists' Convention (notes). April 5-6 2003, Sydney, Australia.

Chapter 8

Your Pet and Jofly Media: two case studies

Lee Duffield PhD, John Flynn and Janice Holland

Janice Holland and John Flynn started their own media businesses, to follow up ideas they'd developed while working in corporate environments. They had the benefit of new technologies making it possible for a sole trader to survive, often under strongly competitive and demanding conditions. After a full year each talks about making the change, and about survival, stimulus and satisfaction in a new phase of professional life. Janice had been studying small magazines especially street press publications styled for specialised segments of the market and distributed free. She had an idea, to bring out a quality publication for pet lovers, and set to work, investigating markets, organising production, and then bringing out the first editions of Your Pet. It's been a success, building a good base of support among readers and advertisers. John was one of the first video journalists, with a commercial television network, enjoying the exhausting work of a reporter-with-camera, and learning that extending his range with new technology could be empowering. Becoming an independent, he has found a key outlet in online sports reporting and multi-media. He still shoots video, but in the confines of present online accessibility to audiences does more work with still photography, and reports from events all over Australia.

Janice Holland founder of *Your Pet*

Introduction

This is a report on the magazine start up process and on the production of the first four issues of the Brisbane-based publication *Your Pet*, in 2005. It considers achievements, challenges that were faced, and the impact of technology on the manufacture of such publications, which loosely go together with the free 'street press' phenomenon as an aspect of new media and citizen media. It also considers the future for *Your Pet*.

The magazine itself became known to readers in Brisbane, the Gold Coast and Sunshine Coast, (especially those who might visit pet-friendly places such as a veterinary surgery, pet shop or RSPCA animal shelter), as a high quality, full colour glossy quarterly, A4 size with 32 pages, featuring an adventurous layout with many pictures. *Your Pet* has insisted on best practice in design and printing, an independent editorial position and strong aesthetic, on the premise that a polished product recommends itself well. Circulation was initially based on a print run of 30,000 each edition (with plans to increase this as the business grows). Its cover pictures indicate the broad range of interests: a dog, a cat, a bird, a picture from the film *Must Love Dogs*. That is significant as magazines about animals have tended to specialise by species, e.g. on dogs, racehorses, or livestock for the grazing industry. *Your Pet* enlisted the participation of industry figures, such as the veterinarians Dr Paddy Batch and Dr Cam Day, but steers away from an emphasis on 'how to' sections, like how to care for your hamster in Winter, towards general interest features, e.g. features on certain popular breeds, Council policies on walking your dog, or psychology of pet owners ('Why we love pets so much'). It includes helpful information, e.g. about pet day care and holidaying with pets, and even obituaries for special departed friends. .

Background

About the owner and editor, Janice Holland, and why she wanted to undertake this project: Janice began with twenty years experience in marketing and communications; was a former freelance writer; a speech and media writer for the Queensland State Government, and an editor of business and industry magazines, where she learned a good deal about business start-ups. She says:

I have always loved the aesthetic aspect of magazines; I had begun my career working on The Open Road magazine, published by the automobile club, the NRMA; I noticed the increase of street press and wanted to explore the trend. Furthermore I am passionate about the creative industries being valued at the economic level, where aesthetics and good design will really count in the marketplace; I have a love of animals, and animals as pets, and have a desire to contribute something positive to community. I considered this would be at heart a creative process, and was influenced by some writers, viz John Howkins.

Following a review of the street press and exploration of ideas about new/citizen media, the aims of the undertaking were determined to be: to create a successful, commercially viable product; and to demonstrate how creativity can lead to jobs and have an economic value. The project was in two distinct stages: The start-up, with business planning, marketing, editorial work, production and distribution of the first issue; then a process of marketing, advertising sales, editorial, production and distribution of issues 2, 3 and 4.

A conceptual basis for this was provided by the writer John Howkins, in *The Creative Economy: how people make money from ideas* (2002:16), where the creative process is defined as a 'five-fold mix of dreams and analysis, intuitive jumps and cold-blooded calculation', called 'RIDER':

1. *Review* the process of taking stock of things...curiosity, asking why
2. *Incubation*; letting our ideas sort themselves out, this can take a few hours or several months
3. *Dreams* are the unconscious wanderings, the explorations of myth and symbol and magic and stories
4. *Excitement* is the adrenaline that powers intuitive jumps and half-calculated sideways movements...the trick is NOT to look before you leap.
5. *Reality checks*; analysis and measurement to ensure dreams and intuitions have not taken us too far away.

Howkins outlines conditions for the embodiment of creativity in a tradable product, to accrue commercial value. It would require a marketplace with active sellers and buyers, some ground rules on laws and contracts and some conventions about what constitutes a reasonable deal.

The idea

The initiating idea was to establish a free pet lifestyle magazine distributed directly to pet lovers *via* pet-related outlets, to be funded through advertising. Initial research was conducted, involving brain storming with various colleagues on magazine content; looking through other 'street press' (e.g. music, lifestyle); assessment of existing pet publications at the time (e.g. *DogsLife, Pet NZ*); and analysis of growth in the pet industry, (revealing almost $2.3 billion on pet care annually, on figures from The Australia Institute). Project planning would then follow, started with a 'Howkins' *Review*.

Stages of Growth

Stage 1 – Start up

This stage was a period of intense activity focused on getting out the vital first edition, upon which the rest of the operation would depend, as a model for production, and exemplar for prospective advertisers and contributors. *Your Pet* had no staff at the beginning apart from its editor; each process had to begin from the 'ground up'. The 'start-up' phase entailed business planning, marketing and public relations work, advertising, setting up distribution, and then the task at the core of the entire enterprise, the 'editorial' work and production, i.e. the actual journalism. Notes on stage 1:

Business planning
1. Establish and register the company, and business name, (meetings with solicitor)
2. Protect intellectual property (IP); (register a trade mark and magazine name)
3. Develop a revenue plan including advertising rates, printing quotes, production costs and budget; (continue comparisons with other pet magazines and street press, as artifacts and models; meetings with accountant)
4. Develop administrative processes and information management systems
5. Obtain a post box, telephone, bank account, credit card facilities, GST reporting templates
6. At this point the process has reached the second, *Incubation* stage of the Howkins RIDER process; providing a guide to ensure steps are in a workable order, and essentials are all included.

Marketing and public relations; advertising

1. Identify and segment readership, (access Council data on dog registrations; meet veterinarians, industry representatives)
2. Determine the style, format and name of the magazine, (check other magazines / 'artifacts')
3. Determine the logo and key messages
4. Appoint and brief a designer
5. Purchase marketing/promotional materials, (information kit, rate card, stationery, stickers, banner)
6. Devise a marketing and public relations / media plan
7. Set up the web site, (an awareness phase for the site, targeted to advertisers)
8. Attend a major Brisbane pet trade show, for exposure; magazine launch there by a celebrity veterinarian
9. Identify and approach targeted advertisers

Distribution

1. Identify distribution outlets
2. Determine the print run, and how the magazines will be distributed

Editorial and production of issue 1

1. Decide on the editorial content, sections and page plan
2. Make the production schedule/timeline
3. Select and contract a printer
4. Approach and appoint industry experts who will appear in the magazine
5. Write copy or appoint and brief writers
6. Photography options, (obtain access to stock picture services, and set up an agreement with a commercial photographer)
7. Sub-edit contributions
8. Design, layout and proofing

For Janice Holland as the 'sole trader' responsible for the birth and survival of *Your Pet*, the actual writing, laying out, printing and distribution of the first issue was a milestone in a process for which the 'Howkins' formula was a steady reference. That process had come to the Howkins section on *Dreams*. The actual phase recognised as 'production' was still to follow, as it entailed the crucial issues of marketing the product now established in a material form.

Stage 2 – Production

Marketing

1. Mail the magazine and information mailed directly to potential advertisers
2. Send out the magazine and media release to media outlets
3. Upgrade the website to provide greater value to advertisers (banner advertisements) and to readers (more resources)

Advertising sales

1. Develop an advertiser database
2. Appoint an advertising account manager
3. Ongoing revision/updating of marketing materials

Editorial and production of issues 2, 3 and 4

1. Review the production schedule/timeline
2. Write copy or appoint and brief writers including appointment of a sub-editor
3. Liaise with industry experts, (a new avian veterinarian joins)
4. Photography options, (further work with professional photographer)
5. Sub-edit contributions
6. Design, layout and proofing, (a new designer appointed from issue 3)

Distribution

1. Broadening of distribution; reassess distribution (i.e. libraries versus pet outlets; need for advertising / company representatives to see the magazine)
2. Distribution team appointed
3. Mail out to advertisers directly from printers
4. Monitoring circulation issues in industry press

Business planning

1. Ongoing monitoring of what other magazines are doing
2. Ongoing budgeting and planning

Figures 1.1-4 (next page) The cover art for Your Pet's first four editions.

Following the completion of issue 3, the ongoing viability of *Your Pet* was assessed. The initial editions had made a huge impact on resources of capital and time, but as a perusal of the magazine would show, advertisers were starting to take up the magazine amid strong industry awareness and a warm response from readers, and advertising commitments were in place for future issues. The decision was made to proceed. The *Your Pet* diary noted that the stage called *Excitement* had been reached, in Howkins' RIDER. The issue 3 assessment considered achievements and challenges.

Stage 3 – Evaluation

Achievements

1. Production of four high-quality magazines
2. Successful carriage of an idea to reality
3. Overwhelmingly positive responses from readers and industry

4. The advertising sales trend is upwards, (issue 3 broke even, issue 4 presented a profit)
5. Advertising commitments secured for the next four issues.

Challenges

1. Resources and financial commitments
2. Risk and attitude to risk
3. Size of project and time constraints to get everything done
4. Hard news versus entertainment/infotainment
5. Advertising versus editorial, (a 'no advertorial' policy had been adopted, provoking questions about juxtaposing of material)
6. Editorial and advertising policy for future editions
7. Production schedules, accommodating time constraints versus commitment of time to ensure quality content
8. 'Educating the industry', a totally new concept for a specialist publication working closely with industry interests including experts in their field; how to get common understandings about communication issues with the public?
9. The diversity of industry, from large pharmaceutical companies to small, family-run businesses
10. Industry politics, (engagement of animal welfare organizations and others)
11. Staffing; identification of roles, choice of personnel, remuneration plans
12. New pet magazines on the market, the recurring prospect of competition (*The Australian*, 27.10.05)

The enterprise in context

Histories

As mentioned above part of the inspiration for *Your Pet* was culturally somewhat different in its subject matter, the alternative or 'street press' movement, though there was much common ground, for example the search for specialised readerships, free distribution, and ambivalence on advertising or advertorial issues. To survey the field Janice Holland began with an historical approach, turning over the history of magazines, notably in the United States; beginning with the publisher Benjamin Franklin in 1741, and his rival Andrew Bradford. Magazines flourished for two decades after the US Civil War, up to the start of the mass circulation era in the 1890s; an outgrowth of change to an industrial economy, with new technologies improving the printing process, transport and the mails. Magazines turned to specialised publishing in a major way after World War II, e.g. news magazines, cars, photography, for some time enjoying the benefits of economic expansion, and side-stepping competition from the new television medium. Between 1950 and 1960 magazine circulation in America actually increased 21% and advertising revenue increased 86%. In more recent decades magazines have continued to prosper, in still more specialized forms, e.g. consumer magazines, special interest, custom, business, professional, in-flight (Click and Baird, p 2-11,1990).

Evolution of street press

The street press of today followed on from publications justifiably known as 'alternative' media, according to Liam Dennis (2004):

The forerunners of current street press publications include Richard Neville's Oz, Go Set and Revolution titles...the main Sydney street press publications (Drum Media, Revolver, 3D World) are independently owned, separating them from the highly concentrated mainstream press in which the main players bear the familiar names of Murdoch, Packer and Fairfax... Publications are available for essentially any pop phalanx, ranging from indie/alternative music (Drum Media, Revolver), gay and lesbian issues (Capital Q) and dance (3D World), each often serving as a de facto cultural unifier. These attributes are embodied in perhaps the most successful and enduring publication in the industry, Drum Media which for the purposes of this analysis serves as a case study to examine the typicalities (sic) of the street press medium.

Characteristics of the alternative and street press: These are alternatives to mainstream media; when Richard Neville and others launched *Oz* magazine in 1963, carrying social satire and serious socio-political content, before much time had passed the editors were charged under obscenity laws. Many street publications are music and film industry-related (focusing on creative, independent aspects of these industries); they are published on newsprint; are free and accessible; depend on advertising and classified revenue for survival; and today the titles are fast becoming a mix of traditional and consumer magazine characteristics. *Your Pet* is definitely a hybrid of different types. The mixing of characteristics can work to the advantage of publishers, for example *B&T* magazine noting the Perth-based weekly *X-Press*, with a CAB circulation figure of 40,000, had 'marketed itself along the lines of consumer press since inception 16 years ago'. (*B&T*, 30.3.04). Some issues being faced by the street press include major growth in newspaper inserted magazines (NIMs), which may come to produce strong competition, and municipal authorities taking an interest in regulating free distribution, with Sydney Council already foreshadowing a policy to be in place by 2007.

Impact of technology

Observation of the field of 'street' publishing and its derivatives such as *Your Pet* shows the imprints of technological change. Access to production tools friendly to smaller print runs has been a key factor. Advances in printing methods along with the ability to design magazines digitally allow small-scale publishing to survive. These changes encourage the sole operator and/or home business, and in the present case *Your Pet* operated for its first year *via* a 'virtual office', i.e. voluntary and paid staff are home based with unique email addresses and telephone numbers, working off an online database.

With new media or citizen media, technology is facilitating the circulation of independent opinion, and independent publishing. In print, such publications can work on an expansion of traditional 'letters to the editor', to take in contributions of full articles/opinion pieces making up the broader content of the magazine, i.e. free magazines operating as a free and inter-active forum. Citizen media appears to have additional strength because of its heavy online focus. To some observers, says Macnamara (2005), web logs, or blogs, are regarded as 'the birth of a new genre of mass media which they are calling Consumer Generated Media or Citizen Media.' Others see the new trend forcing a shake-up in all journalism:

> *Journalism finds itself at a rare moment in history where, for the first time, its hegemony as gatekeeper of the news is threatened by not just new technology and competitors but, potentially, by the audience it serves. Armed with easy-to-use web publishing tools, always-on connections and increasingly powerful mobile devices, the online audience has the means to become an active participant in the creation and dissemination of news and information. And it's doing just that on the Internet ... Key trends shaping the future of media and journalism and impact on the Internet include: the democratisation of media due to low barriers to entry; challenges to media's hegemony; a redefinition of credibility – who has it and what it takes to create it; the rise of new experts and watchdogs; changes to the economic models for media companies; and the new expectations and demands of the consumer in the journalistic process. (Bowman and Willis, 2005).*

To many consumers, as in this commentary on an opinion website, from writer Kym Durance, a plethora of messages, flexibility, and above all inter-activity are welcome developments:

The level of interactive debate on social, cultural and political matters is steadily growing thanks in large part to alternative forms of media. News and commentary have never been more interesting and diverse than they are today under the influence of independent media. Today there are blogs and web-based media outlets of all kinds covering a broad range of interests and issues. Some would argue that many of them are instruments of the mainstream media. Well they may be, but a growing number of them are not, and what most of them offer regardless of their origin is a rich mix of immediacy and interactivity – a marked point of difference -- and accessibility. And regardless of the political or cultural stance an alternative media outlet might take, it is those flexible characteristics that make up part of its growing appeal.' (Durance, 2005).

Is citizen media the next evolutionary step for street press? It can well be that the definitions of these media forms will be decided, and expressed, in terms of the technologies to be applied. If it is a question of online or print, most magazines already have an online presence where they post a portion of the print magazine, provide basic content and demographic information, or provide a fully interactive, additional resource for readers. Online has the advantage of lower production costs, without the burdens of print design, printing and distribution; growing accessibility to households and other places, and immediacy. Print provides a tangible artifact, which will be of value to the reader; it offers a strong aesthetic, a well produced, even small publication being 'nice to look at'; utility, magazines being easy to carry around, convenient to handle; and small magazines meet a need for specialist, segmented publications.

Your Pet quickly realized that cross-over to the popular online option was expected, and advantageous on many fronts. Its website moved during the first year from an awareness raising and information site for advertisers, to a source of information for both readers and advertisers. It now offers such features as online competitions and an online calendar of events, all designed to generate traffic and increase hits. This promises greater value to advertisers who also get banner advertisements on the site. The next question is whether to provide more participation through setting up a *Your Pet* weblog: to blog or not to blog? Visit *Your Pet* at any time: www.yourpetmagazine.com.au, (accessed 30.12.05).

The future for *Your Pet*

If we go back to John Howkins' creative process, at the end of 2005 *Your Pet* reached the stage that he calls the *Reality Check* (Howkins, 2005:16). The magazine is operating well and with ongoing advertising bookings and increased awareness, publication continues; but in a dynamic society and mass media marketplace, *Your Pet* should already be thinking of its own evolution and long-term options. As a by-product of the experience of starting up this publication, *Your Pet* may even publish a magazine start-up guide, on CD-ROM. It will have a rich set of experiences to draw on.

John Flynn, proprietor of Jofly Media

Introduction

John Flynn casts himself as a freelance video journalist and photo journalist who is carving a living at the margins of the mainstream media, filling a few of the gaps left by the corporate giants. His background included a lengthy apprenticeship as a television news journalist in regional Queensland and the Northern Territory, before diversifying into the role of a 'VJ', video journalist, with Network Ten. He is still active as an occasional camera operator on the late night shift, but now works for himself, and most of his time is spent traveling Australia covering adventure sport / cycling events. Much of the work sits beyond the scope of the newspapers and free to air broadcasters, servicing a diverse base of clients including sporting websites and magazines. He is one of the truly diversified talents of the modern media industry, whose journalistic and photographic skills are used in print, broadcast and web media.

Story of a change

Here John Flynn gives a glimpse into the reasons behind his decision to break out of the conventional journalistic stereotype and make a living as an independent operator, and the name behind 'Jofly Media'. He writes about how his work progressed, and reflects on changes now affecting media users in general and journalists in particular.

Breaking the shackles

With the benefit of hindsight, looking back on the past year since going solo, I can't help but feel like one of those characters ripped from the pages of an airport paperback: the one who gives up the big money and corporate largesse to work for the underprivileged.

That's it in a roundabout way; leaving the world of the 'mass media' to work for the 'content starved'. It is a theme I will develop during this chapter. A glimpse at the diary for the month ahead brings more than a hint of excitement and anticipation. First there's Adelaide to cover the National Track Cycling Championships, Melbourne for the Women's Cycling World Cup, Margaret River W.A. for The Raid Adventure Race World Cup, then back to Kooralbyn in Queensland for a 24-hour mountain bike event. It might all dry up in a month's time, but right now I'm living the dream, reporting on events I enjoy, for an international audience that both craves and deserves the intellectual nourishment. To be sure I'm earning a lot less money than in my previous job with Network Ten, but the boss is a great bloke!

Why go it alone?

When the time came, it was a relatively simple decision, requiring volumes of judgment, but in eventuality, remarkably little reflection. After fifteen years I had tired of the mainstream world of broadcast news, the hype, drama, beat-ups and ego-stroking in the rarefied environment of television. Television news can be a 'hard-core existence'. Most of my working life in the industry was spent in remote postings from Cairns to Alice Springs to the Gold Coast, living life from a front-row seat. Come 2005, I had spent more time at the front line of television news than most of the newsroom, working around the clock in an adrenalin-charged environment. It became distressingly apparent towards the end that the vast majority of 'punters' loathed us. You would get spat at by schoolchildren while covering a school visit by a politician. The teachers would not discourage it. The standing of Australia's television news media appeared to have dropped to the 'lawyers and used car salesmen' level, and as I saw it, we had no-one to blame but ourselves. A tabloidisation of television news and current affairs over recent years took our industry down a dark path and it was time to jump from the runaway train, whatever the injuries or cost. In life you have choices and in a technologically driven world there were new media opportunities to explore. It was time to get out and make use of the skills I had spent the past fifteen years developing.

Working at the parish pump

The early part of my career was spent as a cadet / junior reporter working the regional sports round in Queensland's provincial city of Cairns. Regional television news is a bit like the old 'parish pump'. If a couple of flies were crawling up a wall, and blokes were betting on it, it passed the requisite test of being sport and the local news would surely be there to cover it! Suffice to say, the local sport rounds never lacked variety. We covered the big name sports of rugby league, AFL, basketball (which is huge in regional Australia), and cricket, but unlike in the capital cities, the local sports coverage wasn't limited to these. So-called lower tier sports like hockey, soccer, triathlon, road cycling, mountain biking, horse racing, boxing, athletics, water skiing and more, would regularly feature on the local news and helped contribute to a sense of community. In time, I suppose you might say, I became passionate about servicing the news needs of these sporting viewers and when I returned to big cities, I had become one of these lower tier sporting nuts myself!

Regional television is a great training ground for young journalists. There's no story chasing out of newspapers or being dictated to by thug producers. You generate your own material for the most part, learn to cultivate contacts, to hunt news and write concise copy quickly. If you make a mistake, or go over the top with a beat-up, the community backlash is generally rapid. Also, sooner or later most regional journalists find themselves at the centre of a major breaking story. Some capital city producers are even reluctant to hire former regional journalists; perhaps those journalists are used to autonomy and less likely to conform to a big news room's *status quo*.

The capital city curse

In truth, the day I started work in a so-called 'cap city' newsroom was the day I stopped being a journalist and became a 'reporter'. Invariably, the 'news agenda' would be decided by producers who read newspapers and press releases with the news director over coffee. The chief-of-staff would quote the page number of my story for the day. I would be expected to rehash what was in the article, even without new angles. Having come from a regional environment, I felt the reporters had suffered a loss of will to chase news, through not being able to work up enough new story ideas.

Life as a video journalist

I was hesitant to share the paragraphs above but it is background information for the next phase, my career as a video journalist (VJ). The powers that be within the industry would see it that video journalism is a concept which has been tried now and failed. I would take an alternative view but having spent five years trying to develop the VJ position, my viewpoint could be seen as being slanted. I started with it in October 1999 as one of three people in the Gold Coast Bureau – staffed by nine today. It required much dedication and ridiculous hours; the sort of commitment I could never again make to any corporate enterprise, even my own business! Twenty-four-hour days on the road were not unusual (32 hours was my longest day; the carnage I will never forget), such was the busy nature of Australia's most competitive news market.

Every other day would be spent trying to trump my allocated newspaper story with something fresh and new. As a video journalist in a remote bureau I had more flexibility than most others, so I chased the action rounds hard. (Any excuse to get out of sitting on the politician Cheryl Kernot's front doorstep or stalking the grieving family of an accident victim, whose life story was already splashed all over the local rag.) Frustratingly, even if I did come up with something original, invariably it would be traded with our so-called 'rival' networks for something which head office had 'missed'.

Still I enjoyed the 'in your face' nature of video journalism. You could be all over a story, in among the action, getting the money shots, asking the right questions and have the story in the can before the competition even arrived. If you had shot the pictures and asked the questions, it made the story easier to write and while you were sometimes dog tired from having to do everything, the result was generally of a decent standard.

Learning new skills

After almost four years on the Gold Coast I went to Cairns to set up the network's new North Queensland bureau. It was even closer to the cutting edge: Shooting on a consumer standard camera, editing on a laptop computer and exploring ways of getting vision from remote places utilising file-transfer protocol. I could see this technology was taking me into the world of multimedia, though my network had other ideas. In my eyes, the web was the greatest tool ever invented for value-adding to network news product; my then-head saw the web more as a competitor and there was little interest in developing web enterprises as a means of news content delivery. After coming some distance with new forms of production, it was again time for me to move on.

Working with the Web

My introduction to on-line journalism came through a site known as cyclingnews.com, first as a reader and cycling enthusiast, then as an occasional contributor. Today *Cyclingnews* is one of my biggest clients and cycling journalism, one of my specialty areas. I am self-employed and I shoot mostly stills and write copy for this expanding publication. In the beginning, I never envisaged web journalism becoming a significant part of my career focus, but how times have changed and how quickly they have changed!

To give some background, today, *Cyclingnews* is one of the internet's great success stories and it's no wonder why. At various times, *Cyclingnews* has been rated by industry publications as being among the top ten most popular independent sporting sites world wide, even the top 100 sites for men. It is unclear if these tags were based so much on figures or the 'vibe' the site creates. *Cyclingnews* was originally set up in 1995 by an Australian, Professor Bill Mitchell of Newcastle University, who was, to put it simply, a cycling enthusiast. Professor Mitchell had previously lived in Europe, and like many of those who followed the sport in Australia, found it difficult to access results from Europe's major cycling races. Sure, the Tour de France received some coverage Down Under, but beyond that, many of Europe's major cycling events, The Tour of Flanders, Paris-Roubaix, Milan-San Remo among them, were largely overlooked.

It may seem hard to fathom by today's standards of communication, but as late as the mid 1990s it was not unusual for Australian cycling enthusiasts to wait up to three weeks for the results of major races to filter through, *via* niche market publications. Australian newspapers had access to these results almost instantly and were being sent images of events under standard overseas supply contracts, yet nothing went to air or to print. The sport was not considered to be relevant to a 'mass market'. For those at the margins, the web would become their salvation. *Cyclingnews* immediately hit a nerve among the cycling public, not just in Australia, but the English speaking world in general, and in mainland Europe itself. As the site developed it worked on a simple formula: race results delivered in a timely format, methodical journalism and high quality images of the major events.

Cyclingnews went further though, capitalising on one of the key points of distinction of the internet, a lack of content restriction. Contributions from far afield would be welcomed; smaller events in remote places generally received a decent run and there was even a section for club race results from every corner of the globe. In a sense, the site's creators had developed a parish pump on a global scale, or to be more correct a system of parish pumps connected by a pipeline which guaranteed a constant flow of information. The challenge was to keep the reservoir topped up and the taps running. Today, *Cyclingnews* is considered the definitive source for cycling results and news on the web and utilises a system of global correspondents in mainland Europe, the UK, Asia, North and South America, Australia and New Zealand, among other destinations where the sport enjoys popularity. The site is owned by Sydney businessman Gerard Knapp, a long-standing journalist of 25 years with a sound knowledge of on-line media, who keeps a close eye on quality control. Perhaps this is one of the key differences between the site and a proliferation of cycling related web blogs. There is a focus on journalistic method, a discipline of verification, copy is normally edited before it is published, and so high standards are maintained.

The figures on site visitations are staggering. On the last available audited summary from 2004, *Cyclingnews* received 238 million individual page impressions, made up of readers from 90 countries. On a day-to-day basis, the site has encountered 400,000 individual user sessions per day. It continues to grow at the rate of 300 per cent per annum, and the figures, once collated and independently verified for 2005, are expected to dwarf those for 2004. These results have come amid a broader trend of readers and viewers defecting to the internet for their daily diet of news. The readers choose the material which interests them, rather than being fed a generic diet of what their newspaper or other major service will give.

My role in online journalism

A typical assignment for a site such as *Cyclingnews* is straight-forward. As a journalist you do as always: attend the event, cover your angles, the winners, the hard-luck stories and most importantly, the results and the pictures which tell the story. Normal practice is to forward the results to the site webmaster immediately the race ends, along with a very brief report of up to three paragraphs, and perhaps a photograph of the winner. The main report and race photography can follow; there is really no restriction to the length. There are several schools of thought on the best way of constructing internet news reports, and the nature of the report can be dependent on the structure of the site.

I'm a major supporter of web photo galleries to accompany stories. Many professional photographers are still learning to deal with the web and will typically provide their best three or four images to accompany a story, as they would for a story in print. But the web is different. To me, if you have thirty decent shots (not unusual for a day spent shooting a cycling event), why not put them together in a thumbnail gallery? The web is a content-rich environment and the more variety of content, the more site visitations it will generate. Having watched people reading web pages I think they can become bored with masses of copy, but pictures bring a different reaction.

Technology is a wonderful aide with this sort of work. Laptop computers and mobile phones make accessing the web on the run a breeze and new generation digital SLR cameras can provide high quality images for upload to the site in an instant. In remote locations, with access to tools such as satellite broadband, the world is at your fingertips with just a few keystrokes. Perhaps it sounds easy, but doing all of this in a hurry can be a challenge. Other than wanting everything yesterday, Internet webmasters provide no official deadlines. The sooner the story gets on line the better. After all, immediacy is the name of the game; otherwise it wouldn't be called 'news'. Here training kicks in. What I have learnt over the years is that most people can write, many extremely well. Presenting information quickly, assembling facts on the run, though, requires a special set of skills I loosely call the 'journalistic method'.

Can anyone be a web journalist?

The emergence of the World Wide Web poses an interesting question. Can anyone be a journalist? It can be argued that in Western societies almost anyone has access to the internet, but can observing or taking part in this interactive medium of itself be called journalism? Let me suggest a definition of a journalist: *a person who presents factual information in a structured format and conveys this information, via a medium, to an audience.* It is a liberal definition, admitting anyone capable of assembling a set of facts surrounding an event and presenting them to an audience through a structured method.

Getting back to the web, does this mean members of a cycling club who participate in an online forum about their favourite ride are indulging in journalism? Not really. In the case of a web forum, points of view are being expressed, information is being passed back and forth and some of this information may indeed be fact. Yet there is not necessarily a structured format, or a method to the presentation of the information; it also lacks a central tendency – an ability to give a good summary of what has been going on.

Taking it one step further, the cycling club web page, where the club secretary lists recent results and up coming events, might pass the test of journalism. It is by definition an on-line newsletter, a presentation of facts, however raw it may be in its delivery.

What about the method?

Journalism requires method, to bring everything together, in time. Professional journalists could easily be accused of believing they are chosen ones, a privileged few nominated to keep the public informed. Certainly the role can carry a great deal of responsibility, but it is by no means limited to those paid to do it. Every day, millions of people are using the web for the purpose of distributing information; often there is much method to their efforts; if it is something more than just online chatter, it could loosely be termed journalism. Yet I have found one of the real benefits of a person such as me, a trained journalist with above average camera skills crossing over to the web, has been that my work tends to stand out and be used well. Why should that be? Perhaps it is because I write what is perceived by readers to be interesting copy, or the words work together well with the pictures, or because the talent is quoted properly. All of these things come down to training and experience. It's not rocket science; I'm not so special. A recurring response when I contribute work for a web-based publication is that copy and images are on time; the copy is fluid, and there is a lack of spelling mistakes.

In research for this article, I have checked various sports sites. Some are blogging sites where people have their say on equipment and races, or whatever they like, really. Internet forums and chat pages where members of various user groups get talking are probably of value in a world where people don't know their neighbours. Still I wonder how much better they could be, if those involved in organising their construction were a little better trained as writers for the web. Journalism can be thought of as a way of thinking, and doing. It is easy enough to realise the usefulness of a journalist's preparation – being trained to meet deadlines and show due diligence making the product.

(Please see Appendix for a run-down on some key sports websites.)

Making a living at the margins

'Has it been worth it financially? Are you making a buck out of it?' These are the questions I receive most often from former colleagues intrigued at my decision to venture alone into the world of multi-media journalism. I worked on a plan that in the first year, the business would run at a loss and this has proven true. It's a simple fact you can't just generate work from nowhere. It's a case of working contacts, picking up one gig at a time, holding onto the jobs you have, generating repeat business so you don't have to work so hard generating business next year. So far so good. As a freelance photo journalist I have managed to hold onto the clients I have serviced so far, mainly website clients and magazines, along with some event managers for whom I provide a packaged suite of event media services.

There are the add-ons of course. Sales of still photographic images have become a small but not insignificant part of my income base. There is growing pressure to do more 'mum and dad' event photography, but when you work in editorial, that style of photography can drive you nuts. There have been good decisions and bad decisions. At the start I invested heavily in high-end DV camera equipment, anticipating most of my work would come from freelance broadcast video journalism. This was probably a mistake. I have kept the DV equipment in anticipation that online video will become a bigger part of the web mix, but it is not happening rapidly.

The constraints on datacasting within Australia, both in terms of technology and legislative hurdles are perhaps a topic for another time. It should enjoy a significant growth phase when most people gain access to high-speed internet. In the meantime, my only observation (as one of the independents whose right to trade is affected by this legislation) is that the ACMA (Australian Communications and Media Authority) licensing system for datacasting within Australia is extremely restrictive. Without discussing matters held to be commercial-in-confidence, several web-based clients I have dealt with have become frustrated by Australia's datacasting restrictions.

The upshot is that, without an outlet for quality independent online video, still photography has become a significant component of the presentation of online news. In my situation this has resulted in the need to keep up with the latest entries onto the market of digital SLR cameras, purchase new higher grade lenses, do anything to improve the quality of the images which are forwarded to clients and published. When you are providing pictures for commercial sale, clients look for the best standard. The technology seems to be moving at a faster rate than I can keep up with, but compared with even a few years ago the equipment is reasonably priced.

More broadly, equipment required at entry level for on-line journalism has never been cheaper. The first tool of trade, necessary for any multi-media journalist / photographer is a decent laptop computer. Mine is a garden variety, Dell Multi Media powerhouse notebook. It comes complete with wireless network capability, enough 'grunt' to edit digital video or masses of still photos on the run, DVD burning capability, and usual 'bells and whistles'. At around $2,000 these are technical gems, delivering the same quality of product hardly obtainable in a television edit suite for $100,000 only five years ago. Best of all they are highly portable and with just a *Blue Tooth* key and a mobile phone, offer the capability of uploading just about anywhere.

Reflection and conclusions

Working single-handed leaves little time to think about all the implications of present-day trends in journalistic practice. All the standard practices apply, like getting the story right; making sure of the facts. There is not great pressure to objectify your treatment in a field like adventure sports, but audiences can be very critical; we do not move far

182

away from standard texts, like Kovach and Rosenstiel (2002:71), and the recommended evidentiary approach:

The essence of journalism is a discipline of verification ... While not standardised in any code, every journalist operates by relying on some often highly personal method of testing and providing information ... Practices such as seeking multiple witnesses to an event, disclosing as much as possible about sources, and asking many sides for comment are, in effect, the discipline of verification.

Ethical considerations

Nevertheless, things change; new circumstances bring up new issues to deal with. All forms of journalism produce their individual set of ethical considerations and in this time, working as an independent photo journalist for the web has its challenges. Sometimes the lines between journalism and spin can become blurred. In my case, more often than not, I am employed by a web news publisher to provide independent copy of an event.

It can often be the case that the website is also a key sponsor of the event, or that the event managers have provided accommodation for an event at a remote location for the web news organisation. It is important in these situations to remember your code of ethics. Don't feel you owe anyone favourable copy for providing you with a roof over your head for the night. Alternatively, I now find myself in situations where I am working for an event promoter providing packages of images and copy for distribution to web outlets and magazines. It is important in terms of ethics in these situation to work in a transparent fashion, so that all people involved are aware of specifically who the journalist is working for.

The road ahead

It cannot be classified as a 'living' just yet. My income remains subsidised by, among other things, midnight to dawn shifts shooting news and the occasional general freelance television news job. The bottom line however is that the business is growing from one month to the next and the medium I have chosen as my main business target is growing exponentially. The avenue of work I am pursuing would simply not have been possible even a handful of years ago and it is empowering to provide news to a market which was previously disenfranchised. We can guess at what may happen in the future. 'Uncle Rupert' and others must no doubt try to buy the web, given it cannot be beaten, just as they did with suburban and regional newspapers. Anyone with a site generating significant hits is susceptible to a takeover. Large players, if they cannot buy it, may well try to burn it in some way, but the web may just be a bridge too far – an elusive adversary too difficult to define. As sole traders we may continue to prosper, or at any rate survive, and hope to see to it that the parish pump springs eternal!

Appendix – Sports Websites (notes by John Flynn)

1. www.cyclingnews.com A search under my by-line John Michael Flynn or John Flynn in the site search engine will bring up much of my work.

2. www.sleepmonsters.com Another site I do work for. An adventure racing site managed out of the UK, which is news based, though not with the same quality controls as *Cyclingnews*. It allows the person filing the report to have just about complete control of what goes on the site, hence not all of it is quality journalism, or edited to any great extent. The site does have a huge following as do its child sites all over the globe. Very adventure racing specific.

3. www.farkin.net This grew up as a blog site for mountain bike riders in Australia, but is trying to legitimise itself more with good layout and a newsier look.

4. www.mtbdirt.com.au Very much a parish pump blog site for mountain bike riders in South East Queensland. It relies a lot on threads and forums to generate traffic. I supply photographs from some local events, which they also sponsor.

Some internationals to have a look at also to get some scope:

1. www.solobike.it An Italian Mountain Bike site, which has a good newsy feel. I supply material from some Australian events.

2. www.pianetamountainbike.it Another Italian site which is the main competitor of *solobike*. Interesting to see how the two compete.

3. www.rower.com A Polish cycling site, which is trying to create more international coverage for its own readers. Interestingly, cycling has developed a huge following in Poland and the Czech Republic and due to financial constraints and lack of infrastructure in the broadcast world, the web seems to have become a big force.

4. www.radsport-forum.de A look at how the Germans do it. My experience is they take a very professional approach to web news at the higher end.

5. http://212.227.38.137/web/bike-sport-news/index.php *Bikesport* news, another prominent German site for bicycle related news.

Obviously several of these sites, particularly the blog sites, have links to a lot of other similar ones.

References

B& T magazine, 30.3.04, http://www.bandt.com.au

Bowman S. and Willis C., *We Media: how audiences are shaping the future of news and information*, for the Media Centre, American Press Institute, *http://www.americanpressinstitute.org/*; 30.12.05.

Click J. W. and Baird R. N. (1990), *Magazine Editing and Production*, 5th edition, Wm. C. Brown, USA. Pages 2-11

Dennis L., http://www.users.fl.net.au/~lyndenal/DRUM.htm, circa 2001.

Denniss, Richard, The Australia Institute, *Overconsumption of pet food in Australia*, July 2004.

Durance K., http://www.onlineopinion.com.au/author, asp?id=3792, 26.4.05.

Howkins J. (2002), *The Creative Economy: how people make money from ideas*, London, Penguin.

Kovach B and Rosenstiel T (2001), *The Elements of Journalism*, New York, Three Rivers Press

Macnamara J. http://www.pria.com.au/news/id/56 'New media challenging and changing PR' 01.09.05

The Australian, 27.10.05 Media and Marketing Section, p17, 'Pet periodicals get a bigger paw print'

www.yourpetmagazine.com.au, 30.12.05

Chapter 9

Conclusions ... or a new beginning

Lee Duffield, PhD and John Cokley, PhD

I, Journalist marks a beginning, a *first statement* of definitions of journalism for new times, part of a process unlikely to be resolved or completed for many years.

We are plainly arguing here that a definitive statement about the state of journalism at any point of time from now on can no longer be seriously attempted.

Things are too much on the move, and practitioners in every corner of journalistic activity are having to reflect on their situation and recapitulate on their purposes.

However, we suggest right now that this is a valuable and useful predicament in which journalism should find itself because it suggests the potential for growth.

Every other aspect of human endeavour which today calls itself a profession – especially law, medicine, pharmacy, accountancy and engineering to name but a few – started from a similar point (and not so long ago) working as a trade, training apprentices but then discovering along the way that there was more involved.

Why should journalists think they were any different, or should be? We envision the journalists of the 21st century as professionals in the same mould, who are able to train and reflect on their practice, develop a way of doing things which sets them apart, and offer their services to communities as individual practitioners; sole traders.

Further, we envision journalists "putting up their shingles" in towns, communities of interest (physical or online), as businesses, then going about the tasks for which they have prepared at university and in the work environment.

It will be obvious that this is not the "old-fashioned journalist" described by old media news proprietors, especially newspaper owners, who would harp on about journalism graduates not fitting the traditional mould of the investigative gumshoe, hat perched jauntily on *his* head, cigarette dangling, sleeves rolled up ready to take on any comers.

This was the journalism environment many cut their teeth on, but ongoing life experience, the opportunity to research, think and write about journalism, its faults as well as it good points, and especially the questioning input of our students, have led us to recognise the inevitable: who among audiences today *wants* or *needs* to hark back to a journalism represented by the grumpy old guy with the funny hat, anyway?

And this is why we have compiled this book, which takes in aspects of our life experience and our research, combined with the new research and findings by students, past and present. It includes also the innovative work of our colleague Dr Mark Hayes, who chooses "to boldly go" to some of the remotest audiences on earth to illustrate fundamental principles of our business.

All of our contributors see journalists having to accommodate themselves to new circumstances that bear the hallmarks of crisis, by which we mean a heightened presence of the two elements of danger and opportunity.

The key environmental factors of the "new economy" about which we write are its sensitivity to creative input in design and communication, and new digital technologies, making possible – actually forcing – a merger (*convergence*) of media to cause the birth of new kinds of products.

The "new economy" is an ideal home for new elements in society, the "creative classes", attached to the technologies for communication.

Therefore we have a growing cadre of citizens who are equipped and skilled to engage in interactive media, media that are powerful enough to replicate conventional mass media services, and able to innovate beyond that, providing the new kinds of media products.

They might go into new ventures – as in the model of online producers or podcasters.

They might interact with journalists, identified in this context as professionals in the mass-media field, who derive their principal livelihood from it; making a career of it.

Journalists can expect to function in inter-active situations with customers well and truly engaged in all aspects of the job – conducting surveillance for news, reporting on it, producing artifacts, communicating the messages, commentary, feedback, evaluation, preparation for what's next.

Journalists are evolving into the world's *change monitors*, who inform us when the goal posts change, when people alter their positions, or even simply when the weather turns.

They can expect to have to reform their existing practices quickly, hence our interest in the preparedness to change, or lack of it, on the part of elite practitioners found in international news or television current affairs.

They will operate on a global scale, be it as international reporters turning the technological revolution to their advantage, or as affiliates of a thousand media systems.

The operations of Tuvalu media in the mid-Pacific highlight some of the local-and-global possibilities.

These journalists of the 21st century also may break out of the corporate confines which are still characteristic of the way most do their work.

Some might find the corporations loosening constraints, looking for fresh and original input as a benefit from more intense and varied communication activity in the world at large (yet in different departments they may continue just as they are now).

Other journalists will be sole traders, of which there should be many more than before, considering the availability now of affordable and highly productive tools; a culture of abundant entrepreneurial activity in the economy, many small enterprises operating in communication-related fields; potentially very responsive audience members inundated with information of all kinds but looking for the stimulus of more; heightened awareness on their own part and capacity to realise on the possibilities of being a key player, a journalist, in this new kind of world.

We looked for self-descriptions of such journalists when investigating developments in freelance journalism, and providing the entrepreneurial case studies built on Jofly Media and *Your Pet*.

Putting all of the above observations together, we perceive the profession of journalist to be very strategically placed, at a kind of cross-roads of communication skills, social engagement and knowledge of society, technological mastery, applied creativity, amenability to cultures, and – as always – the drive for sense-making in potentially a very confusing universe.

We therefore have arrived at the essential definition of journalists of our time: they are defined by the way they think.

That statement brings us to restate what has been said in the body of the book, that journalists cope well with the materials of life, work and communication; they are programmed to craft the kinds of products in demand in our time.

They have distinguishing conceptual abilities, mastery of practice, and capacity to deliver product – wetware, software, skills.

Put in this light everybody might enjoy becoming a journalist to some degree, and profit from it.

Hard and fast change leaves us without convictions about how any of this will develop, except to say what is all too obvious: directions of change so far can be identified, but must be monitored all the time; change is now exponential and can radically alter course; possibilities are open; each day is a new start.